Should
TREES
Have Standing?

and other essays on

law, morals and the environment

by
Christopher D. Stone

OCEANA PUBLICATIONS
Dobbs Ferry, New York

Stone, Christopher D.
    Should trees have standing? : and other essays on law, morals, and the environment / by Christopher D. Stone.
    182 p.   26cm.
Includes bibliographical references.
ISBN 0-379-21381-8 (pbk. : alk. paper)
    1. Nature conservation--Law and legislation. 2. Environmental law. 3. Nature conservation--Moral and ethical aspects. 4. Environmental protection--Moral and ethical aspects. I. Title.
K3478. S764   1996
344' .046 - - dc20
[342.446]   96-35448
                                                                              CIP

About The Author

Christopher D. Stone is Roy P. Crocker Professor of Law at the University of Southern California. He did his undergraduate work in Philosophy at Harvard, received his law degree at Yale, and was a fellow in Law and Economics at the University of Chicago before practicing with the New York law firm of Cravath, Swaine & Moore. He has written in a variety of areas including the environment, white collar and corporate crime, legal philosophy, and United States alternate energy policy. He is past Chairman of the Committee on Law and Humanities of the Association of American Law Schools, and has served on or worked under the auspices of a variety of government agencies including the President's Commission on Communications Policy, the Energy Research and Development Administration, the National Institute of Mental Health, the National Science Foundation, the United States Sentencing Commission, and the Department of Energy, as well as the Canadian Institute for Advanced Research. He is a Trustee of the Center for International Environmental Law (CIEL) and Advisor to the Foundation for International Environmental Law and Development (FIELD), in London. He served as Rapporteur for the American Bar Association's Intersectional Committee on International Law and the Environment in preparation for the Rio Earth Summit (1992).

Professor Stone's articles have appeared in a wide range of scholarly and popular publications. His books include *Law, Language and Ethics, Where the Law Ends: The Social Control of Corporate Behavior, Earth and Other Ethics: The Case for Moral Pluralism,* and most recently, *The Gnat is Older Than Man: Global Environment and Human Agenda.* He is currently examining the legal, moral, and cultural dimensions of global environmental degradation.

TABLE OF CONTENTS

INTRODUCTION

THE ROOTS OF "TREES"

It has been twenty-five years since I wrote *Should Trees Have Standing? — Towards Legal Rights for Natural Objects*. It has since assumed a modest but apparently enduring place in contemporary environmental law and ethics, quite out of proportion to its actual impact on the courts. People have asked where did I "get the idea." I am not sure in what sense anyone ever "gets" any idea; and, at any rate I was later to be assured by readers—one should always be prepared to discover one's unoriginality—that the central notion had been floated about as far away as India* and as close to home as California.** The odd thing is, that in this case I can assign a time, not much more than a moment, when the idea and I met up.

My thoughts were not even on the environment. I was teaching an introductory class in Property Law, and simply observing that societies, like human beings, progress through different stages of growth and sensitivity. In our progress through these stages the law, in its way, like art and literature, in theirs, participates. Our subject matter, the evolution of property law, was illustration. Throughout history, there have been shifts in a cluster of related property variables, such as *what things*, at various times, were recognized as ownable (land, movables, ideas, other persons (slaves)); *who* was deemed capable of ownership (individuals, married women); the powers and privileges ownership conveyed (the right to destroy, the immunity from a warrantless search); and so on.[1] It was easy to see how each change shifted the locus and quality of power. But there also had to be an internal dimension, each advance in the law-legitimated concept of "ownership" fueling a change in consciousness, in the range and depth of feelings. For example, how did the innovation of the will—of the power to control our property after death—affect our sense of mortality, of our selves? I myself find all

---

*   Rod Macdonald, then Dean of Magill Law school, wrote to tell me I had missed Mullick v. Mullick, L.R. 52 Ind. App. 245 (Privy Council 1925). (East Indian family dispute regarding custody of an idol reversed with orders that, on retrial, counsel be appointed for the idol.)

** It turned out that the idea of a dog having "rights" had made an early appearance in California, although neither case put the dog's standing in issue and in both the court took the suggestion as an invitation to humor. One judge noted: "It may be that 'every dog has his day'; but if so, it is only a 'dog day' and does not entitle him to claim the rights of persons." People v. Fimbres, 107 Cal. App. 778, 781, 228 P. 19, 20 (1930). The other said of the claim: "though rather *dog*-magically asserted, we think no one of ordinary experience in the common, all-around affairs of this mundane sphere will hesitate to con-*cur*." *In re* Ackerman, 6 Cal. App. 5, 13; 91 P. 429, 433 (1907) (emphasis by court).

this stuff engrossing. But we were approaching the end of the hour. I sensed that the students had already started to pack away their enthusiasms for the next venue. (I like to believe that every lecturer knows this feeling.) They needed to be lassoed back.

"So," I wondered aloud, reading their glazing skepticisms, "what would a radically different law-driven consciousness look like? . . . One in which Nature had rights," I supplied my own answer. "Yes, rivers, lakes, ..." (warming to the idea) "trees . . . animals. . ." (I may have ventured "rocks"; I am not certain.) How would such a posture *in law* affect a community's view *of itself?*

This little thought experiment was greeted, quite sincerely, with uproar. And the end of the hour, none too soon. I stepped out into the hall and asked myself, "What did you just say in there? How could a tree have '*rights*'?" I had no idea.

The wish to answer my question was the starting point of *Should Trees Have Standing?* It launched as a vague if heartfelt conclusion tossed off in the heat of lecture. My initial motive was to restore my credibility. I set out to demonstrate that, whatever other criticisms might be leveled at the idea of Nature having legal rights, it was not incoherent.

But this was the hurdle: what were the criteria of an entity "having its own legal rights"? The question is complicated, because the law lends its mantle to protect all sorts of things, but not in a manner that would lead us to say that the thing has rights. Under conventional law, if Jones lives next to a river, he has a property right to the flowing water in a condition suited for his domestic or at least agricultural use. If an upstream factory is polluting, Jones may well be able to sue the factory. Such a suit would protect the river indirectly. But no one would say the law was vindicating the river's rights. The rights would be Jones'. The suit would occur under conditions that Jones' interest in the river—its law-assured usefulness *to him*—were violated.

So, then, what would be the criteria of a river having "its own" rights? One would have to imagine a legal system in which the rules (1) empower a suit to be brought against the factory in the name of the river (through a guardian or trustee); (2) hold the factory liable on the guardian's showing that, without justification, the factory changed the river to the detriment of its ecology (for example, from oxygenated and teeming with fish to lifeless) irrespective of the economic consequences of the change on any human; and (3) the judgment would be for the benefit of the river; for example, if repairing the pollution—making the river "whole" called for reoxygenating the river and restocking it with fish, the costs would be paid by the polluter into a fund that the guardian would draw from.

I jotted down these three criteria on a yellow legal pad. If the notion were ever to be more than a vague sentiment, I had to find some pending case in which this Nature-centered conception of rights might make a difference in outcome. Could there be such?

I phoned my library reference desk, transmitted the criteria, and asked if they could come up with any litigation that fit this description. I did not expect a quick response.

But within a half hour I got a call back: there was a case involving Mineral King in the California Sierra Nevada. Perhaps it might fit my needs. . ?

Sierra Club v. Morton

The case the library had found, at the time entitled *Sierra Club v. Hickel*, had been recently decided by the Ninth Circuit Court of Appeals. The U.S. Forest Service had granted a permit to Walt Disney Enterprises, Inc. to 'develop' Mineral King Valley, a wilderness area in California's Sierra Nevada Mountains, by construction of a $35 million complex of motels, restaurants, and recreational facilities. The Sierra Club, maintaining that the project would adversely affect the area's esthetic and ecological balance, brought suit for an injunction. But the Ninth Circuit reversed. The key to the Ninth Circuit's opinion was this: not that the Forest Service had been right in granting the permit, but that the Sierra Club Legal Defense Fund had no 'standing' to bring the question to the courts. After all, the Ninth Circuit reasoned, the Sierra Club itself

> "does not allege that it is 'aggrieved' or that it is 'adversely affected' within the meaning of the rules of standing. Nor does the fact that no one else appears on the scene who is in fact aggrieved and is willing or desirous of taking up the cudgels create a right in appellee. The right to sue does not inure to one who does not possess it, simply because there is no one else willing and able to assert it."

This, it was apparent at once, was the ready-made vehicle to bring to the Court's attention the theory that was taking shape. Perhaps the injury to the Sierra Club was tenuous, but the injury to Mineral King—the park itself—wasn't. If the courts could be persuaded to think about the park itself as a jural person—the way corporations are 'persons'—the notion of nature having rights would here make a significant operational difference—the difference between the case being heard and (the way things were then heading) being thrown out of court. In other words, if standing were the barrier, why not designate Mineral King, the wilderness area, as the plaintiff "adversely affected," let the Sierra Club be characterized as the attorney or guardian for the area, and get on with the merits? Indeed, that seemed a more straightforward way to get at the real issue, which was not what all that gouging of roadbeds would do to the Club or its members, but what it would do to the valley. Why not come right out and say—and try to deal with—that?

It was October 1971. The Sierra Club's appeal had already been docketed for review by the United States Supreme Court. The case would be up for argument in November or December at the latest. I sat down with the editor of the *Southern California Law Review,* and we made some quick estimates. The next issue of the *Review* to go to press would be a special Symposium on Law and Technology, which was scheduled for publication in late March or early April. There was no hope, then, of getting an article out in time for the lawyers to work the idea into their briefs or oral arguments. Could something be published in time for the Justices to see it before they had finished deliberating and writing their opinions? The chances that the case would still be undecided in April were only slim. But there was one hope. By coincidence, Justice Douglas (who, if anyone on the Court, might be receptive to the notion of legal rights for natural objects) was scheduled to write the Preface to the Symposium issue. For this reason he would be supplied with a draft of all the manuscripts in December. Thus he would at least have the idea in his hands. If the case were long enough in the deciding, and if he found the theory convincing, he might even have the article available as a source of support.

We decided to try it. I pulled the piece together at a pace that, as such academic writings go, was virtually breakneck, and the law review wedged it into a Symposium in which it did not belong. The manuscripts for the Symposium issue went to the printer in late December, and then began a long wait, all of us hoping that—at least in this case—the wheels of justice would turn slowly enough that the article could catch up with the briefs. It did.

The Supreme Court upheld the Ninth Circuit, a four justice plurality affirming that "the 'injury in fact' test requires more than an injury to a cognizable interest. It requires that the party seeking review be himself among the injured."[2] But Justice Douglas opened his dissent with warm endorsement for the theory that had just then made its way into print:

> "The critical question of 'standing' would be simplified and also put neatly
> in focus if we . . . allowed environmental issues to be litigated . . . in the
> name of the inanimate object about to be despoiled, defaced, or invaded
> . . . Contemporary public concern for protecting nature's ecological
> equilibrium should lead to the conferral of standing upon environmental
> objects to sue for their own preservation. See *Should Trees Have Standing?*
> . . . . This suit would therefore be more properly labeled as Mineral King
> v. Morton."

Justices Blackmun and Brennan favored a liberal construction of available precedent to uphold the Sierra Club on the pleadings it submitted; but in the alternative they would have permitted the "imaginative expansion" of standing for which Douglas was willing to speak.

EARLY REACTIONS

Boosted by Douglas's endorsement, the media got onto *Trees* overnight. It is not unusual for justices to cite law review articles. But there was something, if not prophetic, at least amiably zany about a law professor who "speaks for the trees"—and gets a few Justices to listen. Writing in the Journal of the American Bar Association one practicing lawyer took to verse for rejoinder:

If Justice Douglas has his way —

    O come not that dreadful day —

We'll be sued by lakes and hills

    Seeking a redress of ills.

Great mountain peaks of name prestigious

    Will suddenly become litigious.

Our brooks will babble in the courts,

    Seeking damages for torts.

 How can I rest beneath a tree

    If it may soon be suing me?

Or enjoy the playful porpoise

    While it's seeking habeas corpus?

Every beast within his paws

    Will clutch an order to show cause.

The courts, besieged on every hand,

    Will crowd with suits by chunks of land.

Ah! But vengeance will be sweet

    Since this must be a two-way street.

I'll promptly sue my neighbor's tree

    for shedding all its leaves on me.[3]

The style—a reluctance to confront us natural object advocates head-on, prose to prose—spread. In disposing of a 1983 suit by a tree owner to recover from a negligent driver for injuries to the tree, the Oakland, Michigan County Appeals Court affirmed dismissal with the following opinion in its entirety:

"We thought that we would never see

A suit to compensate a tree.

A suit whose claim in tort is prest

Upon a mangled tree's behest.

A tree whose battered trunk was prest

Against a Chevy's crumpled chest.

A tree that may forever bear

A lasting need for tender care.

Flora lovers though we three

We must uphold the court's decree."[4]

On the tide of such interest, the article was brought out in book form utterly without reedit[5]—essentially photocopied, in fact—and sold briskly. Most reactions were favorable. The Berkeley Monthly, for one, took "Trees" as a sign of better times to come. Others were critical, either of my ideas, or of nearly unrecognizable mutations which the writers proceeded to connect, at their convenience, I thought, with my name. I might have expected to considered a Born Again Pantheist, but not, as one reviewer initiated, that my agenda was transparently communistic. (The gist, as I recall, was that if we couldn't own things—and, after all, what else was there?—the whole institution of ownership was done for). My name, and little chatty, uncritical versions of the idea began to embellish the sort of journals that carry pictures. A revised mass-market paperback edition was issued by Avon Books, unsentineled by scholarly footnotes.

I had not been an environmental lawyer, and the focus of my attentions soon settled back to other things. But the Nature-rights movement was rolling along and lawyers began to file suits in the name of nonhumans. Early named plaintiffs included a river (the Byram),[6] a marsh (No Bottom),[7] a brook (Brown),[8] a beach (Makena),[9] a national monument (Death Valley),[10] a town commons (Billerica),[11] a tree,[12] and an endangered Hawaiian bird (the Palilla).[13]

But I am getting ahead of the story. Let me return to the post-*Trees* developments in the Epilogue.

ENDNOTES

1. Even in these observations I was quickly to learn that I was a late second. A law student at Chicago introduced me to Aldo Leopold's wonderful A *Sand County Almanac* (1966), with its wonderful analogy between modern attitudes towards land and Ulysses' attitude towards his slave girls—both as "property" .

2. Sierra Club v. Morton, 405 U.S. 727 (1972).

3. John Naff, 58 A.B.A. J. 820 (1972).

4. Fisher v. Lowe, No. 60732 (Mich. CA), 69 A.B.A. J., 436 (1983).

5. William Kaufmann, the publisher of Trees' first edition (1974), arranged for a gracious foreword by the biologist Garret Hardin.

6. Byram River v. Village of Port Chester, 12 E.L.R. 20816 (D. Conn., Aug. 21, 1974). (Suit in name of river and other plaintiffs to enjoin pollution by municipal sewage treatment plant dismissed for lack of in personam jurisdiction and transferred to S.D. N.Y., with no reservations expressed, however, regarding the River's designation as party plaintiff.). Ultimately, a stipulation of settlement was approved, 6 E.L.R. 20467 (S.D. N.Y. Jan. 8, 1976) (defendant undertaking to conduct and monitor the project in environmentally protective manner.)

7. Sun Enterprises v. Train, 394 F. Supp. 211 (S.D.N.Y., *aff'd*, 532 F.2d 280 (2d. Cir. 1976). (Suit in the name of Brown Brook and No Bottom Marsh, among others, unsuccessfully challenging Environmental Protection Agency issuance of sewage disposal permits.)

8. See note 7 above.

9. Complaint, Life of the Land, Inc., v. Bd. of Water Supply (2d Cir. Hawaii), (filed Nov. 24, 1975). (Complaint listing Makena Beach as one of several plaintiffs in action against Water Supply Board for failure to assess the environmental impact of the construction of water storage and transmission facilities and violation of state environmental policy.)

10. Complaint, Death Valley Nat'l Monument v. Dept. of the Interior (N.D. Cal.) (filed Feb. 26, 1976). (Complaint filed by environmental groups in name of National Monument, and other plaintiffs, alleging failure to fulfill a trust obligation to protect the monument by permitting strip mining operations by private concerns within the Death Valley Monument, in violation of the Wilderness Act of 1964 and the National Environmental Policy Act of 1969.)

11. Hookway, Whelan et al. and The Billerica Commons v. United States Department of Transportation (D.C. Mass.). (Complaint to enjoin road realignment that would affect town common in violation of N.E.P.A.; the action was not filed after press conference and threat of suit persuaded Department to modify its plans.)

12. See Ezer v. Fuchsloch, 99 Cal.App.3d 849, 160 Cal. Rptr. 486 (1979). Strictly speaking, the tree was not here a party plaintiff. The action was by landowners for injunctive relief against a neighbor based on a restriction recorded by their predecessors in interest providing that no shrub, tree or other landscaping would obstruct any lot's view. The trial court granted a mandatory injunction requiring both defendants to trim their pine trees to afford their neighbors a view of the ocean. On appeal, the defendants argued that the trial court failed to consider the rights of the pine trees to exist untrimmed independent of the inter-human rights created by the restrictive covenant. Judge Jefferson ultimately rejected the argument, invoking a passage from *Trees* at 457-58 as consistent with the court's action: "to say that the environment should have rights is not to say that it should have every right we can imagine, or even the same body of rights that human beings have. Nor is it to say that everything in the environment should have the same rights as every other thing in the environment." 99 Cal. App.3d at 864.

13. Palilla v. Hawaii Dept. of Land & Natural Resources, 471 F.Supp. 985 (D. Hawaii 1979). (Suit in name of endangered bird species, and others, against state resources agency for allowing feral sheep and goats to endanger birds' critical habitat; held: declaratory and injunctive relief granted.)

CHAPTER 1

SHOULD TREES HAVE STANDING?:
TOWARD LEGAL RIGHTS FOR NATURAL OBJECTS

INTRODUCTION: THE UNTHINKABLE

In *Descent of Man*, Darwin observes that the history of man's moral development has been a continual extension in the objects of his "social instincts and sympathies." Originally each man had regard only for himself and those of a very narrow circle about him; later, he came to regard more and more "not only the welfare, but the happiness of all his fellow-men"; then "his sympathies became more tender and widely diffused, extending to men of all races, to the imbecile, maimed, and other useless members of society, and finally to the lower animals. . . ."[1]

The history of the law suggests a parallel development. Perhaps there never was a pure Hobbesian state of nature, in which no "rights" existed except in the vacant sense of each man's "right to self-defense." But it is not unlikely that so far as the earliest "families" (including extended kinship groups and clans) were concerned, everyone outside the family was suspect, alien, rightless.[*] And even within the family, persons we presently regard as the natural holders of at least some rights had none. Take, for example, children. We know something of the early right-status of children from the widespread practice of infanticide—especially of the deformed and female.[2] (Senicide,[**] as among the North American Indians, was the corresponding rightlessness of the aged).[†] Maine tells us that as late as the Patria Potestas of the Romans, the

---

[*] See DARWIN, supra note 1, at 113-14:

> . . . No tribe could hold together if murder, robbery, treachery, etc., were common; consequently such crimes within the limits of the same tribe "are branded with everlasting infamy"; but excite no such sentiment beyond these limits. A North-American Indian is well pleased with himself, and is honored by others, when he scalps a man of another tribe; and a Dyak cuts of the head of an unoffending person, and dries it as a trophy... It has been recorded that an Indian Thug conscientiously regretted that he had not robbed and strangled as many travelers as did his father before him. In a rude state of civilization the robbery of strangers is, indeed, generally considered as honorable.

See also Service, *Forms of Kinship* in MAN IN ADAPTATION 112 (Y. Cohen ed. 1968).

[**] There does not appear to be a word "gericide" or "geronticide" to designate the killing of the aged. "Senicide" is as close as the Oxford English Dictionary comes, although, as it indicates, the word is rare. 9 OXFORD ENGLISH DICTIONARY 454 (1933).

[†] See DARWIN, supra note 1, at 386-93. WESTERMARCK, supra note 2, at 387-89, observes that where the killing of the aged and infirm is practiced, it is often supported by humanitarian justification; this, however, is a far cry

father had *jus vitae necisque*-the power of life and death-over his children. A fortiori, Maine writes, he had the power of "uncontrolled corporal chastisement; he can modify their personal condition at pleasure; he can give a wife to his son; he can give his daughter in marriage; he can divorce his children of either sex; he can transfer them to another family by adoption; and he can sell them." The child was less than a person: an object, a thing.[*]

The legal rights of children have long since been recognized in principle, and are still expanding in practice. Witness, just within recent time, *In re Gault*,[3] guaranteeing basic constitutional protections to juvenile defendants, and the Voting Rights Act of 1970.[4] We have been making persons of children although they were not, in law, always so. And we have done the same, albeit imperfectly some would say, with prisoners,[**] aliens, women (especially of the married variety), the insane,[5] Blacks, foetuses,[†] and Indians.

---

from saying that the killing is requested by the victim as his right.

[*] H. MAINE, ANCIENT LAW 153 (Pollock ed. 1930). Maine claimed that these powers of the father extended to all regions of private law, although not to the Jus Publicum, under which a son, notwithstanding his subjection in private life, might vote alongside his father. Id. At 152. WESTERMARCK, supra note 2, at 393-94, was skeptical that the arbitrary power of the father over the children extended as late as into early Roman law.

[**] See Landman v. Royster, 40 U.S.L.W. 2256 (E.D. Va., Oct. 30, 1971) (eighth amendment and due process clause of the fourteenth amendment require federal injunctive relief, including compelling the drafting of new prison rules, for Virginia prisoners against prison conduct prohibited by vague rules or no rules, without disciplinary proceedings embodying rudiments of procedural due process, and by various penalties that constitute cruel and unusual punishment). See Note, *Courts, Corrections and the Eighth Amendment: Encouraging Prison Reform by Releasing Inmates*, 44 S. CAL. L. REV. 1060 (1971).

[†] See note 10 and accompanying text infra. The trend toward liberalized abortion can be seen either as a legislative tendency back in the direction of rightlessness for the foetus—or toward increasing rights of women. This inconsistency is not unique in the law of course; it is simply support for Hohfeld's scheme that the "jural opposite" of someone's right is someone else's "no-right." W. HOHFELD, FUNDAMENTAL LEGAL CONCEPTIONS (1923).

Consider in this regard a New York case in which a settlor S established a trust on behalf of a number of named beneficiaries and "lives in being." Desiring to amend the deed of trust, the grantor took steps pursuant to statute to obtain "the written consent of all persons beneficially interested in [the] trust." At the time the grantor was pregnant and the trustee Chase Bank advised it would not recognize the proposed amendment because the child *en ventre sa mere* might be deemed a person beneficially interested in the trust. The court allowed the amendment to stand, holding that birth rather than conception is the controlling factor in ascertaining whether a person is beneficially interested in the trust which the grantor seeks to amend. In re Peabody, 5 N.Y.2d 541, 158 N.E.2d 841 (1959).

The California Supreme Court has recently refused to allow the deliberate killing of a foetus (in a non-abortion situation) to support a murder prosecution. The court ruled foetuses not to be denoted by the words "human being" within the statute defining murder. Keeler v. Superior Court, 2 Cal. 3d 619, 87 Cal. Rptr. 481, 470 P.2d 617 (1970). But see note p.13 and accompanying text infra.

Some jurisdictions have statutes defining a crime of "feticide"— deliberately causing the death of an unborn child. The absence of such a specific feticide provision in the California case was one basis for the ruling in Keeler. See 2 Cal. 3d at 633 n.16, 87 Cal. Rptr. At 489 n.16, 470 P.2d at 625 n.16.

Nor is it only matter in human form that has come to be recognized as the possessor of rights. The world of the lawyer is peopled with inanimate right-holders: trusts, corporations, joint ventures, municipalities, Subchapter R partnerships,[6] and nation-states, to mention just a few. Ships, still referred to by courts in the feminine gender, have long had an independent jural life, often with striking consequences.[*] We have become so accustomed to the idea of a corporation having "its" own rights, and being a "person" and "citizen" for so many statutory and constitutional purposes, that we forget how jarring the notion was to early jurists. "That invisible, intangible and artificial being, that mere legal entity" Chief Justice Marshall wrote of the corporation in *Bank of the United States v. Deveaux*[7]- could a suit be brought in its name? Ten years later, in the *Dartmouth College* case,[8] he was still refusing to let pass unnoticed the wonder of an entity "existing only in contemplation of law."[9] Yet, long before Marshall worried over the personifying of the modern corporation, the best medieval legal scholars had spent hundreds of years struggling with the notion of the legal nature of those great public "corporate bodies," the Church and the State. How could they exist in law, as entities transcending the living Pope and King? It was clear how a king could bind himself—on his honor—by a treaty. But when the king died, what was it that was burdened with the obligations of, and claimed the rights under, the treaty his tangible hand had signed? The medieval mind saw (what we have lost our capacity to see)[**] how unthinkable it was, and worked out the most elaborate conceits and fallacies to serve as anthropomorphic flesh for the Universal Church and the Universal Empire.[†]

It is this note of the unthinkable that I want to dwell upon for a moment. Throughout legal history, each successive extension of rights to some new entity has been, theretofore, a bit unthinkable. We are inclined to suppose the rightlessness of

---

[*]   For example, see United States v. Cargo of the Brig Malek Adhel, 43 U.S. (2 How.) 210 (1844). There, a ship had been seized and used by pirates. All this was done without the knowledge or consent of the owners of the ship. After the ship had been captured, the United States condemned and sold the "offending vessel." The owners objected. In denying release to the owners, Justice Story cited Chief Justice Marshall from an earlier case: "This is not a proceeding against the owner; it is a proceeding against the vessel for an offense committed by the vessel; which is not the less an offense. . .because it was committed without the authority and against the will of the owner." 43 U.S. at 234, quoting from United States v. Schooner Little Charles, 26 F. Cas. 979 (No. 15,612) (C.C.D. Va. 1818).

[**]   Consider, for example, that the claim of the United States to the naval station at Guantanamo Bay, at $2,000-a-year rental, is based upon a treaty signed in 1903 by Jose Montes for the President of Cuba and a minister representing Theodore Roosevelt; it was subsequently ratified by two-thirds of a Senate no member of which is living today. Lease [from Cuba] of Certain Areas for Naval or Coaling Stations, July 2, 1903, T.S. No. 426; C. BEVANS, 6 TREATIES AND OTHER INTERNATIONAL AGREEMENTS OF THE UNITED STATES 1776-1949, at 1120 (U.S. Dep't of State Pub. 8549, 1971).

[†]   O. GIERKE, POLITICAL THEORIES OF THE MIDDLE AGE (Maitland transl. 1927), especially at 22-30. The reader may be tempted to suggest that the "corporate" examples in the text are distinguishable from environmental objects in that the former are comprised by and serve humans. On the contrary, I think that the more we learn about the sociology of the firm—and the realpolitik of our society—the more we discover the ultimate reality of these institutions, and the increasingly legal fictiveness of the individual human being. See note p.37 and accompanying text *infra*.

rightless "things" to be a decree of Nature, not a legal convention acting in support of some status quo. It is thus that we defer considering the choices involved in all their moral, social, and economic dimensions. And so the United States Supreme Court could straight-facedly tell us in *Dred Scott* that Blacks had been denied the rights of citizenship "as a subordinate and inferior class of beings, who had been subjugated by the dominant race. . . ."*

In the nineteenth century, the highest court in California explained that Chinese had not the right to testify against white men in criminal matters because they were a "race of people whom nature has marked as inferior, and who are incapable of progress or intellectual development beyond a certain point. . .between whom and ourselves nature has placed an impassable difference."** The popular conception of the Jew in the 13th Century contributed to a law which treated them as "men *ferae naturae*, protected by a quasi-forest law. Like the roe and the deer, they form an order apart."† Recall, too, that it was not so long ago that the foetus was "like the roe and the deer." In an early suit attempting to establish a wrongful death action on behalf of a negligently killed foetus (now widely accepted practice), Holmes, then on the Massachusetts Supreme Court, seems to have thought it simply inconceivable "that a man might owe a civil duty and incur a conditional prospective liability in tort to one not yet in being."[10] The first woman in Wisconsin who thought she might have a right to practice law was told that she did not, in the following terms:

> The law of nature destines and qualifies the female sex for the bearing and
> nurture of the children of our race and for the custody of the homes of
> the world. . .[A]ll life-long callings of women, inconsistent with these
> radical and sacred duties of their sex, as is the profession of the law, are

---

*   Dred Scott v. Sandford, 60 U.S. (19 How.) 396, 404-05 (1856). In Bailey v. Poindexter's Ex'r, 56 Va. (14 Gratt.) 132, 142-43 (1858) a provision in a will that testator's slaves could choose between emancipation and public sale was held void on the ground that slaves have no legal capacity to choose:

> "These decisions are legal conclusions flowing naturally and necessarily from the one clear, simple, fundamental idea of chattel slavery. That fundamental idea is, that, in the eye of the law, so far certainly as civil rights and relations are concerned, the slave is not a person, but a thing. The investiture of a chattel with civil rights or legal capacity is indeed a legal solecism and absurdity. The attribution of legal personality to a chattel slave,- legal conscience, legal intellect, legal freedom, or liberty and power of free choice and action, and corresponding legal obligations growing out of such qualities, faculties and action-implies a palpable contradiction in terms."

**   People v. Hall, 4 Cal. 399, 405 (1854). The statute there under interpretation provided that "no Black or Mulatto person, or Indian shall be allowed to give evidence in favor of, or against a white man," but was silent as to Chinese. The "policy" analysis by which the court brings Chinese under "Black. . .or Indian" is a fascinating illustration of the relationship between a "policy" decision and a "just" decision, especially in light of the exchange between Hart, *Positivism and the Separation of Law and Morals*, 71 HARV. L. REV. 593 (1958) and Fuller, *Positivism and Fidelity to Law—A Reply to Professor Hart*, id. At 630.

†   Schechter, *The Rightlessness of Medieval English Jewry*, 4 JEWISH Q. REV. 121, 135 (1914) quoting from M. BATESON, MEDIEVAL ENGLAND 139 (1904). Schechter also quotes Henry de Bracton to the effect that "a Jew cannot have anything of his own, because whatever he acquires he acquires not for himself but for the king. . ." Id. At 128.

departures from the order of nature; and when voluntary, treason against it. . .The peculiar qualities of womanhood, its gentle graces, its quick sensibility, its tender susceptibility, its purity, its delicacy, its emotional impulses, its subordination of hard reason to sympathetic feeling, are surely not qualifications for forensic strife. Nature has tempered woman as little for the juridical conflicts of the court room, as for the physical conflicts of the battlefield. . . .*

The fact is, that each time there is a movement to confer rights onto some new "entity," the proposal is bound to sound odd or frightening or laughable.** This is partly because until the rightless thing receives its rights, we cannot see it as anything but a *thing* for the use of "us"—those who are holding rights at the time.† In this vein, what is striking about the Wisconsin case above is that the court, for all its talk about

---

*   In re Goddell, 39 Wisc. 232, 245 (1875). The court continued with the following "clincher":

"And when counsel was arguing for this lady that the word, person, in sec. 32, ch. 119 [respecting those qualified to practice law], necessarily includes females, her presence made it impossible to suggest to him as *reductio ad absurdum* of his position, that the same construction of the same word. . .would subject woman to prosecution for the paternity of a bastard, and. . .prosecution for rape."

Id. At 246.

The relationship between our attitudes toward woman, on the one hand, and, on the other, the more central concern of this article—land—is captured in an unguarded aside of our colleague, Curt Berger: ". . .after all, land, like woman, was meant to be possessed. . . ." LAND OWNERSHIP AND USE 139 (1968).

**   Recently, a group of prison inmates in Suffolk County tamed a mouse that they discovered, giving him the name Morris. Discovering Morris, a jailer flushed him down the toilet. The prisoners brought a proceeding against the Warden, complaining, *inter alia*, that Morris was subjected to a discriminary discharge and was otherwise unequally treated. The action was unsuccessful, on grounds that the inmates themselves were "guilty of imprisoning Morris without a charge, without a trial, and without bail," and that other mice at the prison were not treated more favorably. "As to the true victim the Court can only offer again the sympathy first proffered to his ancestors by Robert Burns. . ." The Judge proceeded to quote from Burns' "To a Mouse." Morabito v. Cyrta, 9 CRIM. L. REP. 2472 (N.Y. Sup. Ct. Suffolk Co. Aug. 26, 1971).

The whole matter seems humorous, of course. But what we need to know more of is the function of humor in the unfolding of a culture, and the ways in which it is involved with the social growing pains to which it is testimony. Why do people make jokes about the Women's Liberation Movement? Is it not on account of- rather than in spite of- the underlying validity of the protests, and the uneasy awareness that a recognition of them is inevitable? A. Koestler rightly begins his study of the human mind, ACT OF CREATION (1964), with an analysis of humor, entitled "The Logic of Laughter." And cf. Freud, *Jokes and the Unconscious*, 8 STANDARD EDITION OF THE COMPLETE PSYCHOLOGICAL WORKS OF SIGMUND FREUD (J. Strachey transl. 1905). (Query too: what is the relationship between the conferring of proper names, e.g., Morris, and the conferring of social and legal rights?)

†   Thus it was that the Founding Fathers could speak of the inalienable rights of all men, and yet maintain a society that was, by modern standards, without the most basic rights for Blacks, Indians, children and women. There was no hypocrisy; emotionally, no one felt that these other things were men.

women, so clearly was never able to see women as they are (and might become). All it could see was the popular "idealized" version of *an object it needed.* Such is the way the slave South looked upon the Black.* There is something of a seamless web involved: there will be resistance to giving the thing "rights" until it can be seen and valued for itself; yet, it is hard to see it and value it for itself until we can bring ourselves to give it "rights"—which is almost inevitably going to sound inconceivable to a large group of people.

The reason for this little discourse on the unthinkable, the reader must know by now, if only from the title of the paper. I am quite seriously proposing that we give legal rights to forests, oceans, rivers and other so-called "natural objects" in the environment—indeed, to the natural environment as a whole.**

---

* "The second thought streaming from. . .the older South [is] the sincere and passionate belief that somewhere between men and cattle, God created a *tertium quid,* and called it a Negro-a clownish, simple creature, at times even lovable within its limitations, but straitly foreordained to walk within the Veil." W.E.B. DuBOIS, THE SOULS OF BLACK FOLK 89 (1924).

** In this article I essentially limit myself to a discussion of non-animal but natural objects. I trust that the reader will be able to discern where the analysis is appropriate to advancing our understanding of what would be involved in giving "rights" to other objects not presently endowed with rights—for example, not only animals (some of which already have rights in some senses) but also humanoids, computers, and so forth. Cf. The National Register for Historic Places, 16 U.S.C. § 470 (1970), discussed in Ely v. Velde, 321 F. Supp. 1088 (E.D. Va. 1971).

As the reader will discover, there are large problems involved in defining the boundaries of the "natural object." For example, from time to time one will wish to speak of that portion of a river that runs through a recognized jurisdiction; at other times, one may be concerned with the entire river, or the hydrologic cycle—or the whole of nature. One's ontological choices will have a strong influence on the shape of the legal system, and the choices involved are not easy. See notes p.13 and p.19 and accompanying text *infra.*

On the other hand, the problems of selecting an appropriate ontology are problems of all language—not merely of the language of legal concepts, but of ordinary language as well. Consider, for example, the concept of a "person" in legal or in everyday speech. Is each person a fixed bundle of relationships, persisting unaltered through time? Do our molecules and cells not change at every moment? Our hypostatizations always have a pragmatic quality to them. See D. HUME, *Of Personal Identity,* in TREATISE OF HUMAN NATURE bk. 1, pt. IV, sec. VI, in THE PHILOSOPHICAL WORKS OF DAVID HUME 310-18, 324 (1854); T. MURTI, THE CENTRAL PHILOSOPHY OF BUDDHISM 70-73 (1955). In LOVES BODY 146-47 (1966) Norman O. Brown observes:

"The existence of the "let's pretend" boundary does not prevent the continuance of the real traffic across it. Projection and introjection, the process whereby the self as distinct from the other is constituted, is not past history, an event in childhood, but a present process of continuous creation. The dualism of self and external world is built up by a constant process of reciprocal exchange between the two. The self as a stable substance enduring through time, an identity, is maintained by constantly absorbing good parts (or people) from the outside world and expelling bad parts from the inner world. There is a continual "unconscious" wandering of other personalities into ourselves.'

Every person, then, is many persons; a multitude made into one person; a corporate body; incorporated, a corporation. A 'corporation sole;' every man a parson-person. The unity of the person is as real, or unreal, as the unity of the corporation."

See generally, W. BISHIN & STONE, LAW, LANGUAGE AND ETHICS Ch. 5 (1972).

In different legal systems at different times, there have been many shifts in the entity deemed "responsible" for

As strange as such a notion may sound, it is neither fanciful nor devoid of operational content. In fact, I do not think it would be a misdescription of recent developments in the law to say that we are already on the verge of assigning some such rights, although we have not faced up to what we are doing in those particular terms.[*] We should do so now, and begin to explore the implications such a notion would hold.

TOWARD RIGHTS FOR THE ENVIRONMENT

Now, to say that the natural environment should have rights is not to say anything as silly as that no one should be allowed to cut down a tree. We say human beings have rights, but—at least as of the time of this writing—they can be executed.[11] Corporations have rights, but they cannot plead the fifth amendment;[12] *In re Gault* gave 15-year-olds certain rights in juvenile proceedings, but it did not give them the right to vote. Thus, to say that the environment should have rights is not to say that it should have every right we can imagine, or even the same body of rights as human beings have. Nor is it to say that everything in the environment should have the same rights as every other thing in the environment.

What the granting of rights does involve has two sides to it. The first involves what might be called the legal-operational aspects; the second, the psychic and socio-psychic aspects. I shall deal with these aspects in turn.

THE LEGAL-OPERATIONAL ASPECTS

What it Means to be a Holder of Legal Rights

There is, so far as I know, no generally accepted standard for how one ought to use the term "legal rights." Let me indicate how I shall be using it in this piece.

First and most obviously, if the term is to have any content at all, an entity cannot be said to hold a legal right unless and until *some public authoritative body* is prepared to

---

harmful acts: an entire clan was held responsible for a crime before the notion of individual responsibility emerged; in some societies the offending hand, rather than a entire body, may be "responsible." Even today, we treat father and son as separate jural entities for some purposes, but as a single jural entity for others. I do not see why, in principle, the task of working out a legal ontology of natural objects (and "qualities," e.g., climatic warmth) should be any more unmanageable. Perhaps someday all mankind shall be, for some purposes, one jurally recognized "natural object."

[*] The statement in text is not quite true; cf. Murphy, *Has Nature Any Right to Life?*, 22 HAST. L. J. 467 (1971). An Irish court, passing upon the validity of a testamentary trust to the benefits of someone's dogs, observed in dictum that "'lives' means lives of human beings, not of animals or trees in California." Kelly v. Dillon, 1932 Ir. R. 255, 261. (The intended gift over on the death of the last surviving dog was held void for remoteness, the court refusing "to enter into the question of a dog's expectation of life," although prepared to observe that "in point of fact neighbor's [sic] dogs and cats are unpleasantly long-lived. . ." Id. At 260-61).

give *some amount of review* to actions that are colorably inconsistent with that "right." For example, if a student can be expelled from a university and cannot get any public official, even a judge or administrative agent at the lowest level, either (i) to require the university to justify its actions (if only to the extent of filling out an affidavit alleging that the expulsion "was not wholly arbitrary and capricious") or (ii) to compel the university to accord the student some procedural safeguards (a hearing, right to counsel, right to have notice of charges), then the minimum requirements for saying that the student has a legal right to his education do not exist.[13]

But for a thing to be a *holder of legal rights,* something more is needed than that some authoritative body will review the actions and processes of those who threaten it. As I shall use the term, "holder of legal rights," each of three additional criteria must be satisfied. All three, one will observe, go towards making a thing count jurally—to have a legally recognized worth and dignity in its own right, and not merely to serve as a means to benefit "us" (whoever the contemporary group of rights-holders may be). They are, first, that the thing can institute legal actions *at its behest;* second, that in determining the granting of legal relief, the court must take *injury to it* into account; and, third, that relief must run to the *benefit of it.*

To illustrate, even as between two societies that condone slavery there is a fundamental difference between S1, in which a master can (if he chooses), go to court and collect reduced chattel value damages from someone who has beaten his slave, and S2, in which the slave can institute the proceedings himself, for his own recovery, damages being measured by, say, his pain and suffering. Notice that neither society is so structured as to leave wholly unprotected the slave's interests in not being beaten. But in S2 as opposed to S1 there are three operationally significant advantages that the slave has, and these make the slave in S2, albeit a slave, a holder of rights. Or, again, compare two societies, S1, in which pre-natal injury to a live-born child gives a right of action against the tortfeasor at the mother's instance, for the mother's benefit, on the basis of the mother's mental anguish, and S2, which gives the child a suit in its own name (through a guardian *ad litem*) for its own recovery, for damages to it.

When I say, then, that at common law "natural objects" are not holders of legal rights, I am not simply remarking what we would all accept as obvious. I mean to emphasize three specific legal—operational advantages that the environment lacks, leaving it in the position of the slave and the foetus in S1, rather than the slave and foetus of S2.

The Rightlessness of Natural Objects at Common Law

Consider, for example, the common law's posture toward the pollution of a stream. True, courts have always been able, in some circumstances, to issue orders that will stop the pollution—just as the legal system in S1 is so structured as incidentally to discourage beating slaves and being reckless around pregnant women. But the stream itself is fundamentally rightless, with implications that deserve careful reconsideration.

The first sense in which the stream is not a rights-holder has to do with standing. The stream itself has none. So far as the common law is concerned, there is in general no way to challenge the polluter's actions save at the behest of a lower riparian—another human being-able to show an invasion of his rights. This conception of the riparian as the holder of the right to bring suit has more than theoretical interest. The lower riparians may simply not care about the pollution. They themselves may be polluting, and not wish to stir up legal waters. They may be economically dependent on their polluting neighbor.* And, of course, when they discount the value of winning by the costs of bringing suit and the chances of success, the action may not seem worth undertaking. Consider, for example, that while the polluter might be injuring 100 downstream riparians $10,000 a year *in the aggregate,* each riparian separately might be suffering injury only to the extent of $100—possibly not enough for any one of them to want to press suit by himself, or even go to the trouble and cost of securing co-plaintiffs to make it worth everyone's while. This hesitance will be especially likely when the potential plaintiffs consider the burdens the law puts in their way:** proving, e.g., specific damages, the "unreasonableness" of defendant's use of the water, the fact that practicable means of abatement exist, and overcoming difficulties raised by issues such as joint casuality, right to pollute by prescription, and so forth. Even in states which, like California, sought to overcome these difficulties by empowering the attorney-general to sue for abatement of pollution in limited instances, the power has been sparingly invoked and, when invoked, narrowly construed by the courts.†

The second sense in which the common law denies "rights" to natural objects has to do with the way in which the merits are decided in those cases in which someone is competent and willing to establish standing. At its more primitive levels, the system protected the "rights" of the property owning human with minimal weighing of any values: *"Cujus est solum, ejus est usque ad coelum et ad infernos."*†† Today we have come more

---

*   For example, see People ex rel. Ricks Water Co. v. Elk River Mill & Lumber Co., 107 Cal. 221, 40 Pac. 531 (1895) (refusing to enjoin pollution by a upper riparian at the instance of the Attorney General of the grounds that the lower riparian owners, most of whom were dependent on the lumbering business of the polluting mill, did not complain).

**   The law in a suit for injunctive relief is commonly easier on the plaintiff than in a suit for damages. See J. GOULD, LAW OF WATERS § 206 (1883).

†   However, in 1970 California amended its Water Quality Act to make it easier for the Attorney General to obtain relief, e.g. one must no longer allege irreparable injury in a suit for an injunction. CAL. WATER CODE § 13350(b) (West 1971).

††   To whomsoever the soil belongs, he owns also to the sky and to the depths. See W. BLACKSTONE, 2 COMMENTARIES 18.

     At early common law, the owner of land could use all that was found under his land "at his free will and pleasure" without regard to any "inconvenience to his neighbour." Acton v. Blundell, 12 Meeson & Welsburg 324, 354, 152 Eng. Rep. 1223, 1235 (1843). "He [the landowner] may waste or despoil the land as he pleases. . ." R. MEGARRY & H. WADE, THE LAW OF REAL PROPERTY 70 (3d ed. 1966). See R. POWELL, 5 THE LAW OF REAL PROPERTY p.725 (1971).

and more to make balances—but only such as will adjust the economic best interests of identifiable humans. For example, continuing with the case of streams, there are commentators who speak of a "general rule" that "a riparian owner is legally entitled to have the stream flow by his land with its quality unimpaired" and observe that "an upper owner has, prima facie, no right to pollute the water."[14] Such a doctrine, if strictly invoked, would protect the stream absolutely whenever a suit was brought; but obviously, to look around us, the law does not work that way. Almost everywhere there are doctrinal qualifications on riparian "rights" to an unpolluted stream.* Although these rules vary from jurisdiction to jurisdiction, and upon whether one is suing for an equitable injunction or for damages, what they all have in common is some sort of balancing. Whether under language of "reasonable use," "reasonable methods of use," "balance of convenience," or "the public interest doctrine,"** what the courts are balancing, with varying degrees of directness, are the economic hardships on the upper riparian (or dependent community) of abating the pollution vis-a-vis the economic hardships of continued pollution on the lower riparians. What does not weigh in the balance is the damage to the stream, its fish and turtles and "lower" life. So long as the natural environment itself is rightless, these are not matters for judicial cognizance. Thus, we find the highest court of Pennsylvania refusing to stop a coal company from discharging polluted mine water into a tributary of the Lackawana River because a plaintiff's "grievance is for a mere personal inconvenience; and. . .mere private personal inconveniences. . .must yield to the necessities of a great public industry, which although in the hands of a private corporation, subserves a great public interest."[15] The stream itself is lost sight of in "a quantitative compromise between two conflicting interests."[16]

The third way in which the common law makes natural objects rightless has to do with who is regarded as the beneficiary of a favorable judgment. Here, too, it makes a considerable difference that it is not the natural object that counts in its own right. To illustrate this point, let me begin by observing that it makes perfectly good sense to speak of, and ascertain, the legal damage to a natural object, if only in the sense of "making it whole" with respect to the most obvious factors.† The costs of making a

---

*   For example, courts have upheld a right to pollute by prescription, Mississippi Mills Co. V. Smith, 69 Miss. 299, 11 So. 26 (1882), and by easement, Luama v. Bunker Hill & Sullivan Mining & Concentrating Co., 41 F.2d 358 (9th Cir. 1930).

** See Red River Roller Mills v. Wright, 30 Minn. 249, 15 N.W. 167 (1883) (enjoyment of stream by riparian may be modified or abrogated by reasonable use of stream by others); Townsend v. Bell, 167 N.Y. 462, 60 N.E. 757 (1901) (riparian owner not entitled to maintain action for pollution of stream by factory where he could not show use of water was unreasonable); Smith v. Staso Milling Co., 18 F.2d 736 (2d Cir. 1927) (in suit for injunction, right on which injured lower riparian stands is a quantitative compromise between two conflicting interests); Clifton Iron Co. V. Dye, 87 Ala. 468, 6 So. 192 (1889) (in determining whether to grant injunction to lower riparian, court must weigh interest of public as against injury to one or the other party). See also Montgomery Limestone Co. V. Bearder, 256 Ala. 269, 54 So. 2d 571 (1951).

†   Measuring plaintiff's damages by "making him whole" has several limitations. These and the matter of

forest whole, for example, would include the costs of reseeding, repairing watersheds, restocking wildlife—the sorts of costs the Forest Service undergoes after a fire. Making a polluted stream whole would include the costs of restocking with fish, water-fowl, and other animal and vegetable life, dredging, washing out impurities, establishing natural and/or artificial aerating agents, and so forth. Now, what is important to note is that, under our present system, even if a plaintiff riparian wins a water pollution suit for damages, no money goes to the benefit of the stream itself to repair its damages.* This omission has the further effect that, at most, the law confronts a polluter with what it takes to make the plaintiff riparians whole; this may be far less than the damages to the stream,** but not so much as to force the polluter to desist. For example, it is easy to imagine a polluter whose activities damage a stream to the extent of $10,000 annually, although the aggregate damage to all the riparian plaintiffs who come into the suit is only $3000. If $3000 is less than the cost to the polluter of shutting down, or making the requisite technological changes, he might prefer to pay off the damages (i.e., the legally cognizable damages) and continue to pollute the stream. Similarly, even if the jurisdiction issues an injunction at the plaintiffs' behest (rather than to order payment of damages), there is nothing to stop the plaintiffs from "selling out" the stream, i.e., agreeing to dissolve or not enforce the injunction at some price (in the example above, somewhere between plaintiffs' damages—$3000—and defendant's next best economic alternative). Indeed, I take it this is exactly what Learned Hand had in mind in an opinion in which, after issuing an anti-pollution injunction, he suggests that the defendant "make its peace with the plaintiff as best it can."[17] What is meant is a peace between them, and not amongst them and the river.

I ought to make it clear at this point that the common law as it affects streams and rivers, which I have been using as an example so far, is not exactly the same as the law affecting other environmental objects. Indeed, one would be hard pressed to say that there was a "typical" environmental object, so far as its treatment at the hands of the law is concerned. There are some differences in the law applicable to all the various resources that are held in common: rivers, lakes, oceans, dunes, air, streams (surface and subterranean), beaches, and so forth.† And there is an even greater difference as

---

measuring damages in this area generally are discussed more fully on pp. 20-25 and accompanying text *infra*.

* Here, again, an analogy to corporation law might be profitable. Suppose that in the instance of negligent corporate management by the directors, there were no institution of the stockholder derivative suit to force the directors to make *the corporation* whole, and the only actions provided for were direct actions by stockholders to collect for damages *to themselves qua* stockholders. Theoretically and practically, the damages might come out differently in the two cases, and not merely because the creditors' losses are not aggregated in the stockholders' direct actions.

** And even far less than the damages to all human economic interests derivately through the stream; *see* pp. 21-22 *infra*.

† Some of these public properties are subject to the "public trust doctrine," which, while ill-defined, might be

between these traditional communal resources on one hand, and natural objects on traditionally private land, e.g., the pond on the farmer's field, or the stand of trees on the suburbanite's lawn.

On the other hand, although there be these differences which would make it fatuous to generalize about a law of the natural environment, most of these differences simply underscore the points made in the instance of rivers and streams. None of the natural objects, whether held in common or situated on private land, has any of the three criteria of a rights-holder. They have no standing in their own right; their unique damages do not count in determining outcome; and they are not the beneficiaries of awards. In such fashion, these objects have traditionally been regarded by the common law, and even by all but the most recent legislation, as objects for man to conquer and master and use—in such a way as the law once looked upon "man's" relationship to African Negroes. Even where special measures have been taken to conserve them, as by seasons on game and limits on timber cutting, the dominant motive has been to conserve them for us—for the greatest good of the greatest number of human beings. Conservationists, so far as I am aware, are generally reluctant to maintain otherwise.* As the name implies, they want to conserve and guarantee our consumption and our enjoyment of these other living things. In their own right, natural objects have counted for little, in law as in popular movements.

As I mentioned at the outset, however, the rightlessness of the natural environment can and should change; it already shows some signs of doing so.

Toward Having Standing in Its Own Right

It is not inevitable, nor is it wise, that natural objects should have no rights to seek redress in their own behalf. It is no answer to say that streams and forests cannot have standing because streams and forests cannot speak. Corporations cannot speak, either; nor can states, estates, infants, incompetents, municipalities, or universities. Lawyers speak for them, as they customarily do for the ordinary citizen with legal problems. One ought, I think, to handle the legal problems of natural objects as one does the problems of legal incompetents—human beings who have become vegetable. If a human being shows signs of becoming senile and has affairs that he is de jure incompetent to manage, those concerned with his well being make such a showing to the court, and someone is designated by the court with the authority to manage the incompetent's affairs. The guardian[18] (or "conservator"[19] or "committee"**—the

---

developed in such fashion as to achieve fairly broad-ranging environmental protection. See Gould v. Greylock Reservation Comm'n, 350 Mass. 410, 215 N.E.2d 114 (1966), discussed in Sax, *The Public Trust Doctrine in Natural Resource Law: Effective Judicial Intervention,* 68 MICH. L. REV. 471, 492-509 (1970).

*   By contrast, for example, with humane societies.

**   In New York State the Supreme Court and county courts outside New York City have jurisdiction to appoint

terminology varies) then represents the incompetent in his legal affairs. Courts make similar appointments when a corporation has become "incompetent": they appoint a trustee in bankruptcy or reorganization to oversee its affairs and speak for it in court when that becomes necessary.

On a parity of reasoning, we should have a system in which, when a friend of a natural object perceives it to be endangered, he can apply to a court for the creation of a guardianship.* Perhaps we already have the machinery to do so. California law, for example, defines an incompetent as "any person, whether insane or not, who by reason of old age, disease, weakness of mind, or other cause, is unable, unassisted, properly to manage and take care of himself or his property, and by reason thereof is likely to be deceived or imposed upon by artful or designing persons." **Of course, to urge a court that an endangered river is "a person" under this provision will call for lawyers as bold and imaginative as those who convinced the Supreme Court that a railroad corporation was a "person" under the fourteenth amendment, a constitutional provision theretofore generally thought of as designed to secure the rights of freedmen.[20] (As this article was going to press, Professor Byrn of Fordham petitioned the New York State Supreme Court to appoint him legal guardian for an unrelated foetus scheduled for abortion so as to enable him to bring a class action on behalf of all foetuses similarly situated in New York City's 18 municipal hospitals. Judge Holtzman granted the petition of guardianship.)† If such an argument based on present statutes

---

a committee of the person and/or a committee of the property for a person "incompetent to manage himself or his affairs." N.Y. MENTAL HYGIENE LAW § 100 (McKinney 1971).

* This is a situation in which the ontological problems discussed in note p. 6 *supra* become acute. One can conceive a situation in which a guardian would be appointed by a county court with respect to a stream, bring a suit against alleged polluters, and lose. Suppose now that a federal court were to appoint a guardian with respect to the large river system of which the stream were a part, and that the federally appointed guardian subsequently were to bring suit against the same defendants in state court, now on behalf of the river, rather than the stream. (Is it possible to bring a still subsequent suit, if the one above fails, on behalf of the entire hydrologic cycle, by a guardian appointed by an international court?)

While such problems are difficult, they are not impossible to solve. For one thing, pre-trial hearings and rights of intervention can go far toward their amelioration. Further, courts have been dealing with the matter of potentially inconsistent judgments for years, as when one state appears on the verge of handing down a divorce decree inconsistent with the judgment of another state's courts. Kempson v. Kempson, 58 N.J. Eg. 94, 43 A. 97 (Ch. Ct. 1899). Courts could, and of course would, retain such natural objects in the res nullius classification to help stave off the problem. Then, too, where (as is always the case) several "objects" are interrelated, several guardians could all be involved, with procedures for removal to the appropriate court- probably that of the guardian of the most encompassing "ward" to be acutely threatened. And in some cases subsequent suit by the guardian of more encompassing ward, not guilty of laches, might be appropriate. The problems are at least no more complex than the corresponding problems that the law has dealt with for years in the class action area.

** CAL. PROB. CODE § 1460 (West Supp. 1971). The N.Y. MENTAL HYGIENE LAW (McKinney 1971) provides for jurisdiction "over the custody of a person and his property if he is incompetent to manage himself or his affairs by reason of age, drunkenness, mental illness or other cause. . ."

† In re Byrn, L.A. Times, Dec. 5, 1971, § 1, at 16, col, 1. A preliminary injunction was subsequently granted, and defendant's cross-motion to vacate the guardianship was denied. Civ. 13113/71 (Sup. Ct. Queens Co., Jan. 4, 1972) (Smith, J.). Appeals are pending. Granting a guardianship in these circumstances would seem to be a more

should fail, special environmental legislation could be enacted along traditional guardianship lines. Such provisions could provide for guardianship both in the instance of public natural objects and also, perhaps with slightly different standards, in the instance of natural objects on "private" land.*

The potential "friends" that such a statutory scheme would require will hardly be lacking. The Sierra Club, Environmental Defense Fund, Friends of the Earth, Natural Resources Defense Counsel, and the Izaak Walton League are just some of the many groups which have manifested unflagging dedication to the environment and which are becoming increasingly capable of marshalling the requisite technical experts and lawyers. If, for example, the Environmental Defense Fund should have reason to believe that some company's strip mining operation might be irreparably destroying the ecological balance of large tracts of land, it could, under this procedure, apply to the court in which the lands were situated to be appointed guardian.** As guardian, it might be given rights of inspection (or visitation) to determine and bring to the court's attention a fuller finding on the land's condition. If there were indications that under the substantive law some redress might be available on the land's behalf, then the guardian would be entitled to raise the land's right in the land's name, *i.e.,* without having to make the roundabout and often unavailing demonstration, discussed below, that the "rights" of the club's members were being invaded. Guardians would also be looked to for a host of other protective tasks, *e.g.,* monitoring effluents (and/or monitoring the monitors), and representing their "wards" at legislative and administrative hearings on such matters as the setting of state water quality standards. Procedures

---

radical advance in the law than granting a guardianship over communal natural objects like lakes. In the former case there is a traditionally recognized guardian for the object- the mother-and her decision has been in favor of aborting the foetus.

* The laws regarding the various communal resources had to develop along their own lines, not only because so many different persons' "rights" to consumption and usage were continually and contemporaneously involved, but also because no one had to bear the costs of his consumption of public resources in the way in which the owner of resources on private land has to bear the costs of what he does. For example, if the landowner strips his land of trees, and puts nothing in their stead, he confronts the costs of what he has done in the form of reduced value of his land; but the river polluter's actions are costless, so far as he is concerned- except insofar as the legal system can somehow force him to internalize them. The result has been that the private landowner's power over natural objects on his land is far less restrained by law (as opposed to economics) than his power over the public resources that he can get his hands on. If this state of affairs is to be changed, the standard for interceding in the interests of natural objects on traditionally recognized "private" land might well parallel the rules that guide courts in the matter of people's children whose upbringing (or lack thereof) poses social threat. The courts can, for example, make a child "a dependent of the court" where the child's "home is an unfit place for him by reason of neglect, cruelty, or depravity of either of his parents. . ." CAL. WELF. & INST. CODE § 600(b) (West 1966). See also id at § 601: any child "who from any cause is in danger of leading an idle, dissolute, lewd, or immoral life [may be adjudged] a ward of the court."

** The present way of handling such problems on "private" property is to try to enact legislation of general application under the police power, see Pennsylvania Coal Co. V Mahon, 260 U.S. 393 (1922), rather than to institute civil litigation which, though a piecemeal process, can be tailored to individual situations.

exist, and can be strengthened, to move a court for the removal and substitution of guardians, for conflicts of interest or for other reasons,[*] as well as for the termination of the guardianship.[21]

In point of fact, there is a movement in the law toward giving the environment the benefits of standing, although not in a manner as satisfactory as the guardianship approach. What I am referring to is the marked liberalization of traditional standing requirements in recent cases in which environmental action groups have challenged federal government action. *Scenic Hudson Preservation Conference v. FPC*[22] is a good example of this development. There, the Federal Power Commission had granted New York's Consolidated Edison a license to construct a hydroelectric project on the Hudson River at Storm King Mountain. The grant of license had been opposed by conservation interests on the grounds that the transmission lines would be unsightly, fish would be destroyed, and nature trails would be inundated. Two of these conservation groups, united under the name Scenic Hudson Preservation Conference, petitioned the Second Circuit to set aside the grant. Despite the claim that Scenic Hudson had no standing because it had not made the traditional claim "of any personal economic injury resulting from the Commission's actions,"[23] the petitions were heard, and the case sent back to the Commission. On the standing point, the court noted that Section 313(b) of the Federal Power Act gave a right of instituting review to any party "aggrieved by an order issued by the Commission;"[24] it thereupon read "aggrieved by" as not limited to those alleging the traditional personal economic injury, but as broad enough to include "those who by their activities and conduct have exhibited a special interest" in the aesthetic, conservational, and recreational aspects of power development. . . . "[**] A similar reasoning has swayed other circuits to allow proposed actions by the Federal Power Commission, the Department of Interior, and the Department of Health, Education and Welfare to be challenged by environmental action groups on the basis of, e.g., recreational and esthetic interests of members, in lieu of direct economic injury.[†] Only the Ninth Circuit has balked, and one of these

---

[*]   CAL. PROB. CODE §1580 (West Supp. 1971) lists specific causes for which a guardian may, after notice and a hearing, be removed.

Despite these protections, the problem of overseeing the guardian is particularly acute where, as here, there are no immediately identifiable human beneficiaries whose self interests will encourage them to keep a close watch on the guardian. To ameliorate this problem, a page might well be borrowed from the law of ordinary charitable trusts, which are commonly placed under the supervision of the Attorney General, See CAL. CORP. CODE §§ 9505, 10207 (West 1955).

[**]   354 F.2d 608, 616 (2d Cir. 1965). The court might have felt that because the New York-New Jersey Trail Conference, one of the two conservation groups that organized Scenic Hudson, had some 17 miles of trailways in the area of Storm King Mountain, it therefore had sufficient economic interest to establish standing: Judge Hays' opinion does not seem to so rely, however.

[†]   Road Review League v. Boyd, 270 F. Supp. 650 (S.D.N.Y. 1967). Plaintiffs who included the Town of Bedford and the Road Review League, a non-profit association concerned with community problems, brought an action to review and set aside a determination of the Federal Highway Administrator concerning the alignment of an

cases, involving the Sierra Club's attempt to challenge a Walt Disney development in the Sequoia National Forest, is at the time of this writing awaiting decision by the United States Supreme Court.[*]

Even if the Supreme Court should reverse the Ninth Circuit in the Walt Disney-Sequoia National Forest matter, thereby encouraging the circuits to continue their trend toward liberalized standing in this area, there are significant reasons to press for the guardianship approach notwithstanding. For one thing, the cases of this sort have extended standing on the basis of interpretations of specific federal statutes—the Federal Power Commission Act,[25] the Administrative Procedure Act,[26] the Federal Insecticide, Fungicide and Rodenticide Act, and others. Such a basis supports environmental suits only where acts of federal acts of federal agencies are involved; and even there, perhaps, only when there is some special statutory language, such as "aggrieved by" in the Federal Power Act, on which the action groups can rely. Witness for

---

interstate highway. Plaintiffs claimed that the proposed road would have an adverse effect upon local wildlife sanctuaries, pollute a local lake, and be inconsistent with local needs and planning. Plaintiffs relied upon the section of the Administrative Procedure Act, 5 U.S.C. § 702 (1970), which entitles persons "aggrieved by agency action within the meaning of a relevant stature" to obtain judicial review. The court held that plaintiffs had standing to obtain judicial review of proposed alignment of the road:

> I see no reason why the world "aggrieved" should have different meaning in the Administrative Procedure Act from the meaning given it under the Federal Power Act. . . . The "relevant statute," *i.e.,* the Federal Highways Act, contains language which seems even stronger than that of the Federal Power Act, as far as local and conservation interests are concerned.

Id. at 661.

In Citizens Comm. for the Hudson Valley v. Volpe, 425 F.2d 97 (2d Cir. 1970), plaintiffs were held to have standing to challenge the construction of a dike and causeway adjacent to the Hudson Valley. The Sierra Club and the Village of Tarrytown based their challenge upon the provisions of the Rivers and Harbors Act of 1899. While the Rivers and Harbors Act does not provide for judicial review as does the Federal Power Act, the court stated that the plaintiffs were "aggrieved" under the Department of Transportation Act, the Hudson River Basin Compact Act, and a regulation under which the Corps of Engineers issued a permit, all of which contain broad provisions mentioning recreational and environmental resources and the need to preserve the same. Citing the *Road Review League* decision, the court held that as "aggrieved" parties under the Administrative Procedure Act, plaintiffs similarly had standing. Other decisions in which the court's grant of standing was based upon the Administrative Procedure Act include: West Virginia Highlands Conservancy v. Island Creek Coal Co., 441 F.2d 231 (4th Cir. 1971); Environmental Defense Fund, Inc. v. Hardin, 428 F.2d 1093 (D.C. Cir. 1970); Allen v. Hickel, 424 F.2d 944 (D.C. Cir. 1970); Brooks v. Volpe, 329 F. Supp. 118 (W.D. Wash. 1971); Delaware v. Pennsylvania N.Y. Cent. Transp. Co., 323 F. Supp. 487 (D. Del. 1971); Izaak Walton League of America v. St. Clair, 313 F. Supp. 1312 (D. Minn. 1970); Pennsylvania Environmental Council, Inc. v. Bartlett, 315 F. Supp. 238 (M.D. Pa. 1970).

[*] Sierra Club v. Hickel, 433 F.2d 24 (9th Cir. 1970), *cert. granted sub nom.* Sierra Club v. Morton, 401 U.S. 907 (1971) (No. 70-34). The Sierra Club, a non-profit California corporation concerned with environmental protection, claimed that its interest in the conservation and sound management of natural parks would be adversely affected by an Interior permit allowing Walt Disney to construct the Mineral King Resort in Sequoia National Forest. The court held that because of the Sierra Club's failure to assert a direct legal interest, that organization lacked standing to sue. The court stated that the Sierra Club had claimed an interest only in the sense that the proposed course of action was displeasing to its members. The court purported to distinguish *Scenic Hudson* on the grounds that the plaintiff's claim of standing there was supported by the "aggrieved party" language of the Federal Power Act.

example, *Bass Angler Sportsman Society v. United States Steel Corp.*[28] There, plaintiffs sued 175 corporate defendants located throughout Alabama, relying on 33 U.S.C. § 407 (1970), which provides:

> It shall not be lawful to throw, discharge, or deposit . . . any refuse matter . . . into any navigable water of the United States, or into any tributary of any navigable water from which the same shall float or be washed into such navigable water . . .[29]

Another section of the Act provides that one-half the fines shall be paid to the person or persons giving information which shall lead to a conviction.[*] Relying on this latter provision, the plaintiff designated his action a *qui tam* action[**] and sought to enforce the Act by injunction and fine. The District Court ruled that, in the absence of express language to the contrary, no one outside the Department of Justice had standing to sue under a criminal act and refused to reach the question of whether violations were occurring.[†]

Unlike the liberalized standing approach, the guardianship approach would secure an effective voice for the environment even where federal administrative action and public lands and waters were not involved. It would also allay one of the fears courts—such as the Ninth Circuit—have about the extended standing concept: if any ad hoc group can spring up overnight, invoke some "right" as universally claimable as the esthetic and recreational interests of its members and thereby get into court, how can a flood of litigation be prevented?[††] If an ad hoc committee loses a suit brought *sub*

---

[*]   33 U.S.C. § 411 (1970) reads:
"Every person and every corporation that shall violate, or that shall knowingly aid, abet, authorize, or instigate a violation of the provisions of sections 407, 408, and 409 of the title shall . . . be punished by a fine . . . or by imprisonment . . . in the discretion of the court, one-half of said fine to be paid to the person or persons giving information which shall lead to conviction."

[**] This is from the latin, "who brings the action as well for the King as for himself," referring to an action brought by a citizen for the state as well as for himself.

[†]   "These sections create a criminal liability. No civil action lies to enforce it: criminal statutes can only be enforced by the government. A qui tam action lies only when expressly or impliedly authorized by statute to enforce a penalty by civil action, not a criminal fine."

324 F. Supp. 412, 415-16 (N.D., M.D. & S.D. Ala. 1970). Other *qui tam* actions brought by the Bass Angler Sportsman Society have ben similarly unsuccessful. See Bass Anglers Sportsman Soc'y of America v. Scholze Tannery, 329 F. Supp. 339 (E.D. Tenn. 1971): Bass Anglers Sportsman's Soc'y of America v. United States Plywood Champion Papers. Inc., 324 F. Supp. 302 (S.D. Tex. 1971).

[††] Concern over an anticipated flood of litigation initiated by environmental organizations is evident in Judge Trask's opinion in Alameda Conservation Ass'n v. California, 437 F.2d 1087 (9th Cir.), *cert. denied*, Leslie Salt Co.v. Alameda Conservation Ass'n, 402 U.S. 908 (1971), where a non-profit corporation having as a primary purpose protection of the public's interest in San Francisco Bay was denied standing to seek an injunction prohibiting a land exchange that would allegedly destroy wildlife, fisheries and the Bay's unique flushing characteristics:

nom. Committee to Preserve our Trees, what happens when its very same members reorganize two years later and sue *sub nom.* The Massapequa Sylvan Protection League? Is the new group bound by res judicata? Class action law may be capable of ameliorating some of the more obvious problems. But even so, court economy might be better served designating the guardian de jure representative of the natural object, with rights of discretionary intervention by others, but with the understanding that the natural object is "bound" by an adverse judgment.[30] The guardian concept, too, would provide the endangered natural object with what the trustee in bankruptcy provides the endangered corporation: a continuous supervision over a period of time, with a consequent deeper understanding of a broad range of the ward's problems, not just the problems present in one particular piece of litigation. It would thus assure the courts that the plaintiff has the expertise and genuine adversity in pressing a claim which are the prerequisites of a true "case or controversy."

The guardianship approach, however, is apt to raise two objections, neither of which seems to me to have much force. The first is that a committee or guardian could not judge the needs of the river or forest in its charge; indeed, the very concept of "needs," it might be said, could be used here only in the most metaphorical way. The second objection is that such a system would not be much different from what we now have: is not the Department of Interior already such a guardian for public lands, and do not most states have legislation empowering their attorneys general to seek relief—in a sort of *parens patriae* way—for such injuries as a guardian might concern himself with?

As for the first objection, natural objects can communicate their wants (needs) to us, and in ways that are not terribly ambiguous. I am sure I can judge with more certainty and meaningfulness whether and when my lawn wants (needs) water, than the Attorney General can judge whether and when the United States wants (needs) to take an appeal from an adverse judgement by a lower court. The lawn tells me that it wants water by a certain dryness of the blades and soil—immediately obvious to the touch—the appearance of bald spots, yellowing, and a lack of springiness after being walked on; how does "the United States" communicate to the Attorney General? For similar reasons, the guardian-attorney for a smog-endangered stand of pines could venture

---

"Standing is not established by suit initiated by this association simply because it has as one of its purposes the protection of the "public interest" in the waters of the San Francisco Bay. However well intentioned members may be, they may not be uniting create for themselves a super-administrative agency or a parans patriae official status with the capability of over-seeing and of challenging the action of the appointed and elected officials of the state government. Although recent decisions have considerably broadened the concept of standing, we do not find that they go this far. [Citation.]

Were it otherwise the various clubs, political, economic and social now or yet to be organized, could wreak havoc with the administration of government, both federal and state. There are other forums where their voices and their views may be effectively presented, but to have standing to submit a "case or controversy" to a federal court, something more must be shown."

437 F.2d at 1090.

with more confidence that his client wants the smog stopped, than the directors of a corporation can assert that "the corporation" wants dividends declared. We make decisions on behalf of, and in the purported interest of, others every day; these "others" are often creatures whose wants are far less verifiable, and even far more metaphysical in conception, than the wants of rivers, trees, and land.[*]

As for the second objection, one can indeed find evidence that the Department of Interior was conceived as a sort of guardian of the public lands.[31] But there are two points to keep in mind. First, insofar as the Department already is an adequate guardian it is only with respect to the federal public lands as per Article IV, section 3 of the Constitution.[**] Its guardianship includes neither local public lands nor private lands. Second, to judge from the environmentalist literature and from the cases environmental action groups have been bringing, the Department is itself one of the bogeys of the environmental movement. (One thinks of the uneasy peace between the Indians and the Bureau of Indian Affairs.) Whether the various charges be right or wrong, one cannot help but observe that the Department has been charged with several institutional goals (never an easy burden), and is currently looked to for action by quite a variety of interest groups, only one of which is the environmentalists. In this context, a guardian outside the institution becomes especially valuable. Besides, what a person wants, fully to secure his rights, is the ability to retain independent counsel even when, and perhaps especially when, the government is acting "for him" in a beneficent way. I have no reason to doubt, for example, that the Social Security System is being managed "for me"; but I would not want to abdicate my right to challenge its actions as they affect me, should the need arise.[32] I would not ask more trust of national forests, vis-à-vis the Department of Interior. The same considerations apply in the instance of local agencies, such as regional water pollution boards, whose members' expertise in pollution matters is often all too credible.[†]

---

[*]   Here, too, we are dogged by the ontological problem discussed on p. 6 *supra*. It is easier to say that the smog-endangered stand of pines "wants" the smog stopped (assuming that to be a jurally significant entity) then it is to venture that the mountain, or the planet earth, or the cosmos, is concerned about whether the pines stand or fall. The more encompassing the entity of concern, the less certain we can be in venturing judgments as to the "wants" of any particular substance, quality, or species within the universe. Does the cosmos care if we humans persist or not? "Heaven and earth . . . regard all things as insignificant, as though they were playthings made of straw." LAO-TZU, TAO TEH KING 13 (D. Goddard transl. 1919).

[**]   Clause 2 gives Congress the power "to dispose of and make all needful Rules and Regulations respecting the Territory or other Property belonging to the United States."

[†]   *See* the L.A. Times editorial *Water: Public vs. Polluters* criticizing:

   ". . . the ridiculous built-in conflict of interests on Regional Water Quality Control Board. By law, five of the seven seats are given to spokesmen for industrial, governmental, agricultural or utility users. Only one representative of the public at large is authorized, along with a delegate from fish and game interests."

   Feb. 12, 1969, Part II, at 8. cols. 1-2.

The objection regarding the availability of attorneys-general as protectors of the environment within the existing structure is somewhat the same. Their statutory powers are limited and sometimes unclear. As political creatures, they must exercise the discretion they have with an eye toward advancing and reconciling a broad variety of important social goals, form preserving morality to increasing their jurisdiction's tax base. The present state of our environment, and the history of cautious application and development of environmental protection laws long on the books,[33] testifies that the burdens of any attorney-general's broad responsibility have apparently not left much manpower for the protection of nature. *(Cf. Bass Anglers,* above.) No doubt, strengthening interest in the environment will increase the zest of public attorneys even where, as will often be the case, well-represented corporate pollutors are the quarry. Indeed, the United States Attorney General has stepped up anti-pollution activity, and ought to be further encouraged in this direction.[34] The statutory powers of the attorneys-general should be enlarged, and they should be armed with criminal penalties made at least commensurate with the likely economic benefits of violating the law.* On the other hand, one cannot ignore the fact that there is increased pressure on public law-enforcement offices to give more attention to a host of other problems, from crime "on the streets" (why don't we say "in the rivers"?) to consumerism and school bussing. If the environment is not to get lost in the shuffle, we would do well, I think, to adopt the guardianship approach as an additional safeguard, conceptualizing major natural objects as holders of their own rights, raisable by the court-appointed guardian.

Toward Recognition of Its Own Injuries

As far as adjudicating the merits of a controversy is concerned, there is also a good case to be made for taking into account harm to the environment–in its own right. As indicated above, the traditional way of deciding whether to issue injunctions in law suits affecting the environment, at least where communal property is involved, has been to strike some sort of balance regarding the economic hardships on *human beings.* Even recently, Mr. Justice Douglas, our jurist most closely associated with conservation sympathies in his private life, was deciding the propriety of a new dam on the basis of, among other things, anticipated lost profits from fish catches, some $12,000,000 annually.** Although he decided to delay the project pending further findings, the reasoning seems unnecessarily incomplete and compromising. Why should the envi-

---

*   To be effective as a deterrent, the sanction ought to be high enough to bring about an internal reorganization of the corporate structure which minimizes the chances of future violations. Because the corporation is not necessarily a profit-maximizing "rationally economic man," there is no reason to believe that setting the fine as high as–but not higher than–anticipated profits from the violation of the law, will bring the illegal behavior to an end.

** Udall v. FPC, 387 U.S. 428, 437 n.6 (1967). See also Holmes, J. in New Jersey v. New York, 283 U.S. 336, 342 (1931): "A river is more than an amenity, it is a treasure. It offers a necessity of life that must be rationed among

ronment be of importance only indirectly, as lost profits to someone else? Why not throw into the balance the cost *to the environment?*

The argument for "personifying" the environment, from the point of damage calculations, can best be demonstrated from the welfare economics position. Every well-working legal-economic system should be so structured as to confront each of us with the full costs that our activities are imposing on society.* Ideally, a paper-mill, in deciding what to produce–and where, and by what methods–ought to be forced to take into account not only the lumber, acid and labor that its production "takes" from other uses in the society, but also what costs alternative production plans will impose on society through pollution. The legal system, through the law of contracts and the criminal law, for example, makes the mill confront the costs of the first group of demands. When for example, the company's purchasing agent orders 1000 drums of acid from the Z Company, the Z Company can bind the mill to pay for them, and thereby reimburse the society for what the mill is removing from alternative uses.

Unfortunately, so far as the pollution costs are concerned, the allocative ideal begins to break down, because the traditional legal institutions have a more difficult time "catching" and confronting us with the full social costs of our activities. In the lakeside mill example, major riparian interests might bring an action, forcing a court to weigh their aggregate losses against the costs to the mill of installing the anti-pollution device. But many other interests–and I am speaking for the moment of recognized homocentric interests–are too fragmented and perhaps "too remote" causally to warrant securing representation and pressing for recovery: the people who own summer homes and motels, the man who sells fishing tackle and bait, the man who rents rowboats. There is no reason not to allow the lake to prove damages to them as the prima facie measure of damages to it. *By doing so, we in effect make the natural object, through its guardian, a jural entity competent to gather up these fragmented and otherwise unrepresented damage claims, and press them before the court even where, for legal or practical reasons, they are not going to be pressed by traditional class action plaintiffs.*** Indeed, one way–the homocentric way–to view what I am proposing so far, is to view the guardian of the natural

---

those who have power over it."

* To simplify the description, I am using here an ordinary language sense of causality, *i.e.,* assuming that the pollution causes harm to the river. As Professor Coase has pointed out in *The Problem of Social Cost,* 3 J. LAW & ECON. 1 (1960), harm-causing can be viewed as a reciprocal problem, *i.e.,* in the terms of the text, the mill wants to harm the river, and the river–if we assume it "wants" to maintain its present environment quality–"wants" to harm the mill. Coase rightly points out that at least in theory (if we had the data) we ought to be comparing the alternative social product of different social arrangements, and not simply imposing full costs on the party who would popularly be identified as the harm-causer.

** I am assuming that one of the considerations that goes into a judgment of "remoteness" is a desire to discourage burdensome amounts of petty litigation. This is one of the reasons why a court would be inclined to say–to use the example in the text–that the man who sells fishing tackle and bait has not been "proximately" injured by the polluter. Using proximate cause in this manner, the courts can protect themselves from a flood of litigation. But once the guardian were in court anyway, this consideration would not obtain as strongly, and courts might be more inclined to allow proof on the damages to remotely injured humans (although the proof itself is an

object as the guardian of unborn generations, as well as of the otherwise unrepresented, but distantly injured, contemporary humans.[35] By making the lake itself the focus of these damages, and "incorporating" it so to speak, the legal system can effectively take proof upon, and confront the mill with, a larger and more representative measure of the damages its pollution causes.

So far, I do not suppose that my economist friends (unremittent human chauvinists, every one of them!) will have any large quarrel in principle with the concept. Many will view it as a *trompe l'oeil* that comes down, at best, to effectuate the goals of the paragon class action, or the paragon water pollution control district. Where we are apt to part company is here–I propose going beyond gathering up the loose ends of what most people would presently recognize as economically valid damages. The guardian would urge before the court injuries not presently cognizable—the death of eagles and inedible crabs, the suffering of sea lions, the loss from the face of the earth of species of commercially valueless birds, the disappearance of a wilderness area. One might, of course, speak of the damages involved as "damages" to us humans, and indeed, the widespread growth of environmental groups shows that human beings do feel these losses. But they are not, at present, economically measurable losses: how can they have a monetary value for the guardian to prove in court?

The answer for me is simple. Wherever it carves out "property" rights, the legal system is engaged in the process of *creating* monetary worth. One's literary works would have minimal monetary value if anyone could copy them at will. Their economic value to the author is a product of the law of copyright; the person who copies a copyrighted book has to bear a cost to the copyright-holder because the law says he must. Similarly, it is through the law of torts that we have made a "right" of—and guaranteed an economically meaningful value to—privacy. (The value we place on gold—a yellow inanimate dirt—is not simply a function of supply and demand—wilderness areas are scarce and pretty too—but results from the actions of the legal systems of the world, which have institutionalized that value; they have even done a remarkable job of stabilizing the price). I am proposing we do the same with eagles and wilderness areas as we do with copyrighted works, patented inventions, and privacy: *make* the violation of rights in them to be a cost by declaring the "pirating" of them to be the invasion of a property interest.[*] If we do so, the net social costs the polluter would be confronted with would include not only the extended homocentric costs of his pollution (explained above) but also to the environment *per se*.

How, though, would these costs be calculated? When we protect an invention, we can at least speak of a fair market value for it, by reference to which damages can be

---

added burden of sorts).

[*]   Of course, in the instance of copyright and patient protection, the creation of the "property right" can be more
        directly justified on homocentric grounds.

computed. But the lost environmental "values" of which we are now speaking are by definition over and above those that the market is prepared to bid for: they are priceless.

One possible measure of damages, suggested earlier, would be the cost of making the environment whole, just as, when a man is injured in an automobile accident, we impose upon the responsible party the injured man's medical expenses. Comparable expenses to a polluted river would be the costs of dredging, restocking with fish, and so forth. It is on the basis of such costs as these, I assume, that we get the figure of $1 billion as the cost of saving Lake Erie.[36] As an ideal, I think this is a good guide applicable in many environmental situations. It is by no means free from difficulties, however.

One problem with computing damages on the basis of making the environment whole is that, if understood most literally, it is tantamount to asking for a "freeze" on environmental quality, even at the costs (and there will be costs) of preserving "useless" objects.[*] Such a "freeze" is not inconceivable to me as a general goal, especially considering that, even by the most immediately discernible homocentric interests, in so many areas we ought to be cleaning up and not merely preserving the environmental status quo. In fact, there is presently strong sentiment in the Congress for a total elimination of all river pollutants by 1985,[37] notwithstanding that such a decision would impose quite large direct and indirect costs on us all. Here one is inclined to recall the instructions of Judge Hays, in remanding Consolidated Edison's Storm King application to the Federal Power Commission in *Scenic Hudson*:

> The Commission's renewed proceedings must include as a basic concern
> the preservation of natural beauty and of natural historic shrines, keeping
> in mind that, in our affluent society, the cost of a project is only one of
> several factors to be considered.[38]

Nevertheless, whatever the merits of such a goal in principle, there are many cases in which the social price tag of putting it into effect are going to seem too high to accept. Consider, for example, an oceanside nuclear generator that could produce low cost electricity for a million homes at a savings of $1 a year per home, spare us the air pollution that comes from burning fossil fuels, but which through a slight heating effect threatened to kill off a rare species of temperature-sensitive sea urchins; suppose further that technological improvements adequate to reduce the temperature to present environmental quality would expand the entire one million dollars in anticipated fuel savings. Are we prepared to tax ourselves $1,000,000 a year on behalf of the sea

---

[*]   One ought to observe, too, that in terms of real effect on marginal welfare, the poor quite possibly will bear
         the brunt of the compromises. They may lack the wherewithal to get out to the countryside—and probably want
         an increase in material goods more acutely than those who now have riches.

urchins? In comparable problems under the present law of damages, we work out practicable compromises by abandoning restoration coats and calling upon fair market value. For example, if an automobile is so severely damaged that the cost of bringing the car to its original state by repair is greater than the fair market value, we would allow the responsible tortfeasor to pay the fair market value only. Or if a human being suffers the loss of an arm (as we might conceive of the ocean having irreparably lost the sea urchins), we can fall back on the capitalization of reduced earning power (and pain and suffering) to measure the damages. But what is the fair market value of sea urchins? How can we capitalize their loss to the ocean, independent of any commercial value they may have to someone else?

One answer is that the problem can sometimes be sidestepped quite satisfactorily, In the sea urchin example, one compromise solution would be to impose on the nuclear generator the costs of making the ocean whole somewhere else, in some other way, e.g., reestablishing a sea urchin colony elsewhere, or making a somehow comparable contribution.* In debate over the laying of the trans-Alaskan pipeline the builders are apparently prepared to meet conservationists' objections half-way by reestablishing wildlife away from the pipeline, so far as is feasible.[39]

But even if damage calculations have to be made, one ought to recognize that the measurement of damages is rarely a simple report of economic facts about "the market," whether we are valuing the loss of a foot, a foetus, or a work of fine art. Decisions of this sort are always hard, but not impossible. We have increasingly taken (human) pain and suffering into account in reckoning damages, not because we think we can ascertain them as objective "facts" about the universe, but because, even in view of all the room for disagreement, we come up with a better society by making rude estimates of them than by ignoring them.**We can make such estimates in regard

---

* Again, there is a problem involving what we conceive to be the injured entity.

** Courts have not been reluctant to award damages for the destruction of heirlooms, literary manuscripts or other property having ascertainable market value. In Willard v. Valley Gas Fuel Co., 171 Cal. 9 151 Pac. 286 (1915), it was held that the measure of damages for the negligent destruction of a rare old book written by one of plaintiff's ancestors was the amount which would compensate the owner for all detriment including sentimental loss proximately caused by such destruction. The court, at 171 Cal. 15, 151 Pac. 289, quoted approvingly from Southern Express Co. v. Owens, 146 Ala. 412, 426, 41 S. 752, 755 (1906):

"Ordinarily, where property has a market value that can be shown, such value is the criterion by which actual damages for its destruction or loss may be fixed. But it may be that property destroyed or lost has no market value. In such state of the case, while it may be that no rule which will be absolutely certain to do justice between the parties can be laid down, it does not follow from this, nor is it the law, that the plaintiff must be turned out of court with normal damages merely. Where the article or thing is so unusual in its character that market value cannot be predicated of it, its value, or plaintiff's damages, must be ascertained in some other rational way and from such elements as are attainable."

Similarly, courts award damages in wrongful death actions despite the impossibility of precisely appraising the damages in such cases. In affirming a judgment in favor of the administrator of the estate of a child killed by defendant's automobile, the Oregon Supreme Court, in Lane v. Hatfield, 173 Or. 79, 88-89, 143 P.2d 230, 234 (1943), acknowledged the speculative nature of the measure of damages:

to environmental losses fully aware that what we are doing is making implicit normative judgements (as with pain and suffering)–laying down rules as to what the society
is going to "value" rather than reporting market evaluations. In making such normative
estimates decision-makers would not go wrong if they estimated on the "high side,"
putting the burden of trimming the figure down on the immediate human interests
present. All burdens of proof should reflect common experience; our experience in
environmental matters has been a continual discovery that our acts have caused more
long-range damage than we were able to appreciate at the outset.

To what extent the decision-maker should factor in costs such as the pain and
suffering of animals and other sentient natural objects, I cannot say; although I am
prepared to do so in principle.* Given, in all events, the conjectural nature of the
"estimates" and the roughness of the "balance of conveniences" procedure where that
is involved, the practice would be of more interest from the socio-psychic point of
view, discussed below, than from the legal-operational.

Toward Being a Beneficiary in Its Own Right

As suggested above, one reason for making the environment itself the beneficiary of a
judgement is to prevent it from being "sold out" in a negotiation among private
litigants who agree not to enforce rights that have been established among themselves.[40] Protection from this will be advanced by making the natural object a party to
an injunctive settlement. Even more importantly, we should make it a beneficiary of
money awards. If in making the balance requisite to issuing an injunction, a court
decides not to enjoin a lake polluter who is causing injury to the extent of $50,000
annually, then the owners and the lake ought both to be awarded damages. The natural
object's portion could be put into a trust fund to be administered by the object's

---

"No one knows or can know when, if at all, a seven year old girl will attain her majority, for her marriage may
take place before she has become twenty-one years of age. . . . Moreover, there is much uncertainty with respect
to the length of time anyone may live. A similar uncertainty veils the future of a minor's earning capacity or
habit of saving. Illness or a non-fatal accident may reduce an otherwise valuable and lucrative life to a burden
and liability.

The rule, that the measure of recovery by a personal representative for the wrongful death of his decedent is
the value of the life of such decedent, if he had not come to such an untimely end, has been termed vague,
uncertain and speculative if not, conjectural. It is, however, the best that judicial wisdom has been able to
formulate."

*   It is not easy to dismiss the idea of "lower" life having consciousness and feeling pain, especially since it is so
difficult to know what these terms mean even as applied to humans. *See* Austin, *Other Minds, in Logic and Language*
342 (S. Flew ed. 1965); Schopenhauer, *On the Will in Nature*, in TWO ESSAYS BY ARTHUR SCHOPENHAUER 193,
281-304 (1889). Some experiments on plant sensitivity–of varying degrees of extravagance in their
claims–include Lawrence, *Plants Have Feelings, Too . . .* ,ORGANIC GARDENING & FARMING 64 (April 1971);
Woodlief, Royster & Huang, *Effect of Random Noise on Planet Growth* 46 J. ACOUSTICAL SOC. AM. 481 (1969);
Backster, *Evidence of a Primary Perception in Plant Life*, 10 INT'L J. PARAPSYCHOLOGY 25 (1968).

guardian, as per the guardianship recommendation set forth above. So far as the damages are proved, as suggested in the previous section, by allowing the natural object to cumulate damages to others as prima facie evidence of damages to it, there will, of course, be problems of distribution. But even if the object is simply construed as representing a class of plaintiffs under the applicable civil rules,[41] there is often likely to be a sizeable amount of recovery attributable to members of the class who will not put in a claim for distribution (because their pro rata share would be so small, or because of their interest in the environment). Not only should damages go into these funds, but where criminal fines are applied (as against water polluters) it seems to me that the monies (less prosecutorial expenses, perhaps) ought sensibly to go to the fund raiser than to the general treasuries. Guardians fees, including legal fees, would than come out of this fund. More importantly, the fund would be available to preserve the natural object as closely as possible to its condition at the time the environment was made a rights-holder.*

The idea of assessing damages as best we can and placing them in a trust fund is far more realistic than a hope that a total "freeze" can be put on the environment status quo. Nature is a continuous theatre in which things and species (eventually man) are destined to enter and exit.** In the meantime, co-existence of man and his environment means that *each* is going to have to compromise for the better of both. Some pollution of streams, for example, will probably be inevitable for some time. Instead of setting an unrealizable goal of enjoining absolutely the discharge of all such pollutants, the trust fund concept would (a) help assure that pollution would occur only in those instances where the social need for the pollutant's product (via his present method of production) was so high as to enable the polluter to cover all homocentric costs, plus some estimated costs to the environment *per se,* and (b) would be a corpus for preserving monies, if necessary, until the feasible technology was developed. Such a fund might even finance the requisite research and development.

(Incidentally, if "rights" are to be granted to the environment, then for many of the same reasons it might bear "liabilities" as well—as inanimate objects did anciently.†

---

*   This is an ideal, of course—like the ideal that no human being ought to interfere with any other human being. *See Dyke, Freedom, Consent and the Costs of Interaction,* and Stone, *Comment,* in IS LAW DEAD? 134-67 (E. Rostow ed. 1971). Some damages would inevitably be *damnum absque injuria.* See note 93 *supra.*

**   The inevitability of some form of evolution is not inconsistent with the establishment of a legal system that attempts to interfere with or ameliorate the process: is the same not true of the human law we now have. *e.g.,* the laws against murder?

†   Holmes, *Early Forms of Liability,* in THE COMMON LAW (1881), discussed the liability of animals and inanimate objects in early Greek, early Roman and some later law. Alfred's Laws (A.D. 871-901) provided, for example, that a tree by which a man was killed should "be given to the kindred, and let them have it off the land within 30 nights." Id. at 19. In Edward I's time, if a man fell from a tree the tree was deodand. Id. at 24. Perhaps the liability of non-human matter is, in the history of things, part of a paranoid, defensive phase in man's development; as humans become more abundant, both from the point of material wealth and internally, they may be willing to allow an advance to the stage where non-human matter has rights.

Rivers drown people, and flood over and destroy crops; forests burn, setting fire to contiguous communities. Where trust funds had been established, they could be available for the satisfaction of judgments against the environment, making it bear the costs of some of the harms it imposes on other right holders. In effect, we would be narrowing the claim of Acts of God. The ontological problem would be troublesome here, however, when the Nile overflows, is it the "responsibility" of the river? the mountains? the snow? the hydrologic cycle?)*

Toward Rights in Substance

So far we have been looking at the characteristics of being a *holder of rights*, and exploring some of the implications that making the environment a holder of rights would entail. Natural objects would have standing in their own right, through a guardian; damage to and through them would be ascertained and considered as an independent factor; and they would be the beneficiaries of legal awards. But these considerations only give us the skeleton of what a meaningful rights-holding would involve. To flesh out the "rights" of the environment demands that we provide it with a significant body of rights for it to invoke when it gets to court.

In this regard, the lawyer is constantly aware that a right is not, as the layman may think, some strange substance that one either has or has not. One's life, one's right to vote, one's property, can all be taken away. But those who would infringe on them must go through certain procedures to do so; these procedures are a measure of what we value as a society. Some of the most important questions of "right" thus turn into questions of degree: how much review, and of which sort, will which agencies of state accord us when we claim our "right" is being infringed?

We do not have an absolute right either to our lives or to our driver's licenses. But we have a greater right to our lives because, if even the state wants to deprive us of that "right," there are authoritative bodies that will demand that the state make a very strong showing before it does so, and it will have to justify its actions before a grand jury, petit jury (convincing them "beyond a reasonable doubt"), sentencing jury, and, most likely, levels of appellate courts. The carving out of students "rights" to their education is being made up of this sort of procedural fabric. No one, I think, is maintaining that in no circumstances ought a student to be expelled from school. The battle for student "rights" involves shifting the answers to questions like: before a student is expelled, does he have to be given a hearing; does he have to have prior notice of the hearing, and notice of charges; may he bring counsel, (need the state provide counsel if he cannot?); need there be a transcript; need the school carry the

---

* *See* note p. 6 *supra*. In the event that a person built his house near the edge of a river that flooded, would "assumption of the risk" be available on the river's behalf?

burden of proving the charges; may he confront witnesses; if he is expelled, can he get review by a civil court; if he can get such review, need the school show its actions were "reasonable," or merely "not unreasonable," and so forth?[42]

In this vein, to bring the environment into the society as a rightsholder would not stand it on a better footing than the rest of us mere mortals, who every day suffer injuries that are *damnum absque injuria*. What the environment must look for is that its interests be taken into account in subtler, more procedural ways.

The National Environmental Policy Act is a splendid example of this sort of rights-making through the elaboration of procedural safeguards. Among its many provisions, it establishes that every federal agency must:

> (c) include in every recommendation or report on proposals for legislation and other major Federal actions significantly affecting the quality of the human environment, a detailed statement by the responsible official on–
>
> > (i) environmental impact of the proposed action,
> >
> > (ii) any adverse environmental effects which cannot be avoided should the proposal be implemented,
> >
> > (iii) alternatives to the proposed action,
> >
> > (iv) the relationship between local short-term uses of man's environment and the maintenance and enhancement of long-term productivity, and
> >
> > (v) any irreversible and irretrievable commitments of resources which would be involved in the proposed action should it be implemented.
>
> Prior to making any detailed statement, the responsible Federal official shall consult with and obtain the comments of any Federal agency which has jurisdiction by law or special expertise with respect to any environmental impact involved. Copies of such statement and the comments and views of the appropriate Federal, State, and local agencies, which are authorized to develop and enforce environmental standards, shall be made available to the President, the Council on Environmental Quality and to the public as provided by section 552 of title 5, United States Code, and shall accompany the proposal through the existing agency review processes;
>
> (d) study, develop, and describe appropriate alternatives to recommended courses of action in any proposal which involves unresolved conflicts concerning alternative uses of available resources;

(e) recognize the worldwide and long-range character of environmental problems and, where consistent with the foreign policy of the United States, lend appropriate support to initiatives, resolutions, and programs designed to maximize international cooperation in anticipating and preventing a decline in the quality of mankind's environment;

(f) make available to States, counties, municipalities, institutions, and individuals, advice and information useful in restoring, maintaining, and enhancing the quality of the environment . . . .[43]

These procedural protections have already begun paying off in the courts. For example, it was on the basis of the Federal Power Commission's failure to make adequate inquiry into "alternatives" (as per subsection (iii), in *Scenic Hudson*, and the Atomic Energy Commission's failure to make adequate findings, apparently as per subsections (i) and (ii), in connection with the Amchitka Island underground test explosion,[44] that Federal Courts delayed the implementation of environment-threatening schemes.

Although this sort of control (remanding a cause to an agency for further findings) may seem to the layman ineffectual, or only a stalling of the inevitable, the lawyer and the systems analyst know that these demands for further findings can make a difference. It may encourage the institution whose actions threaten the environment to really *think about* what it is doing, and that is neither an ineffectual nor a small feat. Indeed, I would extend the principle beyond federal agencies. Much of the environment is threatened not by them, but by private corporations. Surely the constitutional power would not be lacking to mandate that all private corporations whose actions may have significant adverse affect on the environment make findings of the sort now mandated for federal agencies. Further, there should be requirements that these findings and reports be channeled to the Board of Directors; if the directors are not charged with the knowledge of what their corporation is doing to the environment, it will be all too easy for lower level management to prevent such reports from getting to a policy-making level. We might make it grounds for a guardian to enjoin a private corporation's actions if such procedures had not been carried out.

The rights of the environment could be enlarged by borrowing yet another page from the Environmental Policy Act and mandating comparable provisions for "private governments." The Act sets up within the Executive Office of the President a Council on Environmental Quality "to be conscious of and responsive to the scientific, economic, social, esthetic, and cultural needs of the Nation; and to formulate and recommend national policies to promote the improvement of the quality of the environment."[45] The Council is to become a focal point, within our biggest "corporation"— the State—to gather and evaluate environmental information which it is to pass on to our chief executive officer, the President. Rather than being ineffectual, this may be a highly sophisticated way to steer organizational behavior. Corporations—especially recidivist polluters and land despoilers—should have to establish comparable internal reorganization, *e.g.*, to set up a Vice-President for Ecological Affairs. The author is not offering this suggestion as a cure-all, by any means. But I do not doubt that this sort of control over internal corporate organization would be an effective supplement to the traditional mechanisms of civil suits, licensing, administrative agencies, and fines.*

Similarly, courts, in making rulings that may affect the environment, should be compelled to make findings with respect to environmental harm—showing how they calculated it and how heavily it was weighed—even in matters outside the present Environmental Protection Act. This would have at least two important consequences. First, it would shift somewhat the focus of court-room testimony and concern; second, the appellate courts, through their review and reversals for "insufficient findings," would give content to, and build up a body of, environmental rights, much as content and body has been given, over the years, to terms like "Due Process of Law."

Beyond these procedural safeguards, would there be any rights of the environment that might be deemed "absolute," at least to the extend of, say, Free Speech? Here, the doctrine of irreparable injury comes to mind. There has long been equitable support for an attorney-general's enjoining injury to communal property if he can prove it to be "irreparable." In other words, while repairable damage to the environment might be balanced and weighed, irreparable damage could be enjoined absolutely. There are several reasons why this doctrine has not been used effectively (witness Lake Erie).** Undoubtedly, political pressures (in the broadest sense) have had an influence. So, too, has the failure of all of us to understand just how delicate the environmental balance is; this failure has made us unaware of how early "irreparable" injury might be occurring, and, if aware, unable to prove it in court. But most important I think, is that the doctrine simply is not practical as a rule of universal application. For one thing, there are too many cases like the sea urchin example above, where the marginal costs of abating the damage seem too clearly to exceed the marginal benefits, even if the damage to the environment itself is liberally estimated. For another, there is a large problem in how one defines "irreparable." Certainly the great bulk of the environment in civilized parts of the world has been injured "irreparably" in the sense of "irreversible"; we are not likely to return it to its medieval

---

* As an indication of what lower-level management is apt to do, *see* Ehrenreich & Ehrenreich, *Conscience of a Steel Worker*, 213 THE NATION 268 (1971). One steel company's "major concession [toward obedience to the 1899 Refuse Act, was to order the workers to confine oil dumping to the night shift. 'During the day the Coast Guard patrols. But at night, the water's black, the oil's black; no one can tell.'" An effective corporation law would assure that the internal information channels within a corporation were capable of forcing such matters to the attention of high-level officials. Even then, there is no guarantee that the law will be obeyed—but we may have improved the odds.

** In the case of Lake Erie, in addition to the considerations that follow in the text, there were possibly additional factors such as that no one polluter's acts could be characterized as inflicting irreparable injury.

quality. Despite the scientific right to the term, judgments concerning "irreparable injury" are going to have to subsume questions both of degree of damage and of value-of the damaged object. Thus, if we are going to revitalize the "irreparable damages" doctrine, and expect it to be taken seriously, we have to recognize that what will be said to constitute "irreparable damage" to the ionosphere, because of its importance to all life, or to the Grand Canyon, because of its uniqueness, is going to rest upon normative judgments that ought to be made explicit.

This suggests that some (relatively) absolute rights be defined for the environment by setting up a constitutional list of "preferred objects," just as some of our Justices feel there are "preferred rights" where humans are concerned.[46] Any threatened injury to these most jealously-to-be-protected objects should be reviewed with the highest level of scrutiny at all levels of government, including our "counter-majoritarian" branch, the court system. Their "Constitutional rights" should be implemented, legislatively and administratively, by, *e.g.*, the setting of environmental quality standards.

I do not doubt that other senses in which the environment might have rights will come to mind, and, as I explain more fully below, would be more apt to come to mind if only we should speak in terms of their having rights, albeit vaguely at first. "Rights" might well lie in unanticipated areas. It would seem, for example, that Chief Justice Warren was only stating the obvious when he observed in *Reynolds v. Sims* that "Legislators represent people, not trees or acres." Yet, could not a case be made for a system of apportionment which *did* take into account the wildlife of an area?* It strikes me as a poor idea that Alaska should have no more congressmen than Rhode Island primarily *because there are in Alaska all those trees and acres, those waterfalls and forests.*** I am not saying anything as silly as that we ought to overrule *Baker v. Carr* and retreat from one man-one vote to a system of one man-or-tree one vote. Nor am I even taking the position that we ought to count each acre, as we once counted each slave, as three-fifths of a man. But I am suggesting that there is nothing unthinkable about, and there might on balance even be a prevailing case to be made for, an electoral apportionment that made some systematic effort to allow for the representative "rights" of non-human life. And if a case can be made for that, which I offer here mainly for purpose of illustration, I suspect that a society that grew concerned enough about the environment to make it a holder of rights would be able to find quite a number of "rights" to have waiting for it when it got to court.

---

* Note that in the discussion that follows I am referring to legislative apportionment, not voting proper.

** In point of fact, there is no reason to suppose that an increase of Congressmen for Alaska would be a benefit to the environment; the reality of the political situation might just as likely result in the election of additional Congressmen with closer ties to oil companies and other developers.

Do We Really Have to Put It That Way?

At this point, one might well ask whether much of what has been written could not have been expressed without introducing the notion of trees, rivers, and so forth "having rights." One could simply and straight-forwardly say, for example, that (R1) "the class of persons competent to challenge the pollution of rivers ought to be extended beyond that of persons who can show an immediate adverse economic impact on themselves," and that (R2), "judges, in weighing competing claims to a wilderness area, ought to think beyond the economic and even esthetic impact on man, and put into the balance a concern for the threatened environment as such." And it is true, indeed, that to say trees and rivers have "rights" is not in itself a stroke of any operational significance—no more that to say "people have rights." To solve any concrete case, one is always forced to more precise and particularized statements, in which the word "right" might just as well be dropped from the elocution.

But this is not the same as to suggest that introducing the notion of the "rights" of trees and rivers would accomplish nothing beyond the introduction of a set of particular rules like (R1) and (R2), above. I think it is quite misleading to say that "*A* has a right to . . ." can be fully explicated in terms of a certain set of specific legal rules, and the manner in which conclusions are drawn from them in a legal system. That is only part of the truth. Introducing the notion of something having a "right" (simply *speaking* that way), brings into the legal system a flexibility and open-endedness that no series of specifically stated legal rules like *R1, R2, R3. . .Rn* can capture. Part of the reason is that "right" (and other so-called "legal terms" like "infant," "corporation," "reasonable time") have meaning—vague but forceful—in the ordinary language, and the force of these meanings, inevitably infused with our thought, becomes part of the context against which the "legal language" of our contemporary "legal rules" is interpreted.[47] Consider, for example, the "rules" that govern the question, on whom, and at what stages of litigation, is the burden of proof going to lie? Professor Krier has demonstrated how terribly significant these decisions are in the trial of environmental cases, and yet, also, how much discretion judges have under them.[*] In the case of such vague rules, it is *context*—senses of direction, of value and purpose—that determines how the rules will be understood, every bit as much as their supposed "plain meaning." In a system which spoke of the environment "having legal rights," judges would, I suspect, be inclined to interpret rules such as those of burden of proof far more liberally from the point of the environment. There is, too, the fact that the

---

[*] Krier, *Environmental Litigation and the Burden of Proof*, in LAW AND THE ENVIRONMENT 105 (M. Baldwin & J. Page eds. 1970). *See* Texas East Trans. Corp. v. Wildlife Preserves, 48 N.J. 261, 225 A.2d 130 (1966). There, where a corporation set up to maintain a wildlife preserve resisted condemnation for the construction of plaintiff's pipe line, the court ruled that ". . .the *quantum* of proof required of this defendant to show arbitrariness against it would not be as substantial as that to be assumed by the ordinary property owner who devotes his land to conventional uses." 225 A.2d at 137.

vocabulary and expressions that are available to us influence and even steer our thought. Consider the effect that has had by introducing into the law terms like "motive," "intent," and "due process." These terms work a subtle shift into the rhetoric of explanation available to judges; with them, new ways of thinking and new insights come to be explored and developed.[48] In such fashion, judges who could unabashedly refer to the "legal rights of the environment" would be encouraged to develop a viable body of law—in part simply through the availability and force of the expression. Besides, such a manner of speaking by courts would contribute to popular notions, and a society that spoke of the "legal rights of the environment" would be inclined to legislate more environment-protecting rules by formal enactment.

If my sense of these influences is correct, then a society in which it is stated, however vaguely, that "rivers have legal rights" would evolve a different legal system than one which did not employ that expression, even if the two of them had, at the start, the very same "legal rules" in other respects.

THE PSYCHIC AND SOCIO-PSYCHIC ASPECTS

There are, as we have seen, a number of developments in the law that may reflect a shift from the view that nature exists *for men*. These range from increasingly favorable procedural rulings for environmental action groups—as regards standing and burden of proof requirements, for example—to the enactment of comprehensive legislation such as the National Environmental Policy Act and the thoughtful Michigan Environmental Protection Act of 1970. Of such developments one may say, however, that it is not the environment *per se* that we are prepared to take into account, but that man's increased awareness of possible long range effects on himself militate in the direction of stopping environmental harm in its incipiency. And this is part of the truth, of course. Even the far-reaching National Environmental Policy Act, in its preambulatory "Declaration of National Environmental Policy," come out both for "restoring and maintaining environmental quality *to the overall welfare and development of man*" as well as for creating and maintaining "conditions under which *man and nature can exist in productive harmony.*"[49] Because the health and well-being of mankind depend upon the health of the environment, these goals will often be so mutually supportive that one can avoid deciding whether our rationale is to advance "us" or a new "us" that includes the environment. For example consider the Federal Insecticide, Fungicide, and Rodenticide Act (FIFRA) which insists that, *e.g.,* pesticides, include a warning "adequate to prevent injury to living man and other vertebrate animals, vegetation, and useful invertebrate animals."[50] Such a provision undoubtedly reflects the sensible notion that the protection of humans is best accomplished by preventing dangerous accumulations in the food chain. Its enactment does not necessarily augur far-reaching changes in, nor even call into question, fundamental matters of consciousness.

But the time is already upon us when we may have to consider subordinating some human claims to those of the environment *per se.* Consider, for example, the disputes over protecting wilderness areas from development that would make them accessible to greater numbers of people. I myself feel disingenuous rationalizing the environmental protectionist's position in terms of a utilitarian calculus, even one that takes future generations into account, and plays fast and loose with its definition of "good." Those who favor development have the stronger argument—they at least hold the protectionist to a standstill—from the point of advancing the greatest good of the greatest number of people. And the same is true regarding arguments to preserve useless species of animals, as in the sea urchin hypothetical. One *can* say that we never know what is going to prove useful at some future time. In order to protect ourselves, therefore, we ought to be conservative now in our treatment of nature. I agree. But when conservationists argue this way to the exclusion of other arguments, or find themselves speaking in terms of "recreational interests" so consistently as to play up to, and reinforce, homocentrist perspectives, there is something sad about the spectacle. One feels that the arguments lack even their proponents' convictions. I expect they want to say something less egotistic and more emphatic but the prevailing and sanctioned modes of explanation in our society are not quite ready for it. In this vein, there must have been abolitionists who put their case in terms of getting more work out of the Blacks. Holdsworth says of the early English Jew that while he was "regarded as a species of res nullius. . .[H]e was valuable for his acquisitive capacity; and for that reason the crown took him under its protection."[51] (Even today, businessmen are put in the position of insisting that their decent but probably profitless acts will "help our company's reputation and be good for profits.")[*]

For my part, I would prefer a frank avowal that even making adjustments for esthetic improvements, what I am proposing is going to cost "us," *i.e.,* reduce our standard of living as measured in terms of our present values.

Yet, this frankness breeds a frank response—one which I hear from my colleagues and which must occur to many a reader. Insofar as the proposal is not just an elaborate legal fiction, but really comes down in the last analysis to a compromise of *our* interests for *theirs*, why should we adopt it? "What is in it for 'us'?"

This is a question I am prepared to answer, but only after permitting myself some observations about how *odd* the question is. It asks for me to justify my position in the very anthropocentric hedonist terms that I am proposing we modify. One is inclined to respond by a counter: "couldn't you (as a white) raise the same questions about compromising your preferred rights-status with Blacks?"; or "couldn't you (as a man) raise the same question about compromising your preferred rights-status with women?" Such counters, unfortunately, seem no more responsive than the question

---

[*] Note that it is in no small way the law that imposes this manner of speech on businessmen. *See* Dodge v. Ford Motor Co., 204 Mich. 459, 499-505, 170 N.W. 668, 682-83 (1919) (holding that Henry Ford, as dominant stockholder in Ford Motor Co., could not withhold dividends in the interests of operating the company "as a semi-eleemosynary institution and not as a business institution").

itself. (They have a nagging ring of "yours too" about them.) What the exchange actually points up is a fundamental problem regarding the nature of philosophical argument. Recall that Socrates, whom we remember as a opponent of hedonistic thought, confutes Thrasymachus by arguing that immorality makes one miserably unhappy! Kant, whose moral philosophy was based upon the categorical imperative ("Woe to him who creeps through the serpent windings of Utilitarianism"[52]) finds himself justifying, *e.g.*, promise keeping and truth telling, on the most prudential—one might almost say, commercial-grounds.[53] This philosophic irony" (as Professor Engel calls it) may owe to there being something unique about ethical argument.[54] "Ethics cannot be put into words", Wittgenstein puts it; such matters "make themselves manifest."[55] On the other hand, perhaps the truth is that in any argument which aims at persuading a human being to action (on ethical or any other bases), "logic" is only an instrument for illuminating positions, at best, and in the last analysis it is psychological appeals to the listener's self-interest that hold sway, however "principled" the rhetoric may be.

With this reservation as to the peculiar task of the argument that follows, let me stress that the strongest case can be made from the perspective of human advantage for conferring rights on the environment. Scientists have been warning of the crises the earth and all humans on it face if we do not change our ways—radically—and these crises make the lost "recreational use" of rivers seem absolutely trivial. The earth's very atmosphere is threatened with frightening possibilities: absorption of sunlight, upon which the entire life cycle depends, may be diminished; the oceans may warm (increasing the "greenhouse effect" of the atmosphere), melting the polar ice caps, and destroying our great coastal cities; the portion of the atmosphere that shields us from dangerous radiation may be destroyed. Testifying before Congress, sea explorer Jacques Cousteau predicted that the oceans (to which we dreamily look to feed our booming populations) are headed toward their own death: "The cycle of life is intricately tied up with the cycle of water. . .the water system has to remain alive if we are to remain alive on earth."[56] We are depleting our energy and our food sources at a rate that takes little account of the needs even of humans now living.

These problems will not be solved easily; they very likely can be solved, if at all, only through a willingness to suspend the rate of increase in the standard of living (by present values) of the earth's "advanced" nations, and by stabilizing the total human population. For some of us this will involve forfeiting material comforts; for others it will involve abandoning the hope someday to obtain comforts long envied. For all of us it will involve giving up the right to have as many offspring as we might wish. Such a program is not impossible of realization, however. Many of our so-called "material comforts" are not only in excess of, but are probably in opposition to, basic biological needs. Further, the "costs" to the advanced nations is not as large as would appear from Gross National Product figures. G.N.P. reflects social gain (of a sort) without discounting for the social *cost* of that gain, *e.g.,* the losses through depletion of resources, pollution, and so forth. As has well been shown, as societies become more and more "advanced," their real marginal gains become less and less for each additional dollar of G.N.P.[57] Thus, to give up "human progress" would not be as costly as might appear on first blush.

Nonetheless, such far-reaching social changes are going to involve us in a serious reconsideration of our consciousness towards the environment. I say this knowing full well that there is something more than a trifle obscure in the claim: is popular consciousness a meaningful notion, to begin with? If so, what is our present consciousness regarding the environment? Has it been causally responsible for our material state of affairs? Ought we to shift our consciousness (and if so, to what exactly, and on what grounds)? How, if at all, would a shift in consciousness be translated into tangible institutional reform? Not one of these questions can be answered to everyone's satisfactions, certainly not to the author's.

It is commonly being said today, for example, that our present state of affairs—at least in the West—can be traced to the view that Nature is the dominion of Man, and that this attitude, in turn, derives from our religious traditions.

> Whatever the origins, the text is quite clear in Judaism, was absorbed all but unchanged into Christianity, and was inflated in Humanism to become the implicit attitude of Western man to Nature and the environment. Man is exclusively divine, all other creatures and things occupy lower and generally inconsequential stature; man is given dominion over all creatures and things; he is enjoined to subdue the earth. . .This environment was created by the man who believes that the cosmos is a pyramid erected to support man on its pinnacle, that reality exists only because man can perceive it, that God is made in the image of man, and that the world consists solely of a dialogue between men. Surely this is an infantilism which is unendurable. It is a residue from a past of inconsequence when a few puny men cried of their supremacy to an unhearing and uncaring world. One longs for a psychiatrist who can assure man that his deep seated cultural inferiority is no longer necessary or appropriate. . .It is not really necessary to destroy nature in order to gain God's favor or even his undivided attention.[58]

Surely this is forcibly put, but it is not entirely convincing as an explanation for how we got to where we are. For one thing, so far as intellectual influences are to be held responsible for our present state of affairs, one might as fairly turn on Darwin as the Bible. It was, after all, Darwin's views—in part through the prism of Spencer—that gave moral approbation to struggle, conquest, and domination; indeed, by emphasizing man's development as a product of chance happenings, Darwin also had the effect—intended or not—of reducing our awareness of the mutual interdependency of everything in Nature. And besides, as Professor Murphy points out, the spiritual beliefs of the Chinese and Indians "in the unity between man and nature had no greater

36

effect than the contrary beliefs in Europe in producing a balance between man and his environment"; he claims that in China, *tao* notwithstanding, "ruthless deforestation has been continuous."[59] I am under the impression, too, that notwithstanding the vaunted "harmony" between the American Plains Indians and Nature, once they had equipped themselves with rifles their pursuit of the buffalo expanded to fill the technological potential.* The fact is, that "consciousness" explanations pass too quickly over the less negative but simpler view of the situation: there are an increasing number of humans, with increasing wants, and there has been an increasing technology to satisfy them at "cost" to the rest of nature. Thus, we ought not to place too much hope that a changed environmental consciousness will in and of itself reverse present trends. Furthermore, societies have long since passed the point where a change in human consciousness on any matter will rescue us from our problems. More then ever before we are in the hands of institutions. These institutions are not "mere legal fictions" moreover: they have wills, minds, purposes, and inertias that are in very important ways their own, *i.e.,* that can transcend and survive changes in the consciousness of the individual humans who supposedly comprise them, and whom they supposedly serve. (It is more and more the individual human being, with his consciousness, that is the legal fiction.)**

For these reasons, it is far too pat to suppose that a western "environmental consciousness" is solely or even primarily responsible for our environmental crisis. On the other hand, it is not so extravagant to claim that it has dulled our resentment

---

* On the other hand, the statement in text, and the previous one of Professor Murphy, may be a bit severe. One could as easily claim that Christianity has had no influence on overt human behavior in light of the killings that have been carried out by professed Christians, often in its name. *Feng shui* has, on all accounts I am familiar with, influenced the development of land in China. *See* Freedman, *Geomancy,* 1968 PROCEEDINGS OF THE ROYAL ANTHROPOLOGICAL IN STITUTE OF GREAT BRITAIN AND IRELAND 5; March, *An Appreciation of Chinese Geomancy,* 27 J. ASIAN STUDIES 253 (1968).

** The legal system does the best it can to maintain the illusion of the reality of the individual human being. Consider, for example, how many constitutional cases, brought in the name of some handy individual, represent a power struggle between institutions-the NAACP and a school board, the Catholic Church and a school board, the ACLU and the Army, and so forth. Are the individual human plaintiffs the real moving causes of these cases-or an afterthought?

When we recognize that our problems are increasingly institutional, we would see that the solution, if there is one, must involve coming to grips with how the "Corporate" (in the broadest sense) entity is directed, and we must alter our views of "property" in the fashion that is needed to regulate organizations successfully. For example, instead of ineffectual, after-the-fact criminal fines we should have more preventive in-plant inspections, notwithstanding the protests of "invasion of [corporate] privacy."

In-plant inspection of production facilities and records is presently allowed only in a narrow range of areas, *e.g.,* in federal law, under the Federal Food, Drug, and Cosmetic Act, 21 U.S.C. § 374 et seq. (1970), and provisions for meat inspection, 21 U.S.C. § 608 (1970). Similarly, under local building codes we do not wait for a building to collapse before authoritative sources inquire into the materials and procedures that are being used in the construction; inspectors typically come on site to check the progress at every critical stage. A sensible preventive legal system calls for extending the ambit of industries covered by comparable "privacy invading" systems of inspection.

and our determination to respond. For this reason, whether we will be able to bring about the requisite institutional and population growth changes depends in part upon effecting a radical shift in our feelings about "our" place in the rest of Nature.

A radical new conception of man's relationship to the rest of nature would not only be a step towards solving the material planetary problems; there are strong reasons for such a changed consciousness from the point of making us far better humans. If we only stop for a moment and look at the underlying human qualities that our present attitudes toward property and nature draw upon and reinforce, we have to be struck by how stultifying of our own personal growth and satisfaction they can become when they take rein of us. Hegel, in "justifying" private property, unwittingly reflects the tone and quality of some of the needs that are played upon:

> A person has as his substantive end the right of putting his will into any and every thing and thereby making it his, because it has no such end in itself and derives its destiny and soul from his will. This is the absolute right of appropriation which man has over all "things."[60]

What is it within us that gives us this need not just to satisfy basic biological wants, but to extend our wills over things, to object-ify them, to make them ours, to manipulate them, to keep them at a psychic distance? Can it all be explained on "rational" bases? Should we not be suspect of such needs within us, cautious as to why we wish to gratify them? When I first read that passage of Hegel, I immediately thought not only of the emotional contrast with Spinoza, but of the passage in Carson McCullers' *A Tree, A Rock, A Cloud,* in which an old derelict has collared a twelve year old boy in a streetcar cafe. The old man asks whether the boy knows "how love should be begun?"

The old man leaned closer and whispered:

> "A tree. A rock. A cloud."
>
> . . .
>
> . . . "The weather was like this in Portland," he said. "At the time my science was begun. I meditated and I started very cautious. I would pick up something from the street and take it home with me. I bought a goldfish and I concentrated on the goldfish and loved it. I graduated from one thing to another. Day by day I was getting this technique. . . .
>
> . . .
>
> . . . "For six years now I have gone around by myself and built up my science. And now I am a master. Son. I can love anything. No longer do I have to think about it even. I see a street full of people and a beautiful

38

light comes in me. I watch a bird in the sky. Or I meet a traveler on the road. Everything, Son. And anybody. All stranger and all loved! Do you realize what a science like mine can mean?"[61]

To be able to get away from the view that Nature is a collection of useful senseless objects is, as McCullers" "madman" suggests, deeply involved in the development of our abilities to love—or, if that is putting it too strongly, to be able to reach a heightened awareness of our own, and others', capacities in their mutual interplay. To do so, we have to give up some psychic investment in our sense of separateness and specialness in the universe. And this, in turn, is hard giving indeed, because it involves us in a flight backwards, into earlier stages of civilization and childhood in which we had to trust (and perhaps fear) our environment, for we had not then the power to master it. Yet, in doing so, we, as persons, gradually free ourselves of needs for supportive illusions. Is not this one of the triumphs for "us" of our giving legal rights to (or acknowledging the legal rights of) the Blacks and women?*

---

* Consider what Schopenhauer was writing "Of Women," about the time the Wisconsin Supreme Court was explaining why women were unfit to practice law, pp. 4-5 *supra:*

"You need only look at the way in which she is formed, to see that woman in not meant to undergo great labour, whether of the mind or of the body. She pays the debt of life not by what she does, but by what she suffers; by the pains of childbearing and care for the child, and by submission to her husband, to whom she should be a patient and cheering companion. The keenest sorrows and joys are not for her, nor is she called upon to display a great deal of strength. The current of her life should be more gentle, peaceful and trivial than man's without being essentially happier or unhappier."

Women are directly fitted for acting as the nurses and teachers of our early childhood by the fact that they are themselves childish, frivolous and short-sighted; in a word, they are big children all their life long-a kind of intermediate stage between the child and the full-grown man, which is man in the strict sense of the word. . . .

However many disadvantages all this may involve, there is at least this to be said in its favour: that the woman lives more in the present than the man, and that, if the present is at all tolerable, she enjoys it more eagerly. This is the source of that cheerfulness which is peculiar to woman, fitting her to amuse man in his hours of recreation, and, in case of need, to console him when he is borne down by the weight of his cares.

. . . . [I]t will be found that the fundamental fault of the female character is that it has *no sense of justice.* This is mainly due to the fact, already mentioned, that women are defective in the powers of reasoning and deliberation; but it is also traceable to the position which Nature has assigned to them as the weaker sex. They are dependent, not upon strength, but upon craft; and hence their instinctive capacity for cunning, and their ineradicable tendency to say what is not true. *** For as lions are provided with claws and teeth, and elephants and boars with tusks, bulls with horns, and the cuttle fish with its cloud of inky fluid, so Nature has equipped woman, for her defense and protection, with the arts of dissimulation; and all the power which Nature has conferred upon man in the shape of physical strength and reason, has been bestowed upon women in this form. Hence, dissimulation is innate in woman, and almost as much a quality of the stupid as of the clever. . . ."

A. SCHOPENHAUER, *On Women,* in STUDIES IN PESSIMISM 105-10 (T. B. Saunders transl. 1893).

If a man should write such insensitive drivel today, we would suspect him of being morally and emotionally blind. Will the future judge us otherwise, for venting rather than examining the needs that impel us to treat the environment as a senseless object—to blast to pieces some small atoll to find out whether an atomic weapon works?

Changes in this sort of consciousness are already developing, for the betterment of the planet and us. There is now federal legislation which "establishes by law"*

> the humane ethic that animals should be accorded the basic creature comforts of adequate housing, ample food and water, reasonable handling, decent sanitation, sufficient ventilation, shelter from extremes of weather and temperature, and adequate veterinary care including the appropriate use of pain-killing drugs. . .[62]

The Vietnam war has contributed to this movement, as it has to others. Five years ago a Los Angeles mother turned out a poster which read "War is not Healthy for children and other living things."[63] It caught on tremendously—at first, I suspect, because it sounded like another clever protest against the war, *i.e.,* another angle. But as people say such things, and think about them, the possibilities of what they have stumbled upon become manifest. In its suit against the Secretary of Agriculture to cancel the registration of D.D.T., Environmental Defense Fund alleged "biological injury to man and other living things."** A few years ago the pollution of streams was thought of only as a problem of smelly, unsightly, unpotable water *i.e.,* to us. Now we are beginning to discover that pollution is a process that destroys wondrously subtle balances of life within the water, and as between the water and its banks. This heightened awareness enlarges our sense of the dangers to us. But it also enlarges our empathy. We are not only developing the scientific capacity, but we are cultivating the personal capacities *within us* to recognize more and more the ways in which nature—like the woman, the Black, the Indian and the Alien—is like us (and we will also become more able realistically to define, confront, live with and admire the ways in which we are all different).†

The time may be on hand when these sentiments, and the early stirrings of the law, can be coalesced into a radical new theory or myth-felt as well as intellectualized-of

---

* Of course, the phase one looks toward is a time in which such sentiments need not be prescribed *by law.*

** Environmental Defense Fund, Inc. v. Hardin, 428 F.2d 1093, 1096 (D.C. Cir. 1970). Plaintiffs would thus seem to have urged a broader than literal reading of the statute, 7 U.S.C. § 135(z) (2) (d) (1970), which refers to ". . .living man and other vertebrate animals, vegetation, and useful invertebrate animals."

 E.D.F. was joined as petitioners by the National Audubon Society, the Sierra Club, and the West Michigan Environmental Action Council, 428 F.2d at 1094-95 n.5.

† In the case of the bestowal of rights on other humans, the action also helps the recipient to discover new personal depths and possibilities—new dignity—within him or her self. I do not want to make much of the possibility that this effect would be relevant in the case of bestowing rights on the environment. But I would not dismiss it out of hand, either. How, after all, do we judge that a person is, say, "flourishing with a new sense of pride and dignity?" What we mean by such statements, and the nature of the evidence upon which we rely in support of them, is quite complex. A tree treated in a "rightful" manner would respond in a manner that, when described, would sound much like the response of a person accorded "new dignity." *See also* note p. 25 *supra.*

man's relationships to the rest of nature. I do not mean "myth" in a demeaning sense of the term, but in the sense in which, at different times in history, our social "facts" and relationships have been comprehended and integrated by reference to the "myths" that we are co-signers of a social contract, that the Pope is God's agent, and that all men are created equal. Pantheism, Shinto and Tao all have myths to offer. But they are all, each in its own fashion, quaint, primitive and archaic. What is needed is a myth that can fit our growing body of knowledge of geophysics, biology and the cosmos. In this vein, I do not think it too remote that we may come to regard the Earth, as some have suggested, as one organism, of which Mankind is a functional part—the mind, perhaps: different from the rest of nature, but different as a man's brain is from his lungs.

> Ever since the first Geophysical Year, international scientific studies have shown irrefutably that the Earth as a whole is an organized system of most closely interrelated and indeed interdependent activities. It is, in the broadest sense of the term, an "organism." The so-called life-kingdoms and the many vegetable and animal species are dependent upon each other for survival in a balanced condition of planet-wide existence; and they depend on their environment, conditioned by oceanic and atmospheric currents, and even more by the protective action of the ionosphere and many other factors which have definite rhythms of operation. Mankind is part of this organic planetary whole; and there can be no truly new global society, and perhaps in the present state of affairs no society at all, as long as man will not recognize, accept and enjoy the fact that mankind has a definite function to perform within this planetary organism of which it is an active part.

> In order to give a constructive meaning to the activities of human societies all over the globe, these activities—physical and mental—should be understood and given basic value with reference to the wholesome functioning of the entire Earth, and we may add of the entire solar system. This cannot be done (1) if man insists on considering himself an alien Soul compelled to incarnate on this sorrowful planet, and (2) if we can see in the planet, Earth, nothing but a mass of material substances moved by mechanical laws, and in "life" nothing but a chance combination of molecular aggregations.

> . . . As I see it, the Earth is only one organized "field" of activities—and so is the *human person*—but these activities take place at various levels, in different "spheres" of being and realms of consciousness. The lithosphere is not the biosphere, and the latter not the. . .ionosphere. The Earth is not *only* a material mass. Consciousness is not only "human"; it exists at animal and vegetable levels, and most likely must be latent, or operating

41

in some form, in the molecule and the atom; and all these diverse and in a sense hierarchical modes of activity and consciousness should be seen integrated in and perhaps transcended by an all-encompassing and "eonic" planetary Consciousness.

. . . .

Mankind's function within the Earth-organism is to extract from the activities of all other operative systems within this organism the type of consciousness which we call "reflective" or "self"-consciousness—or, we may also say to *mentalize* and give meaning, value, and "name" to all that takes place anywhere within the Earth-field. . . .

This "mentalization" process operates through what we call culture. To each region of, and living condition in the total field of the Earth-organism a definite type of culture inherently corresponds. Each region is the "womb" out of which a specific type of human mentality and culture can and sooner or later will emerge. All these cultures—past, present and future—and their complex interrelationships and interactions are the collective builders of the Mind of humanity; and this means of the *conscious Mind of the Earth.*[64]

As radical as such a consciousness may sound today, all the dominant changes we see about us point in its direction. Consider just the impact of space travel, of world-wide mass media, of increasing scientific discoveries about the interrelatedness of all life processes. Is it any wonder that the term "spaceship earth" has so captured the popular imagination? The problems we have to confront are increasingly the world-wide crises of a global organism: not pollution of a stream, but pollution of the atmosphere and of the ocean. Increasingly, the death that occupies each human's imagination is not his own, but that of the entire life cycle of the planet earth, to which each of us is as but a cell to a body.

To shift from such a lofty fancy as the planetarization of consciousness to the operation of our municipal legal system is to come down to earth hard. Before the forces that are at work, our highest court is but a frail and feeble—a distinctly human—institution. Yet, the Court may be at its best not in its work of handing down decrees, but at the very task that is called for: of summoning up from the human spirit the kindest and most generous and worthy ideas that abound there, giving them shape and reality and legitimacy.[65] Witness the School Desegregation Cases which, more importantly than to integrate the schools (assuming they did), awakened us to moral imperatives which, when made visible, could not be denied. And so here, too, in the case of the environment, the Supreme Court may find itself in a position to award "rights" in a way that will contribute to a change in popular consciousness. It would be a modest move, to be sure, but one in furtherance of a large goal: the future of the planet as we know it.

How far we are from such a state of affairs, where the law treats "environmental objects" as holders of legal rights, I cannot say. But there is certainly intriguing language in one of Justice Black's last dissents, regarding the Texas Highway Department's plan to run a six-lane expressway through a San Antonio Park.[66] Complaining of the Court's refusal to stay the plan, Black observed that "after today's decision, the people of San Antonio and the birds and animals that make their home in the park will share their quiet retreat with an ugly, smelly stream of traffic. . . .Trees, shrubs and flowers will be mown down."[67] Elsewhere he speaks of the "burial of public parks," of segments of a highway which "devour parkland," and of the park's heartland.[68] Was he, at the end of his great career, on the verge of saying—just saying—that "nature has 'rights' on its own account"? Would it be so hard to do?

ENDNOTES

1. C. DARWIN, DESCENT OF MAN 119, 120-21 (2d ed. 1874). See also R. WAELDER, PROGRESS AND REVOLUTION 39 et seq. (1967).

2. See DARWIN, supra note 1, at 113. See also E. WESTERMARCK, 1 THE ORIGIN AND DEVELOPMENT OF THE MORAL IDEAS 406-12 (1912). The practice of allowing sickly children to die has not been entirely abandoned, apparently, even at our most distinguished hospitals. *See Hospital Let Retarded Baby Die, Film Shows*, L.A. Times, Oct. 17, 1971, sec. A, at 9, col. 1.

3. 387 U.S. 1 (1967).

4. 42 U.S.C. §§ 1973 et. Seq. (1970).

5. But see T. SZASZ, LAW, LIBERTY AND PSYCHIATRY (1963).

6. INT. REV. CODE of 1954, § 1361 (repealed by Pub. L. No. 89-389, effective Jan. 1, 1969).

7. 9 U.S. (5 Cranch) 61, 86 (1809).

8. Trustees of Dartmouth College v. Woodward, 17 U.S. (4 Wheat.) 518 (1819).

9. Id. At 636.

10. Dietrich v. Inhabitants of Northampton, 138 Mass. 14, 16 (1884).

11. Four cases dealing with the Constitutionality of the death penalty under the eighth and fourteenth amendments are pending before the United States Supreme Court. Branch v. Texas, 447 S.W.2d 932 (Tex. 1969), *cert. granted,* 91 S. Ct. 2287 (1970); Aikens v. California, 70 Cal. 2d 369, 74 Cal. Rptr. 882, 450 P2d 258 (1969), *cert. granted,* 91 S.

Ct. 2280 (1970); Furman v. Georgia, 225 Ga. 253, 167 S.E.2d 628 (1969), *cert. granted,* 91 S. Ct. 2282 (1970); Jackson v. Georgia, 225 Ga. 790, 171 S.E.2d 501 (1969), *cert. granted,* 91 S. Ct. 2287 (1970).

12. See George Campbell Painting Corp. V. Reiid, 392 U.S. 286 (1968); Oklahoma Press Pub. Co. V. Walling, 327 U.S. 186 (1946); Baltimore & O.R.R. v. ICC, 221 U.S. 612 (1911); Wilson v. United States, 221 U.S. 361 (1911); Hale v. Henkel, 201 U.S. 43 (1906).

13. See Dixon v. Alabama State Bd. Of Educ., 294 F.2d 150 (5th Cir.), *cert. denied,* 368 U.S. 930 (1961).

14. See Note, *Statutory Treatment of Industrial Stream Pollution,* 24 GEO. WASH. L. REV. 302, 306 (1955); H. FARNHAM, 2 LAW OF WATERS AND WATER RIGHTS § 461 (1904); GOULD, supra note 32, at § 204.

15. Pennsylvania Coal Co. Sanderson, 113 Pa. 126, 149, 6 A. 453, 459 (1886).

16. Hand, J. In Smith v. Staso Milling Co., 18 F.2d 736, 738 (2d Cir. 1927) (emphasis added). See also Harrisonville v. Dickey Clay Co., 289 U.S. 334 (1933) (Brandeis, J.).

17. Smith v. Staso, 18 F.2d 736, 738 (2d Cir. 1927).

18. See e.g., CAL. PROB. CODE §§ 1460-62 (West Supp. 1971).

19. CAL. PROB. CODE § 1751 (West Supp. 1971) provides for the appointment of a "conservator."

20. Santa Clara County v. Southern Pac. R.R., 118 U.S. 394 (1886). Justice Black would have denied corporations the rights of "persons" under the fourteenth amendment. See Connecticut Gen. Life Ins. Co. V. Johnson, 303 U.S. 77, 87 (1938) (Black, J. Dissenting): "Corporations have neither race nor color."

21. See CAL. PROB. CODE §§ 1472, 1590 (West 1956 and Supp. 1971).

22. 354 F.2d 608 (2d Cir. 1965), *cert. denied,* Consolidated Edison Co. v. Scenic Hudson Preservation Conf., 384 U.S. 941 (1966).

23. 354 F.2d 608, 615 (2d Cir. 1965).

24. Act of Aug. 26, 1935, ch. 687, Title II, § 213, 49 Stat. 860 (*codified* in 16 U.S.C. § 8251(b) (1970).

25. 16 U.S.C. §§ 791 (a) *et seq.* (1970).

26. 5 U.S.C. §§ 551 *et seq.* (1970).

27. 7 U.S.C. §§ 135 *et seq.* (1970). Section 135b(d) affords a right of judicial review to anyone "adversely affected" by an order under the Act. *See* Environmental Defense Fund, Inc. v. Hardin, 428 F.2d 1093, 1096 (D.C. Cir. 1970).

28. 324 F. Supp. 412 (N.D., M.D. & S.D. Ala. 1970), *aff'd mem., sub nom.* Bass Anglers Sportsman Soc'y of America, Inc. v. Koppers Co., 447 F.2d 1304 (5th Cir. 1971).

29. Section 13 of Rivers and Harbors Appropriation Act of 1899.

30. *See* note p.13 *supra.*

31. *See* Knight v. United States Land Ass'n, 142 U.S. 161, 181 (1891)

32. *See* Flemming v. Nestor, 363 U.S. 603 (1960).

33. The Federal Refuse Act is over 70 years old. Refuse Act of 1899, 33 U.S.C. § 407 (1970).

34. *See* Hall, *Refuse Act of 1899 and the Permit Program,* 1 NAT'L RES. DEFENSE COUNCIL NEWSLETTER i (1971).

35. Cf. Golding, *Ethical Issues in Biological Engineering,* 15 U.C.L.A.L. REV. 443, 451-63 (1968).

36. *See* Schrag, *Life on a Dying Lake,* in THE POLITICS OF NEGLECT 167, at 173 (R. Meek & J. Straayer eds. 1971).

37. On November 2, 1971, the Senate, by a vote of 86-0, passed and sent to the House the proposed Federal Water Pollution Control Act Amendments of 1971, 117 CONG. REC. S17464 (daily ed. Nov. 2, 1971). Sections 101(a) and (a)(1) of the bill declare it to be "national policy that, consistent with the provisions of this Act—(1) the discharge of pollutants into the navigable waters be eliminated by 1985." S2770, 92d Cong., 1st Sess., 117 CONG. REC. S17464 (daily ed. Nov. 2, 1971).

38. 354 F.2d 608, 624 (2d Cir. 1965).

39. N.Y. Times, Jan. 14, 1971. § 1, col. 2, and at 74, col. 7.

40. *See* note 16 *supra.* and note p.21 *supra.*

41. *See* FED. R. Civ. P. 23 and note p.13 *supra.*

42. *See* Dixon v. Alabama State Bd. of Educ., 294 F.2d 150 (5th Cir.), *cert. denied,* 368 U.S. 930 (1961); Comment, *Private Government on the Campus–Judicial Review of University Expulsions,* 72 Yale L.J. 1362 (1963).

43. National Environmental Policy Act, 92 U.S.C. § 4332 (1970).

44. *See* Committee for Nuclear Responsibility Inc. v. Schlesinger, 40 U.S.L.W. 3214 (Nov. 5, 1971) (Douglas, J. Dissent to denial of application for injunction in aid of jurisdiction).

45. 42 U.S.C. § 4342 (1970).

46. *See* for example Justice Reed's opinion for the Court in Kovac v. Cooper, 336 U.S. 77 (1949) (*but see* Mr. Justice Frankfurter's concurring opinion, 3236 U.S. at 89-96), and United States v. Carolene Products, 304 U.S. 144, 152 n.4 (1938).

47. *See* Simpson, *The Analysis of Legal Concepts*, 80 LAW Q. REV. 535 (1964).

48. See Stone, *Existential Humanism and the Law*, in EXISTENTIAL HUMANISTIC PSYCHOLOGY 151 (T. Greening ed. 1971).

49. National Environmental Policy Act, 42 U.S.C. §§ 4321-47 (1970).

50. U.S.C. §§ 135 et seq. (1970).

51. W. HOLDSWORTH, HISTORY OF ENGLISH LAW 45 (5th ed. 1931).

52. I. KANT, PHILOSOPHY OF LAW 195 (Hastie Transl. 1887).

53. I. KANT, *The Metaphysics of Morality*, in THE PHILOSOPHY OF KANT § 1 at 230-31 (J. Watson transl. 1908).

54. Engel, *Reasons, Morals and Philosophic Irony*, in LANGUAGE AND ILLUMINATION 60 (1996).

55. L. WITTGENSTEIN, TRACTATUS LOGICO-PHILOSOPHICUS §§ 6.421, 6.522 (D. Pears & B. McGuinness transl. 1961).

56. Cousteau, *The Oceans: No Time to Lose*, L.A. Times, Oct. 24, 1971, § (opinion), at 1, col. 4.

57. *See* J. HARTE & R. SOCOLOW, PATIENT EARTH (1971).

58. McHarg, *Values, Process and Form*, in THE FITNESS OF MAN'S ENVIRONMENT 213-14 (1968).

59. Murphy, *supra* note p.7, at 477.

60. G. HEGEL, HEGEL'S PHILOSOPHY OF RIGHT 41 (T. Knox transl. 1945).

61. C. MCCULLERS, THE BALLAD OF THE SAD CAFE AND OTHER STORIES 150-51 (1958).

62. The "Purpose of the Legislation" in H.R. Rep. No. 91-1651, 91st Cong., 2d Sess., to the "[Animal] Welfare Act of 1970," 3 U.S. CODE CONG. & ADMIN. NEWS 5103, 5104 (1970). Some of the West Publishing Co. typesetters may not be quite ready for this yet; they printed out the title as "Annual Welfare Act of 1970."

63. *See* MCCALL'S, May, 1971, at 44.

64. FD. RUDHYAR, DIRECTIVES FOR NEW LIFE 21-23 (1971).

65. *See* Stone, note 48 *supra.*

66. San Antonio Conservation Soc'y v. Texas Highway Dep't, *cert. denied,* 400 U.S. 968 (1970) (Black, J. dissenting to denial of certiorari).

67. *Id.* at 969.

68. *Id.* at 971.

CHAPTER 2

THE NONPERSON IN LAW[*]

Implicit in all I have written thus far there runs a major question of *care* and *respect*. What are the things we ought to care about and respect, and in what ways should that attitude be manifested? Our two principal institutions for sorting out and implementing these concerns–morals and law–have been dominated, conventionally, by a Persons[**] orientation. Therefore, increasing regard for Nonpersons requires us to consider how suited our received ways of normative analysis are to resolve or even guide us through the evolving problems of contemporary concern. In what ways, and with what justification, might Nonpersons be accounted for in moral thought and legal rules?

At this point, we have to disengage more carefully the legal aspects of our inquiry from the moral. While law and morals share common roots, functions, and often subject matter, their emphases are different. In morals, the emphasis is on generating and justifying general standards of conduct. In law, the emphasis is on authoritatively implementing some of the standards for which morality has spoken: killing is wrong, therefore murder should be punished.

Assuming a need to divide our inquiry, there are two paths we can pursue. We could start by articulating and defending some general theory of morals, and then try to derive from that theory what sorts of moral claims, including claims to legal treatment, could be raised on behalf of various Nonpersons. Under this approach we would begin by asking on what bases *ought* we to be concerned about the preservation of rivers. We would then ask how any defensible concern could be translated into legal reform. The other approach, that which I adopt, is the reverse. It begins by asking whether giving a river various "legal rights" is intelligible and examining what doing so

---

[*] From EARTH AND OTHER ETHICS: THE CASE FOR MORAL PLURALISM (Harper & Row 1987, Copyright Christopher D. Stone

[**] My term *Persons* is less extensive than the biologist's *homo sapiens*. *Persons* is limited to normal adult beings who, possessing full human faculties and living as neighbors in time and space, are capable of knitting the bonds of a common community. *Person* excludes, for example, humans who have not yet been born, those who live on the other side of the world, and those afflicted with such a serious defect that their capacity to form social bonds is impaired. All these are persons, of course, and worthy of our concern. But they are not the Persons who have been the focal concern of ordinary law and morals—which I am of course questioning. Here we ask, how might we allow for various sorts of Nonpersons, personally—those who cannot assert and waive the sorts of claims needed to govern reciprocal relationships?

would entail. Once the implications are identified, we can then proceed to the moral inquiry: *ought* we to commit ourselves to *that*?

By adopting the second approach, we save ourselves the trouble of evaluating a number of arrangements that are legally unintelligible anyway. For example, we eliminate from further worry whether trees ought to have the vote, because giving trees the vote simply is not a coherent option. But other options, which are not so incoherent, can be identified and the implications assessed. The normative inquiry, thus deferred, acquires a more definite focus. The emphasis is not "Does a river have moral rights, and if so, what legal status can be derived from them?" We ask, "In what legal status might a river intelligibly be placed? And for each such arrangement of the legal system (treating a river *this way*) is it morally defensible?"

The nature of a thing's *legal status*, and, in particular, the relationship between its legal status and its moral status, can be clarified if we confront at the start two popular misconceptions. The first mistake is to suppose that all questions of *legal status* can be conflated into questions of *legal rights*. That is, people tend to identify the question "Can some entity be accorded legal recognition?" with "Can (or does) the entity have a legal right?" In fact, the motive for recognizing something as a legal person may have nothing to do with *its* legal rights. For example, the courts may give a stillborn fetus the status of "person" in order to fulfill a technical prerequisite for the parents to file a malpractice case against the doctors.[1] Giving the fetus its independent legal status is designed to secure the legal rights of the parents, not those of the fetus.

This first misconception is commonly compounded by a second error. This is the view that the only basis on which we can support according a thing a legal right (or other legal recognition) is if we can show it has something like its own moral right, underneath.[*]

Let me begin here by placing *legal rights-holding* in perspective. The short of it is that having a legal right is one way to provide something a concern-manifesting legal recognition. But it is not the only way. When the law criminalizes dog beating it institutionalizes concern for dogs. It does so, however, by creating a prospective

---

[*] This misconception is not surprising. Some of the most fundamental legal protections associated with ordinary humans, including freedom of speech and of worship, are derived from claims of human rights that antedate the constitutional provisions that secure them. The moral right became the basis of the legal right. With such an image in mind there is a temptation, when considering whether an animal or tree or future human should have a legal right (or more subtle, lower levels of legal protection) to suppose that the proponent has the burden of demonstrating that the entity has some independent moral right underneath.

But it is not quite so simple. We justify giving corporations legal rights (and legal liabilities) on the grounds it creates a more favorable environment for capital accumulation, and lower commercial "transaction costs." On a like basis, we can support the legal personification of many nonhuman things, even granting them standing in court, etc., because it is the most sensible way of promoting our own ends, without ever reaching questions about whether the thing possesses an independent "moral right." However, the animal rights movement, "deep ecologists" and others, including the author, do press for a level of protection beyond what homocentric arguments would justify.

liability for the dog beater, who is made answerable to public prosecutors at their discretion. In no accepted sense does such a statute create a "right" in the dog. The same principle is at work in legislation establishing animal sanctuaries, and laws that compel cattle transporters to provide minimally "humane" standards at the risk of losing their certificate. The law is enlisted in an effort to protect Nonpersons, but legal rights are not required. The federal government recently issued regulations requiring fishermen who accidentally land sea turtles on their decks to give them artificial respiration. The technique is set out in detail. But the term *turtle's rights* is never mentioned. Nor need it be. The turtles are provided a measure of legal protection by creating enforceable legal duties *in regard to* them, duties enforceable by others, presumably the Commerce Department and Coast Guard. In like vein, no one is doubting that we could create comparable duties in regard to things indisputably devoid of interests; for example, we can imagine a law making it a misdemeanor to deface some special rock, such as Mount Rushmore.* Nor are relations built on duties the only alternative to those built on rights. We could give an algae colony an immunity from governmental action, say, from the draining of a stream for a federal works project.

This should remind us that while allocating rights is a fundamental way of operationalizing legal concern, and I myself emphasized it in *Trees,* such concern can be implemented through a broad range of arrangements, not all of which can be forced in to the class "rights-holding," or even "duties-bearing," mold. Therefore, let me introduce as the more comprehensive notion *legal considerableness.* A terse operational definition would look like this. Consider a lake. The lake is considerable within a legal system if the system's rules have as their immediate object to affect (as to preserve) some condition of the lake. The law's operation would turn on proof that the lake is not in the condition that the law requires, without any further need to demonstrate anyone else's interests in or claims touching the lake.

We can illustrate by reference to a lake which is being polluted by a factory. Under conventional law, the pollution of the lake can be restrained at some human's behest if the human can show that he has a legally protectable interest in the lake.

Contrast that system to one in which the rules empower a suit to be brought against the factory in the name not of the person, but of the lake, through a guardian or trustee. The factory's liability is established on the showing that without justification, it degraded the lake from one condition, which is lawful, to another, which is not.

In the first system described, the lake is not legally considerable. It has no protection that is not wholly parasitic upon the rights of some person ready and willing to assert them. In the latter system, it is the lake that is considerable, not the person empowered to assert claims on its behalf.

---

* The point that the only intelligible *motive* for protecting Mt. Rushmore would appear to be the benefit of humans, and not the benefit of Mt. Rushmore, is a distinct contention dealt with in Part III of *Earth and Other Ethics.*

Now, if this were intended as a jurisprudence text, we might proceed to unpack legal considerateness into the whole array of terms with which legal philosophers deal: rights, duties, privileges, immunities, no-rights, and all the rest. For our purposes, however, we can simply conceptualize considerateness into two broad categories: *legal advantage* (typified by holding a legal right) and *legal disadvantage* (typified by bearing a legal duty). The question I will pursue, therefore, is to what extent and in what senses we can coherently situate Nonpersons in positions of legal advantage and legal disadvantage (hereinafter Advantage and Disadvantage), respectively.

ARE INTERESTS A REQUIREMENT OF LEGAL CONSIDERATENESS?

At this point, someone is bound to object that all this talk about "positioning" a Nonperson in a position of Advantage or of Disadvantage simply slides over the most serious problem. In regard to legislation touching some Nonpersons—as when we criminalize dog beating, for example—few would deny we are acting for the dog's benefit, *really* advantaging it. But one cannot so plausibly characterize an arrangement that nestles the lake in the protective custody of a guardian as being "for the lake's 'benefit'" in any familiar sense of "benefit." We have simply plugged the lake into the legal system roughly in the place that a person might occupy, to a person's advantage; but it is a place that can be of no advantage to the lake, only to people. The same may be said of whatever we might do concerning many Nonpersons, from ants and aquifers to zoophytes and zygotes. Because they have no self-conscious interests in their own fates (as distinct from our interests in them), it is unclear how notions of Advantage and Disadvantage apply.

How do we respond to this challenge? Inasmuch as we cannot examine all Nonpersons at the same time and with equal emphasis, I will set aside for the moment the most sympathetic cases for the Nonperson advocate to represent—those, for example, of distant persons and higher animals. To examine the general problem, we best concentrate on the most implausible of my Nonperson clients, thereby confronting the most fundamental objections. What space is there in law and morals, what toehold even, for the subset of Nonpersons I will call "Things"—utterly disinterested entities devoid of feelings or interests except in the most impoverished or even metaphorical sense?

There are various classes of these disinterested Things. There are man-made inanimates exemplified by artworks and artificial intelligence. There are Things that were not always so disinterested—corpses—and Things with the potential to be otherwise—embryos and fetuses. There are trees and algae which, while without self-consciousness and preferences, are nonetheless living organisms with biological requirements. There are what we discern as functional systems, but not systems that conform to the boundaries of any organism; for example, the hydrologic cycle. Habitats are of this sort. That is, while the habitat may include higher animals, we may find ourselves wishing to speak for some value not reducible to the sum of the values of the habitat's parts, the various things that the habitat sustains in relation. There are several sorts of natural and conventional membership sets already mentioned: species, tribes, nations, corporations. We might for completeness' sake keep in mind such "things" as in the happenstance of our language are rendered as qualities, for example, the quality of the light in the Arizona desert at sunset. Finally, there are events that might be of legal and moral concern, such as the flooding of the Nile.

Whatever might motivate and justify the lawmakers to try to make some such Thing legally considerable, how can we coherently account for an entity that has no welfare? We can imagine our interlocutor putting it this way. "All right," she says, "let us suppose that somewhere in the text that follows, you will be able to demonstrate at least some rational basis that could motivate us to devise legal rules in which a Thing–a lake, say–is made legally considerable, as you use the term. We will even agree to provide it a court-appointed guardian empowered to get up in court and 'take on' polluters in the lake's name. But now comes the tough part. The lake itself being utterly indifferent to whether it is clear and full of fish or muddy and lifeless, when the guardian for the river gets up to speak, *what is he or she supposed to say?*"

My answer will sound, I am afraid, a bit anticlimactic. As in any situation in which a legal guardian is empowered to speak for a ward, what the guardian says will depend upon what the legal rules touching on the ward provide. By definition a Thing can neither be benefited nor detrimented in the ordinary sense, so that the rules cannot orient to its best interests in the way some rules of child custody enlist "the best interests of the child." But what is implied? Not that no legal rules are imaginable. It only means that the state of the Thing for the preservation or attainment of which the guardian speaks will have to be some state the law decrees without reference to what the choiceless Thing would choose. What we should be asking, then, is this: What states of a disinterested entity (a Thing), of necessity unrooted in its own interests or welfare or preferences, are available for the law to embody in legal rules, and what would be the implications of so embodying them?

INTACTNESS AS A LEGAL ADVANTAGE

To examine what sort of legally defined. Advantages might be conferred on a Thing, and with what implications, let us begin by considering a system that took as its target preserving the lake's intactness. The lawmakers could provide stiff criminal penalties for anyone who polluted the lake in the least degree. They could fortify this "advantaging: by assimilating the lake into the civil-liability rules in a way that approximated constituting the lake a rights holder with guardian. Specifically, the law could provide that in case someone violated established effluent standards, altering the state of the lake, a complaint could be instituted in the name of the lake, as party plaintiff, against the polluter. As I spelled out in *Trees,* this suit could be initiated and maintained–as suits are maintained as a matter of course for infants, the senile, and corporations–by a lawyer authorized to represent it, by *ad hoc* court appointment, or otherwise.[2] Assuming that the guardian had to show damages, the law could simply provide that the lake's legal damages were to be measured by the costs of making the lake "whole" in the sense of restoring the lake to the condition it would have been in had its "legal right" to intactness not been violated. That is, if the defendant's liability were established (if the upstream plant were found to have violated the applicable standards), it would have to pay into a trust fund, for the repair of the river, funds adequate to cover such items as aeration, restocking with fish and aquatic plants, filtering, and dredging.

If anyone considers this farfetched, note that the federal courts have allowed such a suit to be brought in the name of the Byram River (the river that forms part of the interstate boundary between southern Connecticut and New York) against the village of Port Chester, which had been polluting it. And it is certainly plausible that some recent and important federal legislation, including the Federal Water Pollution Control Act (FWPCA) and the Comprehensive Environmental Response, Compensation, and Liability Act of 1980 (CERCLA), will be construed as authorizing comparable results. Units of the federal or state governments are empowered to sue polluters as trustees for the environment and to recover and apply the costs of restorations, even if those costs exceed the actual economic consumption value.

Commonwealth of Puerto Rico v. *SS Zoe Colocotroni*[3] is a striking illustration. In *Zoe Colocotroni,* an oil tanker by that name was allowed by its owners to deteriorate into an unseaworthy condition, to be launched without proper charts, and to be manned, as the courts put it, by a "hopelessly lost" and "incompetent crew." The ship ran aground off Puerto Rico, spilling thousands of tons of crude oil. Puerto Rico, as trustee for its resources, submitted an estimate of damage to an area around a twenty-acre mangrove swamp. The major item was for a decline of 4,605,486 organisms per acre. "This means," the district court said, "92,109,720 marine animals were killed," largely sand crabs, segmented worms, and the like. Trying to get a handle on damages (the court's own can of segmented worms), the judge wrote:

> The uncontradicted evidence establishes that there is a ready market with reference to biological supply laboratories, thus allowing a reliable calculation of the cost of replacing these organisms. The lowest possible replacement cost figure is $.06 per animal, with many species selling from $1.00 to $4.50 per individual. Accepting the lowest replacement cost, and attaching damages only to the lost marine animals in the West Mangrove area, we find the damages caused by Defendants to amount to $5,526,584.20.

There was not a lost of precedent, as the reader can imagine. But the court of appeals affirmed the award, filing an opinion clearly sympathetic to deterring damage to nature–keeping it intact–without too finicky a regard either for human economic value or for the lower court's sympathetic but wondrously coarse technique for approximating the "replacement costs."

> No market exists in which Puerto Rico can readily replace what it has lost. The loss is not only to certain plant and animal life but, perhaps more importantly, to the capacity of the now polluted segments of the environment to regenerate and sustain such life for some time into the future. That the Commonwealth did not intend, and perhaps was unable, to exploit these life forms, and the coastal areas which supported them, for commercial purposes should not prevent a damages remedy in the face of the clearly stated legislative intent to compensate for "the total value of the damages caused to the environment and/or natural resources. . . ." In recent times, mankind has become increasingly aware that the planet's resources are finite and that portions of the land and sea which at first glance seem useless like salt marshes, barrier reefs, and other coastal areas, often contribute in subtle but critical ways to an environment capable of supporting both human life and the other forms of life on which we all depend. The Puerto Rico statute is obviously aimed at providing a damages remedy with sufficient scope to compensate for, and deter, the destruction of such resources, and while we can see many problems in fashioning such a remedy, we see no reason to try to frustrate that endeavor.

The *Zoe Colocotroni* litigation suggests that an intactness standard may "make sense," in the sense that it can be operationalized coherently. But it may not always "make sense" when evaluated as policy. Certainly the policy of making the environment whole will be resisted when the costs of restoration or preservation are vastly out of line with the resource's consumption and use value, and the injury arises from a conscientious miscalculation rather than, as in *Zoe Colocotroni,* from gross, almost willful, negligence. That is, even if one recognizes a moral claim to expend for the resource *some* sum in excess of its beneficial social value (as we do in undertaking the rescue of a trapped miner), one is rightly queasy about committing society to a higher price-tag than any moral theory we can devise will warrant. The issue of overprotection is not peculiar to entities that lack, or take no interest in their well-being. The problem arises from our uncertainty about *preferences*. It is thus one of the common "general theory" problems that has to be faced in connection not only with lakes and forests, but also with some "higher" Nonpersons such as whales, primates, and mental defectives, entities that, while possessing interests and even preferences, are at best restricted in their capacities to express them.[*]

---

[*] See, however, David Lamb, "Animal Rights and Liberation Movements," *Environmental Ethics* 4 (1982): 215, 231 (remarking on potential of nonhumans to communicate preferences to us, particularly as we increase our

To understand the difficulty introduced by the want of preferences, we must consider for a moment the significance of preferences in the legal system in its ordinary operations, that is, as it affects dealings among Persons. As the law develops, a body of rules establishes or confirms certain entitlements, such as the right of a homeowner to his home, or of a car owner to her car. In the familiar interpersonal situations, the existence of legally enforceable claims does not freeze the social ordering. They only establish ground rules for the operation of a primarily consensual, mutually beneficial system.

To illustrate, suppose that I own a house, A, in the downtown area of a city. I value it because it is near my place of work, old friends, favored theaters, and reliable restaurants. Suppose now that Developer comes along with plans to turn my present block into apartment buildings. She is prepared to offer me an amount adequate to purchase another house in the suburbs, B, plus an additional lump sum of $100,000. Although I prefer A to B, I do not prefer the present situation to her package offer; that is, to owning B and pocketing the $100,000. By selling to Developer my rights to the favored house, my interests are advanced (I am better off), her interests are advanced (she is better off), and–presuming that the beneficence of her offer reflected the higher economic use society had for the apartment house over the one-family residences–the whole society emerges better off. The point is, because human preferences are rich, revealable, and negotiable, the initial assignment of a property right to my home (my ownership) does not hinder, and in fact may significantly contribute to, an exchange and redistribution of goods that is advantageous to all.

When we move from voluntary to involuntary exchanges, the mechanisms for adjustment shift, but it remains preferences that shape the system. The person who accidentally or deliberately drives a truck into my car is not, like Developer, coming to me with an offer to negotiate. The truck driver is engaged in what we might consider his own private condemnation of my property, "taking it" from me through the sort of negligence or malice that no right to the quiet enjoyment of my car can prevent. But while the legal system cannot prevent such an occurrence, it can provide that the wrongdoer compensate me. And note how the compensation is arrived at. The ideal is to make the wrongdoer pay whatever it takes to bring me to a position of indifference. That position is the point where I have no valid reason to prefer my pre-accident situation to the situation I find myself in after the accident plus the compensation award. In the case of the damaged car, that would ordinarily mean ordering the defendant to pay me whatever it took (in body-shop costs and other expenses) to return the car to the state it was in before the accident. But this is not always the solution. If the cost of returning the car to its original shape is greater than its

efforts to "listen." See also "Koko's Kitten," *National Geographic,* January 1985, 110 (narrating success in communicating with gorilla via sign language).

replacement cost—the cost of substituting another car—the wrongdoer is obliged to make the substitution payment only.

None of these approaches is guaranteed to leave everyone or even anyone perfectly satisfied. But there is much to be said for them as ways of making the best of the many conflicts inherent in community living. Some corrective justice is achieved; that is, we at least approximate compensation for the victims. At the same time, social efficiency is served. By confronting one another with the prospect of having to make amends for the harms we cause, the rules induce us all to take such care as is warranted in the circumstances (to drive more slowly, to have our brakes checked, etc.)—in essence, to accommodate to one another as sensibly and fairly as possible.

If we return now to the question of distributing legally enforceable claims to Nonpersons, we can see more clearly what the problem is. The problem is not the intelligibility of assimilating Nonpersons, even preference-lacking Things, into the system. We can give them claims, and lawyers to speak for them. The real problem is this. Suppose that the only kind of "advantage" we can dole out to Nonpersons is to preserve them from physical change, to substitute pure physical *intactness* for other measures of value. Once assigned, such an entitlement will not be reallocable to the highest use by ordinary law and market mechanisms. The implication is not just to give some special status to the entity over and above what market evaluations would suggest; it is to withdraw the entity from market accountability entirely. The implication is to impose a sort of freeze on selected aspects of the status quo. That would be ironic, since nothing seems quite as "unnatural" as enduring unchange.*

Comparable postures—rules which remove all costs and benefits from consideration at the judicial and administrative levels—are not unknown in the law. We do not do a cost-benefit analysis every time someone claims a right to free speech; that is what is meant by saying that free speech is (more or less) "absolute." The Fourteenth Amendment's prohibition on racial discrimination cannot be evaded by a showing that enforcing the Constitution imposes an *unreasonable* burden. Several years ago the so-called Delaney Amendment prohibited the inclusion in any foodstuff of any substance that might, in any amount, elevate cancer risks in any degree. Indeed, this is precisely the approach the Endangered Species Act of 1966 sought to implement in its original form. Interpreting that Act in *TVA* v. *Hill* [4] the Supreme Court held that notwithstanding that $100 million which had been spent on a huge dam project, the

---

* Moreover, wherever we were to adopt such a "freeze" position, we would be faced with the further question whether to express it in what we might call the imperative form or a weak form. In the imperative form, the Advantage would be construed as carrying an obligation that we intercede to prevent change from whatever cause, however indirectly *we* may be responsible. For example, if the forests surrounding the Sahara were a full Advantage-holder in this imperative sense, we would have an obligation, on the forests' behalf, to set the Sahara back, even if drought, rather than human intervention, were considered the proximate cause. (What if the Sahara had an Advantage?) I presume that, in regard to most things, the assignment of a status-freezing Advantage in this imperative sense would require some more powerful arguments than I can presently imagine.

whole project had to halt if one endangered species–a snail darter–would be placed at risk of elimination.

Now, we can arrange the system this way, that is, devise rules so that the intactness of certain things is insulated from all influence of market value. But note that in the most celebrated instances where we have approximated such a posture, as with constitutional rights to speech, press, and jury trial, there is a strong and broadly shared political consensus for what we do. In the absence of a comparably widespread concord, rules that originate as flat-out prohibitions tend to erode the more their conflict with prevailing desires becomes apparent. For example, the result of the flap over saccharin was to amend the Food and Drug Acts in such a way as to weaken the Delaney Amendment. After the U.S. Supreme Court reprieved the snail darters, Congress amended the law to provide a "review" process designed to relax the protection accorded endangered species in some circumstances. The point is this. I have not yet demonstrated that there is *any* argument for preserving a Thing intact, a chore to which I will turn in part II. Much less have I shown that any such argument could meet the demands of a valid moral theory. But we can anticipate that if the costs to us of intactness are high, the legal arrangement, if it is not to be diluted and evaded, will require not only a moral argument to back it up, but a fairly sturdy moral argument, at that.

Just as a preliminary intuition, is it possible there are Things on whose behalf a plea of such strength could be made? In *Trees,* I suggested as a possibility the Grand Canyon, which owing to its uniqueness, grandness, and association with national heritage might find support on mixed moral bases for so privileged a position–to be treated like an environmental First Amendment, as it were. But regarding most other Things, even if people are persuaded to sacrifice something for their conservation, the costs of intactness will in many circumstances appear unacceptable–even morally unacceptable. Consider, for example, a proposal to gird a river with a series of small hydroelectric dams that will relieve the need to import $1 million of oil annually. Of course, after damming, the river cannot be exactly the same as it was before. Even if we discern a moral reason to sacrifice *something* to preserve the river intact, we may not feel obligated–it may not be *right*–to forego competing benefits, such as heating the houses of the poor. What, then? Recall that in comparable situations when the "rights" of Persons are conflicted, the law's response is to award the "victim," such as the private owner of land condemned for a public purpose, a lump sum calculated to make him indifferent. But we have no way to judge whether some compromise solution we might offer the river is *fair enough, is compensating.* Are we on the horns of a dilemma so fatal–all or nothing–that the assignment of Advantage to Things has to be regarded as unsupportable in all but the most extraordinary circumstances?

This, I take it, is the central challenge of the legal segment of our inquiry. The implementation of Advantages to Nonpersons threatens to back us into a corner. We would not only be handing them Advantages, but Advantages beyond the reach of compromises merited by our own legitimate claims and needs. What is required are more flexible alternatives.

IMPUTING PREFERENCES

First, while Things have (or "take") no interests by definition, the same concession is not required of all Nonpersons, for example, future and spatially remote humans. We cannot know their preferences with certainty, but we can make some good guesses within reason. Even regarding "higher" animals, we cannot dismiss the feasibility of correctly identifying and imputing at least some preferences. Note that the issue being raised here is not the conventional query of the animal rights literature–whether higher animals have properties essential for possessing moral rights. All we are asking here is whether we can project a Nonperson's preferences confidently enough to allocate it some Advantage, without locking ourselves into a position of utter inflexibility.

To illustrate how a Nonperson's preferences, where available, may be enlisted to support the entity's legal position, let me return to the case of the bowhead whales. I am not certain how clear a picture we have of what whales like, of what welfare economists might call their "preference profile." Presumably a whale's preferences are less richly detailed than a Person's, if only because the richness of many alternatives available to humans–to go bowling or sit in a movie–do not present themselves to animals for reasons both physical and intellectual.* On the other hand, we could say much the same for infants and the mentally disabled, on whose behalf the law constructs rough preferences fairly routinely. Surely, unless one is prepared to deny that whales have intelligence and are capable of exercising choice, it is fair to infer that they prefer their present route through the Beaufort Sea to any other. (If the path is not exhaustively prescribed by instinct, why do they select the variations they do?) True, we cannot be certain *why* and *how much* they would find an alternate route less preferable. Perhaps a more northerly path would take them into less comfortable waters in terms of temperature. Another route would involve a less familiar, more bewildering (anxiety-ridden), path; the food at the greater distances from shoreline, even if comparable nutritionally, might be less palatable.

We are unclear on all the details. But we do know some things about their preferences–and we could learn more. For example, I presume that marine biologists know the whales' favorite foods, and it does not seem beyond our capabilities to determine experimentally what meals they would prefer to whatever they can locate on the northernmost edge of their current journey-route. And let us simplify matters by supposing that none of their favorite fare (krill, plankton, or–God forbid!–snail

---

* On the other fin, a whale swimming in the ocean may routinely mull alternatives that would not occur to a person swimming alongside.

darters) are recognized as legal persons in their own right. The point is, the more we are able to approximate such interests, the more freely we can allocate Advantages to Nonpersons with the assurance that if we need to modify them, we can "compensate" the way we do with Persons. This considerably mitigates the inflexibility problem referred to earlier.

To illustrate how such compensation would work, let us suppose that we do regard the whales as having established an Advantage to their traditional migratory route—something like what the law would call an easement by prior occupancy or prescription. Even if we elevated such an Advantage to equivalent rank of a human's property right, it would still be subject to condemnation, just as the ordinary person's easements (such as a long-established access path across a neighbor's property) can be condemned. To carry out this line of thought, suppose that the government had a higher public use for the whale's easement. The Treasury might realize, say, $10 billion in selling the oil rights. If so, mankind could well stand to proceed with the oil sale and still "pay off" the whales with a trust fund of $1 million for making their new course more comfortable. This could be accomplished by, say, "chumming" the alternate, northerly route with whatever foodstuff whale research indicated was high on the whales' preferences. As an ideal, some such solution would be better for everyone (would constitute, in the academic lingo, an interspecies-pareto improvement). The U.S. citizens would be better off through a reduced tax burden. The oil companies and their customers would be better off through the prospect of new domestic oil reserves. And the whales would be no worse off, tided over by a trust fund expended in a way as to compensate them—and help steer them clear of dangers at the drilling site.

Let me hasten to confirm that I do not know enough of the facts about the whales to know whether such a solution would make sense as a response to the bowhead dilemma, and I offer it as an imaginative illustration. But controversies of this sort are not sheerly fanciful,* and the principle illustrated is significant. The more *interested* we have become in other living things, the more we have been able to discover about their preferences. (Experiments with pigeons have revealed something of their discount rates; that is, their willingness to defer modest present gratifications in exchange for more substantial future rewards.) And the more confidently we can construct Nonperson preferences—that is, adopt their standpoint—the more feasibly we can fit them into rules which, while putting them into positions of Advantage, do not do so inflexibly.

---

* An interesting episode of such a character occurred in Wyoming in 1983-84. A rancher installed a twenty-eight-mile-long fence that cut off the migration route of sixteen hundred pronghorn antelopes to their winter grazing site at Red Rim. All risked death. After a storm of publicity, some talk of legal action, and pleas from the governor, the rancher relented and cut passageways in the fence for the antelope to get through. Query: should a rancher in such a situation bear the costs personally, or should he be compensated from the public till?

BOUNDARIES AND IDEALS

Unfortunately, the feasibility of such a preference-enlisting solution exists only in regard to Nonpersons at the higher end of the intelligence scale. In the case of many Nonpersons, and of all Things, that tactic has no place. They have no preferences. What, then, could comprise a workable solution?

One way to avoid inflexibility is to build some threshold conditions into the rules.* Such boundary-sensitive Advantages would not be out of character with ordinary human "rights." To take an obvious example, people have a right to a jury trial in certain federal civil cases if, but only if, the amount in controversy exceeds (depending on the controversy) twenty or fifty thousand dollars. By analogy, we could assign some monetary value to a Thing we chose to protect, say, $25 million for snail darters. This would mean that we were committed to forgo up to that amount to preserve the species. But if the tangible social benefits of some proposed snail-darter-jeopardizing action exceeded $25 million, then the action could proceed under the condition that that sum would be applied either to mitigate the risk, or else be allocated to some other part of the environment, perhaps to preserve some endangered, closely related species in a nearby biotic community.

Indeed, it remains to be seen whether the current administration will not propose some such construction of the toxic spill legislation discussed in the Introduction. A polluter might be required to return the lake to its pre-pollution condition unless the amount required to restore it exceeded a fixed figure. There is no other response when we are dealing with mishaps that are technologically impossible to repair at any price. Instead of demanding an infinite sum in damages, we have to develop feasible alternative remedies. Something like this occurred in the wake of the notorious discharges of the pesticide Kepone into the James River in 1975. A full dredging of the river bottom would not only have been extravagant in relation to the dangers; many believe that stirring up toxins from the bottom was riskier than just leaving them lie. As a consequence, Allied Chemical agreed to fund an $8 million trust fund with the mandate to mitigate the damage to the river to foster general environmental-health research in the area.[5]

Moreover, we do not have to express boundary parameters in monetary terms. We can employ physical definitions. If, say, a lake's level of dissolved oxygen should fall below so many parts per million (a common measure of biological degradation), or if the aggregate biomass it supports should decline below so many specified tons, then

---

* Even without express threshold conditions, judicial institutions are prone to dismiss complaints on traditionally available grounds when any harm the plaintiff suffered can be regarded as de minimis–beneath the threshold of what the law is prepared to recognize. See United States v. Chevron, 583 F.2d 1357 (5th Cir. 1978). The company was found to have discharged oil into a navigable waterway, which caused a presumption of violation of law; but the only consequence was a "sheen" on the water. The company was allowed to rebut the presumption of illegality by demonstrating that the sheen-causing discharge was "less than harmful."

the guardian would be empowered to invoke some legal remedy, in whatever way specified. A comparable approach is written into the Marine Mammal Protection Act. Individual endangered sea mammals, such as porpoises, are not protected as such. But if a human activity, such as seining for tuna, threatens the "optimum sustainable population" of their habitat, then the courts are authorized to intervene. Indeed, at that point, as the courts have interpreted the law, "balancing of interests between the commercial fishing fleet and the porpoise is irrelevant; the porpoise must prevail."[6]

From boundaries expressed in numerical terms of dollars, parts per million, optimum sustainable population, and so on, it is but a short step to enlist some looser notion of ideals as an alternate device for preserving flexibility. That is, while we cannot orient the law to a Thing's welfare, we can orient it to some ideal state of the Thing, without (as with boundaries) undertaking to express that ideal in a specific set of numbers. An enlisting of ideals is not unfamiliar to law. Certainly there are many circumstances in which the law glosses over what an individual actually desires with normative notions of what he or she most valuably *is* and *can become*. On a parity of reasoning, we can transport into the legal rules that govern our relations with Nonpersons norms that try to capture essences. In regard to a river, rather than using a standard expressed in parts per million, or some opacity index, we would examine the issue in terms of whether the river's "riverhood" was being endangered, just as one may have standing to challenge whether an artwork's "integrity"[7] is in peril.

Within such a loose, ideal-oriented construct there is room for compromise. Suppose that in regard to a habitat, the law adopted something like ecosystem stability as a rough measure of its essential, protectable nature. In that case, the guardian would be warranted to settle a suit against the jeopardizer of one of the habitat's populations if the defendant agreed to stock an alternate species, less endangered by the particular project, but equally well linked into the ecological balance.

There are obvious questions about both the boundaries and the ideals-based alternatives. One is certain to wonder how, in selecting the critical boundary variables or supplying content to the key "ideal" (riverhood, habitathood), we can avoid being, on the one hand, totally arbitrary or, on the other, guilty of smuggling in whatever standard advances our own most "raw" homocentric interests. This is part of a larger issue that I return larger issue that I return to in part III. Here, let me say only that we should not underestimate the capacity of commonsensical intuition, reinforced by ordinary language and an understanding of physical processes, to provide us with coherent notions about the essence of things quite independent of what we *want* those things to be. We are able to speak of the "death of a star," quite aside from what state we want the star to be in, or anything we might do about it. It is true that the classificatory categories selected in biology—whether something has vertebrae, nurses its young, climbs trees—undeniably reflect human "interests" in the broadest sense of what we are curious about. But surely we have a notion of what a genus or species is, independent of our own welfares. Hence, we can talk coherently about the design of arrangements that would preserve mosquitos and tarantulas, quite aside from whether doing so would be a good idea in terms of human welfare.

There is a second objection: at least where ideals are concerned, the concepts are likely to be too vague for courts to work with. How would a judge decide the point at which a river's "riverhood" was being infringed? I doubt that it would be any harder than judging "due process" or "negligence" or many other judgments that lawyers and courts are routinely called upon to make. Closer analogies exist in situations where a ruling will affect humans (albeit, in our terminology, Nonpersons) who are yet-unborn beneficiaries of trusts. The court hears out a guardian ad litem to decide what they, as Persons, probably will–or should–like. In other cases courts deal with those unable to reveal their preferences, such as the comatose accident victim and the severely retarded: Shall we turn off the life support systems, or order painful but life-prolonging therapy? We tend to work our way through these cases by invoking a concept of "personhood" that does not seem to me any less problematical than "riverhood."[*]

Or compare an inquiry into "riverhood" with what is involved in a prisoner's rights case. Some restrictions imposed on an inmate are simply part of what is entailed and intended by the imprisonment. But at some point, the imposition goes to far. Judicial analysis ordinarily pays tribute to "cruel and unusual punishment" because that is the language of the Constitution. But the real issue is whether the prison conditions can be reconciled with the essential respect owed the prisoner as a Person: is some protectable sense of his *personhood* being violated? How does the judge judge when this point is reached? We simply trust her to come to a right result (perhaps informed by precedents that develop over the years), even if we know that at bottom she is being guided by a somewhat intuitive metaphysics and morals. In like view, in regard to the river, there is simply a difference we might trust judges to recognize between ribbing a river with dams but leaving the river's total flow and course intact and, on the other hand, so depleting its waters that it simply peters out and never reaches the sea.

---

[*]   A poignant illustration is Superintendent of Belchertown State School v. Saikewicz, 370 N.E.2nd 417 (1977). There, a profoundly retarded, institutionalized 67-year-old man with an I.Q. of 10 contracted leukemia. Chemotherapy could prolong his life, but the treatment would subject him to pain the reasons for which he would not be able to comprehend. Nor had Saikewicz any long-term projection of a *life*, which might have made short-term suffering bearable. The court settled upon a test based on what Saikewicz would have chosen, *were* he able to understand the choice. How can such a hypothetical reasoning process carry forward without introducing some ideal of personhood into the analysis?
We may also invoke something like a personhood standard in instances involving compensation for a loss, where the losers are suspected of exaggerating their true preferences in order to extract a higher payment than is just, and we wish to establish what they probably *really* want.

ENDNOTES

1. *See* Summerfield v. Superior Court of the State of Arizona, Supreme Court of Arizona, April 24, 1985. *And see* MacDonald v. Time, Inc., 554 F.Supp. 1053 (D.C.N.J. 1983) (libel suit not mooted by plaintiff's death).

2. See *Trees* (Chapter 1), pp. 12-14.

3. 456 F.Supp. 1327 (D.Puerto Rico 1978), *aff'd* 628 F.2d 652 (1st Cir. 1979).

4. 437 U.S. 153 (1978).

5. See Christopher D. Stone, "A Slap on the Wrist for the Kepone Mob," *Business and Society Review* 22 (Summer 1977): 4-11.

6. Committee for Humane Legislation v. Richardson, 540 F.2d 1141, 1151, n. 39 (C.A. D.C. 1976).

7. California Civil Code 989(a)(3)(c).

CHAPTER 3

SHOULD WE ESTABLISH A GUARDIAN
FOR FUTURE GENERATIONS?[*]

BACKGROUND: THE MALTESE PROPOSAL

In 1992, in preparation for the Rio "Earth Summit" (United Nations Conference on Environment and Development (UNCED), the delegation of Malta submitted to the Preparatory Committee a proposal (hereinafter the Proposal) that the world community go beyond the vague declarations of responsibilities towards future generations that are appearing in international documents with increasing frequency,[1] and actually institute an official Guardian to represent posterity's interests.[2] Although visionary, and bedeviled by problems, it is well worth our attention.

As the Proposal contends, just as conventional legal systems typically provide representation for infants, the mentally impaired, and others who cannot adequately speak for themselves,[3] so the world order should provide for:

> "[an authorized person ('guardian') to represent future generations at various international fora . . . whose decisions would affect the future . . . to argue the case on behalf of future generations, hence bringing out the long-term implications of proposed actions and proposing alternatives. His role would not be to decide, but to . . . plead for future generations, [and to counter] the firmly established attitude of our civilization [to discount] the future."[4]

Such a Guardianship, it is claimed, would give our responsibilities to future generations "a practical substance and a concrete form."

The recommendation is distinctly preliminary—an invitation to a dialogue of which this Conference is a part. In this spirit, I will react by raising several overlapping issues that the Proposal inspires, issues that range from considerations of economics and institutional design to fundamental questions of moral philosophy.

---

[*]   This essay is a composite of two presentations, one, in September 1994 at a Conference on *Guardian For Future Generations: Status Under International Law*. The Conference was held at the Foundation for International Studies at the University of Malta and underwritten by UNESCO and UNEP. In November 1994 another version was delivered in Kyoto, Japan, at a Conference on future generations sponsored by the Future Generations Alliance Foundation.

(1) Are Future Persons Really Voiceless?

The proposal is based on the widespread assumption that present generations will deeply discount or even disregard the welfare of their descendants, particularly those whose lives will take place relatively remote in time. This conforms to a social choice perspective, which suggests a tendency of political institutions to slight the unborn, since they lack representation in the legislatures. But the voicelessness of the unborn, even of remote descendants, is easy to exaggerate. There is an impressive body of theoretical and empirical literature, much of it generated by analyses of taxation and public finance, indicating that each generation's empathy for its own immediate successors—its children—provides something like an "infinite horizon."[5] I save (and exercise my political voice to conserve key resources) in order to improve the legacy of my daughters, who will save for their children, and so on. What this suggests is that the function of the Guardian (below) might perhaps be less to affect motivation, as to uncover and publicize information about future perils that would otherwise go unnoticed.

(2) For Whom (or What) Should a Guardian Speak?

The Proposal contemplates that the Guardian would represent future generations of *humans*.[6] Those concerned with the state of the future are not, however, restricted to focusing directly on the well-being of persons. One might consider (as I have proposed) a group of guardians, one for each of several natural objects—for example, a legal spokesperson for marine mammals, another for Antarctic fauna, perhaps others for various great cultural artifacts such as the Sphinx.

Of course, the condition in which we pass along these various nonhuman objects affects the well-being of future generations of persons indirectly. Presumably our progeny would want to receive and enjoy whales as part of their legacy. The future generations guardian would take that into account. But in specific contexts the position that might be taken by the Future Generations Guardian would not be expected to coincide with that which would be taken by a guardian for whales or some other object. A great social project which hazards a species or cultural artifact may appear on balance calculated to improve the welfare of future generations, even allowing for the probability-discounted loss of the object. In those circumstances, a future generations guardian might consent to the project as acceptable for his human principals, while a guardian for, e.g. whales, might steadfastly oppose it as too risky for her cetacean clients.

One might argue that where conflicts exist between the welfare of future persons and the preservation of nonhuman creatures and objects, our choice has to be governed by human preferences. But there is no such easy way out from under our responsibilities. The tastes of future generations are not only unformed; it is our choices that will form them. The value persons remote in time place on the existence of, say, songbirds, is not a *given*, but will be a function of the legacy we leave them. I personally would regard the eradication of all songbirds as a terrible loss for my remote progeny. But they may find the electronic sounds they will be able to create an entirely adequate substitute, particularly if they never have the opportunity to hear live song-birds. In other words, we cannot consistently appeal to their wants in making the very decisions that will, inescapably, form those wants.

One implication is to reinforce the case for Guardians for natural objects and human artifacts (rather than future persons), since our decisions on whether to make, e.g., whales and songbirds planetary heirlooms will strongly influence—we might say, is logically prior to—the value future persons will place on those *things*; the decisions regarding those things might most appropriately be made through decisions informed by thing-specific guardians.

In all events, none of these remarks is intended to undermine the argument to establish a Guardian for Future Generations (of Persons). But we should remember that such a Guardian is not inconsistent with guardians pleading for other interests and values, whose contributions will in some instances carry our concerns along tangent lines of thinking.

(3) Are the Moral Arguments Disparaging the Rights of Future Generations Critical to the Guardianship Proposal?

There is a wide-ranging and impressive body of literature regarding the moral status of future generations. The central inquiry is whether ethics provide any compelling reasons that we sacrifice our welfare in the interests of persons unborn. The answers are controversial and complex. A considerable body of opinion suggests that it is incoherent that we can have a duty towards any person not in being, or, alternatively, that such a person can be said to "hold" (at most, "will hold") a right against us.[7] It does, indeed, seem to deform the ordinary concept of "right" to suppose that rights (that we not store nuclear waste in vulnerable deposit sites, for example) will spring into the hands of those who will live in 2200, long after the possibility of a remedy against us, the violators, has been mooted by our deaths.[8]

One rejoinder is that rights and duties are not the only fabric of which a morality can be woven. Whether or not a starving person in Somalia has a *right* that I aid her, and whether or not I have a *duty* to aid, the state of affairs in which she is aided by me is surely morally superior to the state in which I do not aid her. The Proposal well-advisedly speaks not in terms of our posterity's rights, but of our *responsibilities*, which are typically viewed to run wider, and be less inflexible and imperative, than rights and duties.* Those advocating a Guardianship for Future Generations can thus

---

* If one of your ancestors drank and gambled away the fortune your family had built up until his day, it would be odd to claim that he violated a "duty" to you (or to say that you had a "right" to the uninvaded corpus of the family fortune); but it is not odd to say that he acted "irresponsibly." *See* Daniel A. Farber & Paul A.

locate a moral grounding for their position without miring in some of the most daunting conundrums that the future generations literature debates.

Indeed, let me go a step further. It is quite possible for the Proposal to go forward entirely independent of the moral status of future persons. That is, whether or not posterity possesses moral rights against us, and whether or not we have moral responsibilities towards them, the establishment within the international legal system of a Future Persons Guardian can be defended without ranging beyond the welfare of those presently living. Specifically, imagine that most living people would regard insuring the well-being of future persons as a positive public good (in their own welfare functions). Put otherwise, just as people get benefit from assurances that their homes will not be robbed, so they get benefit from assurances that their descendants will be provided for. In the first instance, because we are happier if public safety is provided, through collective action we establish guardians called police officers; in the second, being happier contemplating a snug posterity, we designate a guardian to speak for them.

Now, this is not to overlook that special moral pleadings in regard to posterity, e.g., an argument that the unborn hold (will hold) rights, or that we have strong duties towards them, will strengthen the argument for establishing a Future Generations Guardian, and be available to expand the powers with which the Guardian ought to be invested. The point is merely that the Guardianship notion need not stand or fall on—or be postponed until resolution of—the most perplexing philosophical objections to rights of the unborn.

(4) Which "Future Generation" is the Guardian's Principal?

Even if we adopt (from consideration of our own interests or of theirs) the Proposal's aim to safeguard future generations directly, and other things—species of animals cultural artifacts, etc.—only indirectly, ambiguities remain. Most of the discussions that invoke "future generations" use the term loosely and not with much consistency. Sometimes it is used to refer to the members of successive, roughly overlapping "waves" of populations twenty-five or thirty years apart; sometimes, to what we might call "remote generations"—people who will not come into existence for hundreds of years. One virtue of a dialogue focused on institutionalizing a Guardian for Future Generations is that it compels us to undertake a more precise identification of whose interests, exactly, are to be protected.

Hemmerbaugh, *The Shadow of the Future: Discount Rates, Later Generations, and the Environment*, 346 Vand. L. Rev. 294-295 (1993). Also, it can be said that the paradigmatic right is relatively detailed (Person *A* has a right that person *B* perform act *q*) whereas a responsibility, such as a parent's responsibility to its child, is more general (to provide an environment not unfavorable for the child's development).

To begin with—the point is obvious, but bears underscoring—we ordinarily imagine individuals, rather than generations, as foci of our concern. Welfare, rights, duties, etc., pertain, in ordinary non-metaphorical parlance, to persons. What we call "generations" are constructed of lives that are continuously overlapping. People die and others are born to replace them. It may be possible to give the term "generation" a special independent status, not reducible to expressions about individuals. But even so, a number of questions would remain about which future generation we were talking about.

To illustrate, consider one credible climate change scenario which (rightly or not) has it that relatively unconstrained use of carbon and other greenhouse gases will, on net, benefit humankind for the next several generations. Our near descendants will gain more in economic growth than they will lose in environmental peril. But at some more remote period—after 200 years, say—the accumulated congestion will trigger a host of nonlinear positive feedback mechanisms with dire consequences for populations then living.

Where such conflicts among future generations are possible—our near descendants pitted against our remote ones—which should the Guardian consider his principal?

(5) Who Should Serve as Guardian?

The Proposal contemplates appointment of ". . . an eminent person, without known prejudices, and having practical wisdom, integrity, moderation and humility, with an ability to feel the pain and share the joy of people who will live at a great distance from us in time."[9]

Obviously there is a problem of obtaining international concordance on which candidate best (or simply suitably) displays these agreeable qualities. And there is the obvious question, whether a single individual, rather than an agency or series of agencies (below) would be better suited to the task. But we also might ask which would be more desirable, specific expertise or the wider vision of each epoch's generalists. The answer turns on the anticipated functions we expect the guardianship to provide.

If the function is simply to speak for the *general* welfare of future persons, the opinions of a generalist are not inappropriate. Such a person, in authority, might aim to moderate present-future wealth imbalances through economic and fiscal measures, such as tempering the effective social rate of discount.* But if the function were to be

---

* On intertemporal allocation (between present and future consumption), *see generally* Amartya K. Sen, *On optimising the Rate of Saving*, 71 Econ. J. 479-496 (1961). Sen indicates why a political decision, of a sort that a Futures Guardian might broker, could result in a higher rate of savings for future generations than would be motivated by individuals each maximizing their personal utilities. *Id.* at 487-88. *See also* William D. Nordhaus's observation, "The key institutions for determining interest rates—central banks—appear more concerned with inflation and

more specific, such as selecting techniques for long-term storage of nuclear waste, highly technical, area-specific questions are raised. One would accordingly desire more specific scientific expertise. To illustrate, my own analogous proposals, favoring a number of distinct guardians for distinct objects (the tropical forests, oceans, whales, etc.), place heavier reliance on scientific expertise inasmuch as each "object" requires distinct bodies of knowledge. In the case of the oceans, one strong candidate would be the joint Group of Experts on the Scientific Aspects of Marine Pollution (GE-SAMP), with lawyer staffing. Such recognized institutional bodies have several advantages. They concentrate and mobilize knowledge; their opinions are therefore authoritative, and readily enjoy a credit that may be denied the speculations of a well-respected generalist. Considering the concern over the long term effects on human life of specific assets and activities, future persons might wish that those who spoke for them had more than practical wisdom and humility.

(6) Where Should a Guardian Be Situated?

The Proposal appears to contemplate a Guardian housed within the United Nations. But there are other options for where a Guardian might be housed. The United Nations provides a prestigious base of operations. Both for reasons of acquiring immediate authority and for symbolic reasons, the U.N. would seem to be the right spot (probably for the U.N. as well as for the Guardian).

But another alternative is to house the Guardian independent of any existing institution. Such a free-standing guardian might be an international body—that is, appointed by and responsible to nation-states. But there would be a weakness. Because the actions that the Guardian would presumably call into question are often those of nation-states, a strong argument can be made for establishing the Guardian as a nongovernmental organization (NGO), thereby providing it a freer hand to criticize and supplement official activities. The Guardian would gain in independence, but lose, probably, in influence.

And, of course, there need not be a single Guardian. One could arrange a cluster of expert but institutionally free-standing guardians. Another alternative would be to establish a number of guardians, each separately housed within such agencies as the central banks,[10] the World Bank, International Atomic Energy Agency, Global Environmental Facility, etc. There is, indeed, much to be said for structuring guardians into vital slots in such existing bureaucracies. Doing so would promote the guardians's access to the flow of critical information and put them in direct contact with those who

---

trade balances than with ethical judgments about the consumption trade-offs between current and future generations." Nordhaus, How Much Should We Invest in Preserving Our Current Climate? p. 263 (Cowles Foundation Paper No. 847, 1993).

are making the decisions the will want to influence. These are strategic advantages that might outweigh the risks "in-house" guardians would be co-opted.

But the most important question that emerges when we put the issue this way is, what, other than name, might a guardian add to the these institutions? The question is not rhetorical, but it is worth keeping in mind that those who run, for example, the World Bank, or the new Commission on Sustainable Development, would be bewildered by the suggestion that they should "start thinking about future generations." It would be a useful exercise for the proponents of a Guardian or guardians to review the performance of such agencies and to indicate the decisions the Guardian, had there been one somewhere on hand, would have done differently.[*]

As a practical matter, the question of guardian location is less likely to be settled by ideal organizational theory than fortuitously, on a case by case basis. We are not likely to see the question of creating a single Guardian with plenary jurisdiction brought to a vote imminently. But as international law takes shape gradually, we have the more realistic prospect of providing guardianship functions through a series of incremental proposals, convention by convention, and institution by institution, as new ones are formed and reformed. Such negotiations provide the opportunity to create context-specific guardians. To illustrate, the question of a special future Guardian might be posed initially in furthering any of the numerous convention that already invokes "future generations" terminology, such as the 1991 Arctic Environmental Protection Strategy, that aims to "safeguard the Arctic environment for future generations . . ."[11], or in the context of establishing or reshaping an institutional arrangement, such as under NAFTA, perhaps as an integral part of the yet-to-be formed Commission for Environmental Cooperation, or in the context of a UNEP Regional Seas Program.

(7) What Official Functions Should the Guardian Serve?

As concerns official functions, the Proposal is clear that nothing beyond "the power of advocacy" is contemplated. "His role would not be to decide but to promote enlightened decisions . . . to put forward arguments on behalf of future generations . . . at various international fora, particularly the United Nations."[12]

As an alternative, the functions of a Guardian might be further specified and expanded. For example, the Guardian might be authorized (i) to appear before the

---

[*]   In regard to all of these institutional questions, while a designated Guardian would be an original and perhaps valuable advance, the basic concept is not entirely novel. For example, in the United States, the Office of Technology Assessment (OTA), the Assistant to the President for Science and Technology, and various official scientific bodies have aimed to extend the time-horizon of the Congress and Executive. Other comparable offices undoubtedly exist in other nations and in international bodies. Where they exist, the availability of such technical advisors does not displace the need for a Guardian with broader ambitions. But we could profitably identify existing agencies that already supply, if not fulfill, future-orienting services and learn what we can from their successes and deficiencies. What functions currently unprovided should a Guardian therefore emphasize?

legislatures and administrative agencies of states considering actions with pronounced, long term implications; (ii) to appear as a special intervenor-counsel in a variety of bilateral and multi-lateral disputes, and, (iii) perhaps most important, even to initiate legal and diplomatic action on the future's behalf in appropriate situations.[13] An example is when there is a threat to a world cultural heritage, e.g., the Pyramids Plateau, and no signatory to the UNESCO Convention for the Protection of the World Cultural and Natural Heritage[14] steps forward to pursue redress. In other words, at another extreme, the Guardian might be empowered to range outside a particular agency, beyond even the United Nations system, even to the point of suing to enjoin activities that damaged the global patrimony.

And there are certainly other possible entry points for the Guardian. Hungary's justification for terminating its international obligations to Czechoslovakia to build a joint canal system included the claim that reforestation and preservation of animal species were not only of "national value," but their preservation for the *future generations* is a moral obligation."[15] Perhaps in a dispute of this sort, destined for a hearing in the World Court,[16] the Guardian could be available as a Master to make special findings.

Another important question involves the Guardian's power to waive rights of its ward. Suppose, for example, that a collective decision has been made that a certain species of dolphin is to be transmitted to posterity. Its continued existence has been made a "right" of future generations, invocable by the Guardian. It subsequently appears that that species hosts a virus, which, if not eliminated, will imperil all marine mammals. The whales must be sacrificed in order to save more of Nature. Will the Guardian be empowered (on certain conditions?) to waive the right—the way in which the guardian for an infant may, in some circumstances, waive a right of the child?

(8) What Should Be the Guardian's Objectives?

Let us put aside how the Guardian is to be initiated, where it is to be housed, and so on. What is the Guardian *to aim for*? One might say that the Guardian, like any hardy advocate, is to urge the living to pass forward to future generations as much wealth, and as few risks, as he can persuade us of. But even special counsel appointed to patrol the interests of an unascertained, unborn beneficiary under a trust is constrained to appeal to certain legal guidelines. In what circumstances will a Guardian be authorized to challenge the living in the presumed interests of his unborn wards?

One might advance as the guiding principle to further equity among all persons, born and unborn, across all generations.[17] But what "equity" demands across generations is controversial even in philosophy, and thus far too-open ended to serve in law.[18] What might the Guardian turn our attention to, as more specific constraints on future-affecting activities?

(a) resource-regarding standards

It has been suggested that the Guardian could aim to leave future generations a fair share of the earth's *resources*.[19] If a per capita share of each conventional natural resource is meant, the proposal is simply silly. Technology (as well as demand) is continuously shifting the value and even the stock of accessible resources. Increased rates of consumption of many nonrenewable resources has been continually more than offset by improved methods of prospecting, recycling, mining (bio-mining), etc.[20] We may be leaving—effectively—more key resources than we inherited. Moreover, in a generation or two, many of these resources that we value—such as coal and copper—may have faded into worthlessness.

(b) utility-regarding standards

Rather than to demand an intergenerational sharing of the earth's physical assets, it would be better to direct the Guardian to monitor *welfare* in some form. After all, whether a stock of resources is or is not a *shortage* depends on the utility the resource represents to those to whom it is available. Thus, if there is to be a Guardian training our thoughts on future persons, the better guide would be to apportion utility, or some near proxy, e.g., wealth, or basic goods, across all persons born and unborn. The implicit equity argument would be that, just as (people in) richer countries might be expected to pay more for safeguarding the atmosphere than (people in) poor countries, so rich generations would be expected to pay more than poor generations. Even more specifically, the Guardian might conceive its role as to forecast trends and to:

(a) raise average utility;

(b) equalize opportunities (according to some appropriate opportunities index);*

(c) disregard averages, but put a floor under basic needs.[21]

(c) efficient level of harm and harm-avoidance

Another approach would be to focus on the intergenerational *effects* of our *activities*. The Guardian's assignment would not be to equalize wealth or utility among generations—he would be willing to let those fall out where they may—but to internalize (negative) externalities that we the living were otherwise shouldering off on the future persons. Analysis of inter-temporal conflict between the living and the unborn would be assimilated to the familiar modeling of conflict between contemporaries, say, two neighboring nations that are polluting across boundaries.

---

*   The outstanding exposition of this approach is Jerome Rothenberg, *Alternative Approaches to Time Comparisons, in* Global Accord 355 (Nazli Choucri ed., 1993).

The literature is replete with analyses of the policy instruments available to assure that the social costs of such activities are set at the right level. But some of the devices we can deploy to moderate inter-temporal disputes, such as tradable emissions permits,[22] are hard to fit to the intergenerational conflict. (Present and future generations cannot "trade" as straightfowardly as can neighbors, e.g., the United States and Canada). On the other hand, The Guardian might regard a tax as an appropriate way to temper intergenerational externalities (no doubt favoring investment of tax proceeds in long-term capital projects).

But, once more, the complications are daunting. One might well object to the Guardian's efforts to disaggregate our economy into distinct activities, selectively internalizing the negative externalities of those (such as a coal-fired plant), that cast a burden forward, and disregarding the benefits we send along with them. After all, partly because of the "savings" on pollution abatement we are leaving a richer legacies of infrastructure, libraries, technology, and so on. How can we be sure that they will not value the marginal benefits of added technology over the marginal costs of the unabated carbon?

(d) precaution against selected calamities and safeguarding specific assets

As we consider lives increasingly remote from our own, it becomes difficult, not only to identify with them morally, but also even to form an opinion about what to desire for them. Considering the complications that would confront a Guardian whose province was general (to patrol resources generally, or the general level of welfare) it makes sense to focus the Guardian's mandate.

One such focused role would have the Guardian restrict its efforts to assuring that future generations are not deprived of the stock of planetary goods and services requisite for an acceptable (somehow defined) human existence. As Joel Feinberg once put it, we have a moral obligation not to leave our progeny the moral equivalent of a used-up garbage heap.[23] An institutional implication is that a Guardian so charged would have to mull not merely questions of science, but genuine wisdom: what is a good life?

Another possibility is to protect the remote unborn from clear peril where the discounted cost/benefit ratios are most compelling. An illustration is the U.S. Department of Energy study examining strategies to warn our remote progeny (whose language may no more resemble ours than ours does that of the Sumerians), away from highly dangerous storage sites.[24] The costs of some such simple measures may be modest; the benefits, if we only have the ingenuity and (prompted by a Guardian) the conscience, great.

Alternatively, the Guardian might promote only such sacrifices as are calculated to avoid the most cataclysmic events. For example, what future generations might most like from us, is that we would have started work on an emergency defense system capable of destroying earth-bound asteroids or comets.[*] Such a project, incidentally, may illustrate the purest form of intergenerational sacrifice: some imagine that the construction and deployment of a defense system would take so long that all of the costs would be borne by, but none of the benefits accrue to, those who built it.[25]

One way to conceive the selected calamities approach is as safeguarding specific assets. We would not oblige ourselves to share all resources ratably, in the sense that we would have to turn over the same amount of cropland, or cropland per capita, as we inherited—or anything as problematical as that. But we would be constrained not to invade, and indeed, to defend, if need be, the corpus of some very critical endowments: including an atmosphere and ozone shield congenial to life, a healthy ocean ecosystem, and so on. It might be under the "and so on" that we would commit to preserve and pass along great cultural artifacts, such as the Sphinx.

Each focusing of Guardian function would help clarify institutional variables, such as staffing, and incidentally simplify the Guardian's task by restricting the number of "causes" in which he would be required to appear.

(e) Avoiding "irreversible harm"

Merely to avoid gross, life-hobbling calamities may be too modest an objective. The Guardian might take a special stand against measures that are "irreversible" (or "irreparable"). On inspection, this concept, too, is unclear. All change is irreversible in the sense that time runs in one direction. A disturbed ecosystem does not "reverse"; it evolves in other ways than, but for our tampering, it would have.

This is not to say that all courses are practically or ethically equivalent. It only underscores that what we are disposed to label an "irreversible harm" must be some sort of change we imagine future generations will deeply regret and ought not to be permitted. But that does little to advance an answer to our original question, which was how to decide which were the harms that were impermissible.[26]

A helpful way to clarify the intuition that (some) irreversible changes should trigger Guardian intervention comes from the notion of *option value*. A social choice displays option value in circumstances where (1) one of the choices is impossible (or extremely costly) to undo and (2) it is reasonable to anticipate, at some future time, improvements in knowledge of the benefits and costs of the outcomes.[27]

---

[*] The probability that a large (1-2 km. in diameter) asteroid will hit the earth has been variously estimated at about one in 500,000 or a million a year—but the effects could be devastating for life. However, with a telescope network in place, a large object headed for earth could be detected several decades or even centuries in advance, *see* Breck Henderson, *Scientists Support Building Telescopes to Protect Earth from Asteroids*, 135 Aviation Week and Space Technology 70 (Oct. 14, 1991), and could be blasted or nudged off course, *see* T. Ahrens & A. Harris, *Deflection and Fragmentation of Near Earth Asteroids*, 360 Nature 429-433 (Dec. 3, 1992) (Reporting an individual's annual probability of death from such an event as on the order of $\sim 5 \times 10^{-10}$—or roughly the chances of losing one's life in a commercial airplane accident; but should it occur could lead to 25% human mortality or more).

Consider, for example, a biological "hot spot" in a rain forest. Its present value converted to farmland is $1000/acre. Its expected present value as a "library" of genetic material for medicinal and industrial purposes is only $700/acre. The highest economic use of the forest is apparently to transform it to agriculture. However, we also know that someday, as our ability to "read" the library and synthesize and exploit the forest's material improves, the forest *may* have a large benefit that present conversion to farmland will make impossible to realize. Option value is the value of not extinguishing that prospect; to put it otherwise, the facial cost of forgoing conversion ($300/acre) may be merited as a sort of "flexibility premium." We bear the costs of postponing development, to "purchase" an option to exploit the possible benefits of a biological "hot spot" if, at some later time, with the advance of knowledge and technology, substantial benefits should materialize. Of course, in any particular case, the price we pay for the option may or may not prove to have been merited. Nonetheless, this could be one of the services the Guardian would perform: to illuminate and speak for the option value of select assets.[28]

CONCLUSION

Just as human activities generate externalities among contemporaries, through space, so they produce externalities among generations, through time. Some of the intertemporal externalities are negative: nuclear waste, an imperilled ozone shield, a burgeoning population (concentrated among the poor), long-term debt, a pillaged biodiversity portfolio, expanded deserts, and a carbon-congested atmosphere. Some other externalities are certainly positive, however. We are leaving those who follow us great libraries, monuments, infrastructure and technology. If the past is an indication, our progeny, barring calamity, will lead on average better lives than those now living, even with some considerable increase in population. If the munificence of rich nations can be expanded, I would be hard put to make a stronger case for our aiding our temporally remote progeny, whose perils are uncertain and who may come off quite well, over spatially remote contemporaries across the globe, whose wretchedness is certain.

Despite my misgivings, I join those who wish to provide a "well-insured" safeguarding of the interests of those trillions who will follow us, if we are not reckless. Yet, even then—even supposing we are inclined to lean over backwards to safeguard the future trillions from profound perils—we do not know what form their perils will take. Many contemporaries worry, on our progeny's behalf, about the risks of global warming. But we are as unlikely to foresee correctly what will be our progeny's highest perils, as our forbearers would have ben trying to foresee ours. (Our descendants may be more worried about global cooling than about warming, as leading Jeremiads were only a few decades ago.)

In these circumstances, the best "insurance" we can write for future persons has to include, as a central element, enhancing their flexibility to deal with risks presently unforeseen. Fortuitously, this means that if we devote added resources to eliminating many of the problems that bother us—including racism, poverty, nuclear weapons, illiteracy, unrestrained population and excessive nationalism—we will go a long way to helping them. One of the best legacies we could leave our descendants would be, aside from (but it should be said) *wealth*, would be a more flexible and adaptable set of economic and social institutions.[29] For example, global arrangements that could overcome barriers to the movement of commodities, people and capital would be one "insurance" against regional crop loss and famine. An improved World Health Organization, with early-warning capabilities, would mitigate the risks of fast-moving lethal viruses.

Even as these institutional improvements are implemented, however, there will linger a residue of concerns. Our increasing power to confer long range benefits on our descendants does not nullify our increasing power to cast an ever-lengthening shadow of risk. It is a shadow that increasingly falls across populations who have no direct say in the decisions that affect them—at least, no electoral voice nor bargaining power nor sword to rattle. Aside from the shield of our extended self-interest (which should not be under-rated), they are at the mercy of our well-informed concern—well-informed morally and scientifically. In this context, the Maltese proposal is absolutely right, and should go forward.

But we need to remember this. Most of the perils that face the remote future—the perils of a nuclear holocaust, and so on—are also problems for the living, which the living already have some (albeit, from the future's perspective, somewhat imperfect) motivation to resolve from simple self-interest. In a way, this makes formulating a role for a Future Generations Guardian easier. It means that the emphasis of the Guardian (or Guardians) might at least initially be concentrated on a relatively narrow range of long term needs most apt to be overlooked politically—for example, long fuse "time bomb" risks not calculated to marshall an effective constituency among the living.

The Guardian might also wish to emphasize development of a corpus of assets, such as well-secured waste storage sites, that no future generation will be tempted to invade. As the Proposal moves forward, it may be useful to keep this relatively modest and manageable model in mind. Building on the idea would be time well spent. Not the less so, because our progeny will never be able to thank us for it.

ENDNOTES

1. For example "Man . . . has the solemn responsibility to protect and improve the environment for present and future generations," Declaration of the United Nations Conference on the Human Environment, U.N. Doc./A Conf. 48/14 (Stockholm 1972) 11 International Legal Materials 1416 (1972). A 1994 search of the term, "future generations" in various international legal material data-bases including WESTLAW (US Treaties database, which includes T.I.A.S. documents beginning June 1979) and LEXIS, (INTLAW library, ILMTY file, which includes treaties and agreements from International Legal Materials, starting with the Jan. 1980 issue of International Legal Materials) identified seven bilateral agreements, fifteen multilateral agreements, and three declarations employing the term—twenty-two of which are within the past fifteen years.

2. Preparatory Committee for the United Nations Conference on Environment and Development, United Nations, *Principles on General Rights and Obligations*, (Working Group III, 4th Session), New York, NY, 2 March - 3 April, 1992; A/CONF.151PC/WG.III/L.8/REV.1/ADD.2, 21 February 1992.

3. Interestingly, while the UNCED (Rio) Declaration recognizes that women, youth, indigenous peoples, and people under oppression, domination, and occupation, need representation in environmental discussions (Principles 20-23) it overlooks future generations as a disadvantaged group for which some especially appealing arguments for a Guardian might be made. *See also* United Nations Conference on Environment and Development, *Statement of Principles for a Global Consensus on the Management, Conservation and Sustainable Development of all Types of Forests, 32* Int'l Legal Materials 881 (1992) (also discussing the need for further representation of various advantaged and disadvantaged parties alive today, disregarding those of the future. (Principle 2(d)).

4. Proposal, §§ 12-13.

5. *See* Robert J. Barro, *Are Government Bonds Net Worth?*, 82 J. Pol. Econ. 1028 (1974); John J. Setear, *Ricardian Equivalence*, 31 J. Econ. Lit. 142, 148-151 (1993).

6. Proposal, § 12 also suggests the *human species* as a client, and § 15 refers to *those yet to be born*. In the context, I assume these variants are intended synonymously—although, as we will see, one might attach distinct significance.

7. *See* R.T. De George, *The Environment, Rights and Future Generations, in* Responsibilities to Future Generations, 157-170. (Ernest Partridge ed., 1981). *But see*, A. Baier, *The Rights of Past and Future Persons, id.* at 171-183, finding no conceptual difficulty in imputing rights to the unborn.

8. Some have supposed that a conception of our duties to them (duties without contemporary rights-holders) is less offensive than the conception of their rights against us (rights without contemporary duties bearers). *See*, for example, H.B. Nickell, *Book Review: In Fairness to Future Generations: International Law, Common Patrimony, and Intergenerational Equity*, 1 Colo. J. Int'l Envtl. L. & Pol'y 202 (1990). The classic general

treatment is in Joel Feinberg, *Legal Moralism and Free-Floating Evils*, 61 Pac. Phil. Q. 122-155 (1980).

9. Proposal § 14.

10. *See* Nordhaus *supra* footnote p. 70.

11. 30 Int' Legal Materials 1621 (1991).

12. Proposal §§ 12-13.

13. See my analogous proposals for an Oceans Guardian in Christopher D. Stone, Healing the Seas Through a Global Commons Trust Fund, *in* Freedom for the Seas in the 21st Century: Ocean Governance and Environmental Harmony 173, (Jon M. Van Dyke & Durwood Zaelk eds., 1993).

14. The Convention provides for the "transmission to future generations" of certain artifacts. For its potential role in litigation, *see* ICSID (W. Bank) Award in Southern Pacific Properties (Middle East) Ltd. v. Arab Republic of Egypt, 32 Int'l Legal Materials 933 (1993) (Egyptian obligation to protect the Pyramids Plateau raised in unsuccessful defense to suit by contractor whose contract to develop the area was breached by Egypt).

15. See *Treaty Concerning the Construction and Operation of the Gabcikovo-Nagymaros System of Locks and Hungarian Termination of Treaty*, 32 Int'l Legal Materials 1247, 1280 (1993) (Emphasis added).

16. Owing to the tight schedule of the ICJ, The Slovak-Hungarian dispute is not expected to be heard before 1996, *CTK National News Wire*, Dec. 2, 1993.

17. Equitable claims, as such, do not exhaust the field. We could be asked to honor duties dictated by reason, such as per the Kantianism that ONora O'Neill brings to bear on analyzing our obligation to the spatially remote poor. *See* O'NEILL, FACES OF HUNGER: AN ESSAY ON POVERTY, JUSTICE, AND DEVELOPMENT (1986).

18. Worse, to invoke "equity" as an intergenerational standard invites the old objection, "what did the future ever do for us?"

19. *See* EDITH BROWN WEISS, IN FAIRNESS TO FUTURE GENERATIONS (1988). Brian Barry opined that an acceptable ethic "should surely as a minimum include the notion that those alive at any time are custodians rather than owners of the planet, and ought to pass it along in no worse shape than they found it in." Barry, Justice Between Generations, *in* LAW, MORALITY AND SOCIETY 284 (1977).

20. *See* WORLD RESOURCES INSTITUTE AND THE INTERNATIONAL INSTITUTE FOR ENVIRONMENT AND DEVELOPMENT, WORLD RESOURCES 1994-95 5-6 (1994-95).

21. On the range of variables, *see generally*, Amartya K. Sen, *Ethical Issues in Income Distribution*, Resources, Values, and Development (1984). Interestingly, empirical experiments provide evidence that actual subjects eschew as a just distributional principle both a maximization of expected utility (Harsanyi) and a maximum of basic goods (Rawls) in favor of a floor constraint of income and wealth. *See* Norman Frohlich & Joe A. Oppenheimer, Choosing Justice: An Experimental Approach to Ethical Theory (1992).

22. An excellent standard treatment of the policy options is William J. Baumol & Wallace E. Oates, The Theory of Environmental Policy (2d ed. 1988).

23. The Rights of Animals and Unborn Generations, *in* Philosophy and Environmental Crisis 51 (William T. Blackstone ed., 1978).

24. *See* Constance Holden, *Omens of Doom for Nuclear Waste Tomb*, 225 Science 489 (1984); T.R. Reid, *Warning Earthlings of Atomic Dumps,* Wash. Post, Nov. 11, 1984, at A1 (Reporting options to forewarn earth's inhabitants of such dangers until at least 12,000 A.D.).

25. "The ease or difficulty of diverting a comet . . . depends on how much time scientists have to prepare. If decades or centuries are available, an orbit in theory can be shifted by placing a nuclear or chemical reactor on the comet's surface." William J. Broad, *Scientists Ponder Saving Planet From Earth-Bound Comet*, N.Y. Times, Nov. 3, 1992, at C1. Incidentally, such a project would also be distinct in that we would be eliminating a peril we did not cause (the way in which we "cause" toxic wastes).

26. Indeed, once we begin to examine an "irreversible harms" model, we eventually return to much the same conversation as under "selected calamities," with the possible exception that less calamitous outcomes would be of the Guardian's concern.

27. *See* Kenneth J. Arrow & Anthony C. Fisher, *Environmental Preservation, Uncertainty, and Irreversibility*, 88 Q. J. Econ. 312-339 (1974); Anthony C. Fisher & W. Michael Hanemann, *Option Value and the Extinction of Species*, 4 Advances Applied Micro-Econ. 169-190 (1986).

28. Each generation might have an obligation to conserve not only physical assets, but "knowledge of natural and cultural systems." *See* Weiss *supra* endnote 19 at 257-295.

29. *See* Lester Lave, *Mitigating Strategies for Carbon Dioxide Problems*, 72 Am. Econ. Rev. 257-261 (1982).

CHAPTER 4

HOW TO HEAL THE PLANET[*]

INTRODUCTION

Across the world, the environment is in peril. Forests are being stripped, stressed and burned. Natural habitats are vanishing. Deserts are advancing. Croplands suffer from waterlogging in some regions, overgrazing and salinization in others. The atmosphere and ozone shield are under assault. The oceans are being loaded with pollutants and swept of marine life. We are sullying the polar regions, perturbing the climate, and eradicating species.

All these alarms, and more, have been widely sounded. There is no reason to belabor them. What we need now are answers. I have two to put forward: a system of Global Guardianships, and a Global Commons Trust Fund. They alone will not *solve* our complex environmental predicaments;[**] but together they would constitute a major stride forward, a foundation for an appreciable "greening" of international law.

To understand these proposals, a good start is to mark the distinction in outlook between the scientist, on the one hand, and the international lawyer and statesperson, on other. Scientists—at least, geophysicists, geochemists, and the like—have the luxury of contemplating the planet from the grand panorama of astronauts. From that remove national boundaries fade and the mind can be struck by the marvelous wholeness of the Earth and the interconnectedness of the globe-spanning phenomena that sustain its tenants: the one great swirling envelope of atmospheric gases, the great body of ocean, and the broad globe-spanning belts of weather and vegetation.

International lawyers and statespersons operate from a more cramped and mundane vista. Ours is an inherited world in which all that grand unity has been disrupted into political territories. We all know that most of these pencilled borders have little to do with the great natural processes that the scientist is drawn to, that they fluctuate, that they are often the legacies of chance, intrigue, vanity, avarice, and military battles that could have gone either way. But for all their caprice and impermanence, the boundaries that mark the diplomats' world, hardened, as they commonly are, by

---

[*] From Greening International Law, Philippe Sands, ed. Earthscan, 1993; copyright Foundation for International Enviromental Law and Development (FIELD), with permission of FIELD.

[**] Those interested in a fuller treatment of these two proposals, and others, are referred to my book, *The Gnat is Older than Man: Global Environment and Human Agenda;* (Princeton, N.J., Princeton Univ. Press, 1993).

pronounced cultural, religious and socio-economic differences, are no less to be reckoned with than carbon.

Broadly speaking, the diplomats' maps (the foundation for received international law) divide the world into two sorts of regions: those which fall under *territorial sovereignty*, and those that lie outside the political reach of any nation state, the *global commons*.

In this view of things, the territorial sovereignty each nation enjoys is co-extensive with its geographic boundaries, extends upwards through its air traffic space, and, in the case of the many nations with coastal borders, extends across an Exclusive Economic Zone (EEZ) running 200 nautical miles seaward.

The global commons refers to those portions of the planet and its surrounding space that lie above and beyond the recognized territorial claims of any nation. That includes the atmosphere, outer space, and the high seas, together with the potentially valuable seabeds and subsurfaces that have yet to be "enclosed" by any coastal state as part of its territorial extension. On some accounts, much the same commons status does or should apply to the resource-rich Antarctic, which comprises 10% of the planet's land mass, and whose ownership is currently in limbo.

Viewed within the constraints of traditional international law, this two-fold division into national territories and commons areas has crucial significance for all efforts to defend the environment. Within its sovereign territory, a nation can (by and large, and absent its consent through some international treaty) do whatever it wants. Each nation, and it exclusively, has the right to pull up its forests, bulldoze habitats, wipe out species, fish, farm, and mine—and not have to answer to any "outside" authority for the repercussions on its own environment.[1]

If the "outside" world wishes to influence some country's internal behavior—to constrain deforestation, for example—its recourse is limited. International organizations can try to persuade a developing country's leaders of the long-term benefits of a scale and pace of development that is environmentally benign. Funding sources, preeminently the World Bank, can withhold support from massive projects that are environmentally disruptive. Wildlife groups have been known simply to pay a country to set aside an exotic habitat as a wildlife reserve, often arranging so-called "debt-for-Nature swaps." But as long as a nation is chewing up only its own insides, it is not, in the eyes of international law, doing anything it can be sued over. It is true there are *declarations* that all the environment, including internal environments, are to be valued;[2] but they are consistently undermined by conflicting declarations that a nation's use of its own resources is a matter of sovereign prerogative.* The stand-off could be

---

*   For example, the "common concern" language, endnote 7, supra, is immediately qualified by the principle, "States have sovereign rights over their own biological resources." Ibid. This is a long standing and continuing Third World theme. "Development is a fundamental right of all peoples and countries." Kuala Lumpur Declaration on Environment and Development, Article 4, reprinted in 22 *Environmental Policy and Law* 266 (August 1992). In particular, forests "are part of the national patrimony to be managed, conserved and

resolved in a "green" direction: that is, conceivably, grave insults to internal environments could someday come to be considered a sort of "ecocide," and, likened to human rights violations, made a violation of international law. But such a development does not appear imminent. In the meantime, "outside" influence is constrained to such tactics as bargaining, loan conditions, and perhaps trade pressures. And as we know all too well—desertification and deforestation continue—thus far neither these tactics nor any others have been able to arrest the degradation of internal environments.

As frustrating as one finds it to affect the "internal" scenarios, the situation in the commons areas is in many regards even worse. All the nations of the world are faced with deterioration of their internal environments, so that resources required for cleaning up the commons have to compete for resources required to clean up at home. This is a competition in which the domestic demands have a clear advantage. When a country's interior deteriorates—as urban area becomes smoggy, or fish die in lakes—there is a least a political constituency of directly aggrieved voters to focus pressure on whichever government, state, federal or local, can provide relief. By contrast, when we turn to the commons, the areas lack, by definition, their own "citizens" to complain, and, in all events, those who do have complaints cannot locate an authority with competence to complain to.

However, the plight of the commons reflects more than the jurisdictional vacuum. Important economic and bargaining considerations reinforce the inclination to give the commons short shrift. When a nation turns its attentions inward, it can select the most pressing problem on its own political agenda, be it water quality or soil treatment. And because a nation has full control over its domestic programs, it can arrange to fund only those projects for which it receives at least a dollar benefit for each dollar it spends. But suppose we ask the same nation to invest a million dollars in mending the commons—to restrict carbon emissions, for example, and thereby reduce the risks of climate change. In expenditures to clean up the commons it stands to capture *some fraction* of the benefits (the reduced risks of climate change). But most of the benefit will be diffused among all 180 or so members of the world community, some of whom will fail to shoulder their proportionate share of the burden.

One can put the point in familiar public finance terms: the maintenance of the commons is a public good, and efforts to provide for the public good are notoriously dogged by the maneuvers of those who wish to "free ride" on the those who

---

developed by each country in accordance with its national plans and priorities in the exercise of its sovereign rights." Id. at Art. 15. The Declaration reaffirms "the sovereign rights of States to use their biological and genetic resources." Id. at Art. 25. "[T]he implementation mechanisms of the [Framework Convention on Climate Change] should fully take into account the sovereign rights of each country to determine its national policies, plans and programmes for sustainable development." Id. at Art. 24.

contribute. Of course, domestic governments face the same problem when they undertake any public finance project: parks, police, and so on. The problem is that combatting strategic behavior and securing cooperation in the international arena is considerably more difficult than overcoming the analogous obstacles in domestic contexts. In domestic democratic societies subject to majority rule, dissenters—potential free-riders—can be simply forced to pay their share by law. But in the international community, a corollary of sovereignty is that no nation can be forced into any agreement to which it does not assent: in essence, unanimity, not majority, is the collective choice rule. As a consequence, every country is leery of getting drawn into a fragile multilateral agreement in which it may find itself under pressure to pay out a larger share of the costs than its benefits warrant. (This is one basis for the United States's reluctance to put teeth into a Climate Change convention). Each nation may incline to mend its own local disorders even when it would make more sense, overall (if cooperation could be ensured), for all the nations of the world to turn their joint attention to more ominous problems they face in common.

This "no man's land" feature of the commons has important implications for the design of institutional remedies. The fact that the degraded area lies outside anyone's exclusive jurisdiction presents impediments to *monitoring* deterioration, and even more serious obstacles to securing legal and diplomatic *relief.*

Invasion of Territories

Speaking realistically, international law does not enter the picture until something a nation does—releasing a radioactive cloud, for example—sweeps across its boundaries and damages a neighboring country. In those circumstances it is generally agreed—at least it is universally verbalized—that the injured neighbor has grounds for diplomatic and legal remedies. In the 1940s the United States successfully sued Canada over sulphur fumes from a Canadian lead smelter that were wafting across the boundary into the state of Washington.[3] The U.S. once even acquiesced to a Mexican diplomatic demand that we eliminate offensive transboundary odors that were blowing south from a U.S. stockyard.* Such results in the transboundary context are frankly rare; but relief is at least a theoretical option that would-be polluters have to consider in the design of factories etc.

When, however, fumes blow across a frontier not into a neighboring nation, but into up into the commons region of higher atmosphere, or out across the sea, however many soft declarations may denounce it,** resort to law becomes appreciably more

---

* Springer A. *The International Law of Pollution;* (Westport, Conn., Quorum Books, 1983). [pp. 150-2.]

** Note that the Stockholm Declaration (1972) of the United Nations Conference on the Human Environment, note 4, supra, denounces in the same terms "damage to the environment of other States" and damage to "areas beyond the limits of national jurisdiction." The point of the text is that *in practice* the sameness of treatment is problematic. In a typical nation-to-nation transboundary conflict, such as the U.S.-Canada case referred to, one can assume there are officials of the injured state on hand at the site of the harm to inspect the damage and determine where it is coming from. In that dispute, the fumes could be characterized as an "invasion" (however modest) of U.S. sovereignty, the sort of thing international law has customarily sought to mend.

By contrast, when the open sea or the atmosphere is degraded, who is on hand to keep watch? Are significant loadings of heavy metals working their way into the deep seas and seabed? If so, are the levels dangerous—are they insinuating their way into the food cycle?—and who is responsible for cleaning them up? To answer these questions, even to gather the relevant facts in a scientifically and internationally credible way, goes beyond any single nation's ordinary motivation and competence; it practically necessitates a multi-national coordinated effort.

Even then, if the appropriate institution could be established, and the monitors (assume) could identify substantial and worrisome changes in the environment, and pin down their source, there would remain judicial obstacles of legal interest and standing. If someone should come onto your yard, and steal your pet turtle from your pond, you would have a suit because it would be a trespass and injury to your property. But if some nation's fleet of fishing vessels, sweeping the high seas with nets, obliterates scores of rare sea turtles or dolphins, customary international law (that is, international law as it stands absent some specially-tailored treaty) is unlikely to grant a remedy to any nation that objects.* Who can prove that the destroyed creatures would have been captured by the objecting nation? On the high seas, because the turtles are no one's, it is unclear that anyone has the legal interest the law requires to complain. Besides, what is the market value (the law would want to know) of turtles and dolphins and such? Where was the legal damage?

Who is Responsible

One should understand that the liberty of each state to impair the commons is not a positive principle that is anywhere proudly declared. There are in fact any number of lofty declarations of international conferences and commentators which solemnly (although usually with saving double-speak qualifications) renounce abuse of the commons areas. There are even scraps of legal doctrine from which a suit to protect the commons areas might be constructed. Some government could argue that a country responsible for a massive injury to the commons had committed a wrong *erga*

not realized.

* Special conventions and resolutions are beginning to address such issues, e.g., the United Nations General Assembly Resolution on Driftnetting discussed in the text below; as explained more fully in the text, the "Guardianship" concept advocated herein is not inconsistent with, but should be integrated with, those ongoing efforts.

omnes (crime against the community of nations), a notion historically invoked to legitimate the power of any nation to punish piracies on the high seas. But the fact is, aside perhaps from the special case where the complaining nation was able to show that the wrongdoer violated an express agreement (such as a treaty), no claim arising out of commons despoliation has yet to be pressed, and the prospects of such a suit would have to be regarded at present as rather doubtful.[*]

Thus, whatever lip service environmental diplomats will pay the commons areas at great Earth Summits, nations still find it expedient to let vast proportions of their pollutants simply blow away into the global atmosphere or run off untreated into the open sea. Each year, humankind pumps into the atmosphere over eight billion tons of carbon, together with hundreds of millions of tons of nitrogen oxides, sulfur dioxide, particulate, and other such airborne junk. Into the oceans, their marine life already pillaged by modern fishing technology, go hundreds of millions of tons of sewage, dredge spoils, agricultural run-off and industrial wastes. To this we add millions of tons of marine litter—no longer your ordinary biodegradable garbage, either. Each year, tens of thousands of marine mammals, turtles, and seabirds die from entanglement with or ingestion of plastics and abandoned fishing gear ("ghost nets"), some of which will not disintegrate for centuries.

Some of the stuff that has been dumped is even worse. Sitting on the seabed right now are hundreds of thousands of tons of World War II munitions, including unfired chemical weapons,[4] to which we have more recently added untold canisters of nuclear waste that were deposited in the sea for "safe storage," and are already showing signs of fatigue.[5] An ex-Soviet official recently admitted that for nearly thirty years the Soviet military had been jettisoning its nuclear wastes (including thousands of canisters, twelve old reactors and one damaged submarine) into the Arctic Sea in the most heedless way imaginable.[6] The important thing now is, no one is responsible for cleaning the whole mess up.

This does not mean that the commons are utterly undefended. While no nation can be compelled to protect the commons without its consent, various protective conventions and declarations have garnered the cooperation of enough countries to check the rate of deterioration. The 1985 Vienna Convention on Substances that Deplete the Ozone Layer is achieving a dramatic reduction in the release of ozone-depleting agents. The 1991 U.N. General Assembly Resolution against Driftnetting is, technically, no more than that—a legally nonbinding "resolution." Yet, the announced willingness of the major driftnetting nations, Japan, Taiwan and Korea, to respect it is a promising development of some significance. And there is a whole patchwork of other conventions in other areas, each with its own aspirations and attainments. These

---

[*]   It is worth recalling, in this context, a major if perhaps unfortunate theme in international law: the suggestion that anything not specifically *prohibited* is ipso facto *permitted*. See *S.S. Lotus (France v. Turkey)* (PCIJ Ser. A. No. 10 (1927).

include the ban on weapons testing in space, the International Whaling Convention (IWC), the Antarctic treaty system, and the London Convention on the Prevention of Marine Pollution by Dumping of Wastes.

The present picture, as best as can be summarized, is this: if one looks behind the various lofty declarations, and examines the prevailing practices—the law in action—one finds that, aside from a few areas provided for by special treaty, much of the commons is at best only partially and feebly protected. In essence, just as the commons are unowned for purposes of wealth exploitation—anyone can sweep it for fish or scoop up deep sea-bed minerals without answering to the world community—questions about the pollution of the commons are going unanswered. What is to be done?

A VOICE FOR THE ENVIRONMENT: GLOBAL COMMONS GUARDIANS

One approach is to negotiate more and stronger multinational treaties specially tailored to protect designated portions of the commons, along the lines of the Ozone Agreements, and the more recent, still nebulous framework conventions on climate change that emerged from the Earth Summit at Rio. Those efforts deserve further support.

Yet, there is another approach—in some ways bolder, in some ways integral and supplementary to the treaty efforts. As we saw, one of the reasons for over-exploitation of the commons is the lack of a plaintiff clearly qualified to demonstrate both standing and injury. Hence, the first proposal: to establish a system of Guardians who would be legal representatives for the natural environment. The idea is similar to the concept of legal guardians (sometimes "conservators") in familiar legal systems. Presented with possible invasions of the interests of certain persons who are unable to speak for themselves, such as otherwise unrepresented infants, the insane, and the senile, courts are empowered to appoint a legal guardian to speak for them. So, too, guardians can be designated to be the legal voice for the otherwise voiceless environment: the whales, the dolphins, important habitats, and so on.

The guardians could either be drawn from existing international agencies that have the appropriate focus, such as the United Nations Environment Program (UNEP) and the World Meteorological Organization (WMO), or from the many nongovernmental organizations (NGOs), such as Greenpeace or the Worldwide Fund for Nature (WWF). Certainly the Guardians would not be given plenary and unreviewable powers to halt any activity they disapproved of. Rather, the guardian would be built into the institutional process to ensure that environmental values were being identified and accounted for. Take the oceans, to illustrate. To assure that oceanic ecosystems were being adequately accounted for, an Ocean Guardian might be designated, perhaps GESAMP, the Joint Group of Experts on the Scientific Aspects of Marine Pollution, with supplementary legal staffing.

As guardian, its first chore would be to *monitor*. It would review ocean conditions not just to gather facts "scientifically," but with a specific eye towards assuring compliance with conventions already in place. One of the weakness of the 1972 London Dumping Convention (LDC) and many fishing agreements is that compliance depends almost entirely on "self-monitoring," without any independent effort to survey the activities of signatories. The Guardian could provide it. By doing so, it would improve the willingness of every state to comply, for each country will be less hesitant that if it observes the rules, it will just be the one nice, law-abiding "sucker." Everyone would benefit from the mutual assurances.

Second, the Guardian would exercise *legislative functions*, not as a legislative body, but as part of the complex web of global policy-making institutions. In exercising the monitoring function it would undoubtedly come across problems uncovered by existing agreements, which would prompt it to recommend and stimulate formation of new multinational agreements. It could appear before international agencies and even the domestic legislatures and administrative agencies of nations considering ocean-impacting actions to counsel moderation and to suggest alternatives on behalf of its "client."

Third, it could be authorized to appear as a special *intervenor-counsel* for the unrepresented environmental "victim" in a variety of bilateral and multi-lateral disputes. For example, whenever there is a proposal to dam an international river, one or more of the nations along the river may initiate international negotiations to assure the fair division of the water flow, electric and irrigation benefits, etc. But we have learned—often too late and to our chagrin—that such dam projects inevitably affect the environment, including life in the oceans to which they feed. The ocean guardian would appear as a "third party" before the appropriate body to assure, not necessarily that the viability of ocean environment was the conclusive issue, but at least that it was raised in the most strenuous and effective manner possible.[7]

The final function simply takes the intervenor concept one step further. International treaties should endow the Guardian with standing to initiate legal and diplomatic action on the ocean ecosystem's behalf in appropriate situations—to sue at least in those cases where, if the ocean were a sovereign state, the law would afford it some prospect of relief. The law could be arranged so that, even if a violating nation refused to appear, the Guardian could secure a declaratory judgment that the conduct in question was indeed unlawful. Such a judicial pronouncement is far less steely than an injunction, but is not the sort of thing members of the world community would simply brush off, either.

The notion of legal standing for nature is hardly far-fetched. Indeed, many guardianship functions are currently recognized in U.S. environmental laws on a more modest scale. For example, under the Superfund Legislation, the National Oceanic and Atmospheric Administration (NOAA) is designated trustee for fish, marine mammals, and their supporting ecosystems within the U.S. fisheries zone. NOAA has authority to institute suits to recover restoration costs against any party that injures its "ward."[8]

A major law-suit is presently proceeding in federal court in Southern California, in which NOAA attorneys are suing local chemical companies allegedly responsible for seepage of PCBs and other chemicals into the coastal water ecosystem.[9] There is no reason such a system could not be replicated internationally.

A Case for Seals

A recent case in Germany even invoked the guardianship concept in a case with global commons implications.[10] In 1988, approximately 15,000 dead seals mysteriously washed up on the beaches of the North and Baltic Seas. Widespread alarms were sounded, amid considerable concern that the massive deaths were a portent of an impending ecological disaster. The most flagrant insult to the North Sea's chemistry was widely considered to be titanium and other heavy metals that were being produced by incineration and dumping on the high seas by permit of the West German government.

Conceivably, any of the states bordering the sea might have tried to challenge Germany's actions. But recall that, so long as the harm was being done on, or affecting life only in, the high seas, the authority of any nation to sue was (and is) doubtful. For Poland, say, to trace through a legally compensable injury would have been nearly hopeless. From the point of view of national fishing interests, the reduction—even elimination—of the seals might even have been regarded as an economic *benefit*. (The harbor seals involved, unlike fur seals, are themselves commercially valueless but compete with fishermen for commercial fish stocks.) Moreover, all the sea-bordering nations were contributing to the pollution, and thus, had any of them objected their case might have been be met by Germany with an "unclean hands" defense: "you can't complain, because you're are guilty as we are."

Who then, was to speak for the seals—and, in so doing, represent all the elements of the ecological web whose hazarded fortunes were intertwined? In comparable situations in the United States, courts have shown willingness to interpret the Administrative Procedure Act and other laws as giving a public interest group standing to challenge the government's actions. German law, however, is much more stringent about allowing "citizen's suits."

The solution was for a group of German environmental lawyers (with the encouragement and advice of the author) to institute an action in which the North Sea Seals were named the lawsuit's principal plaintiffs, with the lawyers appearing essentially as guardians, speaking for them. And what better plaintiffs? No one could accuse the seals, surely, of unclean hands (or flippers). And the injury to them did not appear as problematical as—it was one step less removed from—the harm that the other littoral nations might have raised.

The German administrative law court rejected the seals' standing on the grounds that seals were not "persons" and no specific legislation had authorized standing on their behalf. There were two lessons. First, the very filing of the case and attendant news media coverage was considerable and favorable. When the time came for the government to renew the ocean dumping permit, the authorities who initially gave their permission were forced by a kindled public opinion to revoke it. Germany has committed to constrict or phase out disposal of heavy metals in the North Sea. The seals lost the battle in court, but won the war.

Second, the seals lost because the guardianship application was ad hoc. Any system for commons Guardians should be institutionalized in advance. When local (länder) statutes so provide, even German courts will allow specially designated environmental groups to challenge forest-threatening actions. In the international context, formal recognition of commons guardians could be achieved though reforms within existing legal frameworks—for example, appropriate amendments of the charters of the United Nations and of the International Court of Justice.

The institutionalization of Guardians would have the virtue of designating one responsible voice for each part of the environment. There is at least one drawback that grows out of that virtue, however. The more power a Guardian were to have, and the more exclusively its voice were made to be the voice that counted, the greater would be the political pressures to compromise its scientific and legal integrity.

Furthermore, while a system of commons guardians would be a step forward, it would be no panacea for biosphere degradation. Those commons areas that were placed under guardianships, such as living ocean resources, would be elevated to a legal and diplomatic standing on a par with a sovereign. But unfortunately, under present law the powers even of sovereign states are limited when it comes to protecting themselves from transfrontier pollution. Hence, the success of a guardianship regime would depend not only upon legitimation and institutionalization of the Guardians as legal representative, but upon significant changes in the substantive law which the Guardian would be empowered to invoke—for example, conventions proscribing levels of pollution hazardous to sea life. The oceans not only need their own independent voice; they need the world community to adopt more diligently protective standards.

FINANCING THE REPAIR:
THE GLOBAL COMMONS TRUST FUND

Supporting a system of guardianships—indeed, any counterattack on global degradation—will cost money. Where will it come from? I have already observed the understandable inclination of political leaders to give priority to their hard-pressed domestic agendas before they address the commons areas. If any nation unilaterally and voluntarily lays out a hundred million dollars to clean up the ocean floor or atmosphere, it just relieves the pressure on other nations to ante up, if they can bank on getting a "free ride" on the benefits of our expenditures. Meager or noncooperation becomes a dominant strategy.

Of course, as noted above, problems of "free-riding" confront any domestic society when it plans the provision of any public goods, such as the payment for police and fire protection, and the maintenance of public parks. But the difference, once more, is this: domestic democratic societies have the power to tax. When the majority decides on a program for the general welfare, it can compel a raising of the needed funds. The world community enjoys no comparable power to levy a "world tax" for world public welfare. While One World idealists have proposed such a tax, it is not presently a viable alternative.

There already exists one financial mechanism to tackle the job without appeal to taxes: the Global Environment Facility (GEF). The GEF is a pilot program originally conceived to support energy conservation, preserve ecological diversity, arrest depletion of the ozone shield, and protect the marine environment. It has been able to garner $1.3 billion in voluntary financial commitments from the industrialized countries for the years 1991, 1992 and 1993. But as a financial mechanism, purely voluntary contributions are not a dependable basis on which to build a stable infrastructure. In fact, the pilot phase of GEF is soon to expire and its future level of funding is highly uncertain.

Exacerbating the GEF's problems has been a continuous conflict over how the fund is to be governed. The developed countries, as donors, want a proportionately stronger voice. They therefore favor governance somewhat along the lines of the World Bank, which allots each nation voting power in proportion to its contributions. In 1987, the World Bank formula gave the United States 19.47% of the voting power; Egypt had just .52%. Such a weighted-voting plan may be explained on pragmatic grounds: it induces the wealthy to keep giving. But the unevenness rankles the Third World as clearly undemocratic, and unresponsive to a pattern of historical wrongs that make wealth transfers now a matter of compensation and obligation, not of largesse. Hence, Third World countries resist transporting the same standards into the environmental field; even more specifically, they fear any such formula will slant funding towards projects favored by the developed countries, such as ozone depletion, and away from the more immediate concerns of the Third World, notably desertification and clean water. All parties have agreed in principle to come up with "some other" formula. But friction over the issue, and the continued inability of anyone to produce a mutually acceptable alternative, is one more impediment to GEF's long-range viability.

Implementing a Global Commons Trust Fund

These considerations suggest the advantages of a fund that is not wholly dependent on voluntary giving. More specifically, a financial mechanism that sought levies in legal obligations would both make the flow of funds relatively dependable from year to year, and, by removing the present element of "largesse," perhaps deflate the governance quandaries that arise out of donor-donee frictions. That is what my proposed Global

Commons Trust Fund (GCTF) aims to achieve. The idea is that to finance the repair of the global commons, we look to levies on uses of the commons areas themselves.

Let us expand on how this might be accomplished. As I have already observed, under present practice all the commons areas can be used and abused with relative impunity—free of charge. If we were to rectify this practice, and charge even a fraction of the fair worth for the various uses to which nation-states put the global commons, we would advance two goals at once. The charges would dampen the intensity of abuse, and at the same time underwrite the costs of providing public order, such as marine resources management and the repair of environmental damages. Because the resources raised would not be grounded on "largesse" but on what could be presented as legitimate obligations, the supply of funds would be relatively more stable from year to year.

The revenue, while difficult to estimate, is potentially enormous. Consider some rough projections.

The Oceans

The world harvests 185 billion pounds of marine fish annually. A tax of a mere one tenth of one percent the commercial value would raise approximately $200 million for the proposed fund.[11] The same token rate on oil and gas produced in the EEZs would add perhaps $80 million more.[12] As for the use of the oceans as a dump-site, the official figures, almost certainly under-reported, amount to 212 million metric tons of sewage sludge, industrial wastes, and dredged materials yearly.[13] A tax of only a dime a ton would raise an additional $20 million. And a charge on ocean transport—particularly uses such as tanker traffic that imperil waters and beaches—would swell the fund further.[14]

The Atmosphere

By burning fossil fuels and living forests, humankind thrusts 22 billion metric tons of carbon dioxide into the atmosphere annually.[15] A CO_2 tax of only 10 cents a ton would raise $2.2 billion each year, thirty times the current budget of the United Nations Environmental Program (UNEP). Taxing other GHGs such as nitrous oxides at a comparably modest (dime-a-ton) rate, indexed to their "blocking" equivalent to CO_2, would bring the total to $3.3 billion.[16] The same ten cents a ton tax could be levied on other (non-GHG) transfrontier pollutants; a sulphur dioxide levy, for example, would produce $16 million more.

Space

Tapping the wealth of the planets may still be far off, but the rights to "park" satellites in the choice slots is a potential source of enormous wealth right now. Most valued are points along the "geostationary orbit," the volume of space 22,300 miles directly above the earth's equator in which a satellite can remain in a relatively fixed point relative to the surface below. The number of available points is restricted by minimal distances required between satellites to avoid interference. Rights to spots directly above the Earth's equatorial belt are also valued because they are exposed to exceptionally long hours of sunlight, and are therefore ideally situated for production of energy from solar radiation, as a support for special operations such as high-tech gravity-free manufacturing, and perhaps ultimately for commercial redirecting to earth.

These positions, and ancillary frequencies in space, "the most precious resource of the telecommunication ages"—worth to users an estimated $1 trillion globally over the next decade—are now parcelled out free of charge in a system that can only be labelled absurd. The tiny island nation of Tonga, after being awarded 3-6 orbital positions gratis, turned right around and put them up for auction, recently striking a deal with a satellite company for $2 million a year "rental." And it is reportedly seeking more such deals. Why should the rights to any of these slots and spectrum positions, a limited resource that is the legacy and province of all Humankind, and potentially worth billions of dollars to users, be doled out like free lottery tickets, while those who would mend the planet are severely limited by a lack of resources? An auction of slots and frequencies would yield several hundred millions annually.

Biodiversity

I am a little more ambivalent about including biodiversity as part of the Common Heritage of Humankind in the sense of making it a tax base for the fund. While tuna are (often) in the high seas, beyond any nation's jurisdiction, most biological riches lie within the territories of nations. Of course, when we talk of biotechnological potential, we are not talking about seizing physical matter from those forests, trees, and so on, as much as copying and exploiting *genetic information*. But that presumably makes small difference to the biologically rich nations such as Columbia and Brazil, who would regard global demands to share the good luck of their biological wealth about the same way the Saudis would react to arguments that the world should co-own its oil. The proposal may simply intrude too far into their sovereign space and prerogatives, which is why the Rio negotiators rejected labeling biodiversity part of the Common Heritage in favor of the limper "common concern."

On the other hand, perhaps a compromise could be worked out whereby the industrial world's pharmaceutical companies, which will presumably manage the exploitation of the potential, would pay a royalty into the GCTF.

Even if we do not include biological diversity in the base, the total thus far: about 4 billion dollars a year. And that is before adding the yield of a surcharge on uneliminated ozone depleting agents, on toxic incineration at sea, or on the liquid wastes that invade the oceans from rivers. Consider also fees on the minerals that someday will be harvested from the sea and seabed, and, perhaps, depending upon the staying power of the conservation movement, which is fighting the efforts, the Antarctic.[17]

Another way to bolster the fund would be to make it the receptacle for legal judgments assessed under various commons-protecting treaties. For example, the oils spills conventions could easily be amended to provide that some measure of ecological damages to the high seas (and not merely local waters) be paid into the trust fund and marked for the benefit of the environment. There are precedents. The Exxon Corporation established an environmental repair fund in the wake of the Exxon Valdez disaster in Alaska. After the spill of the highly dangerous pesticide Kepone into the James River in the United States, Allied Chemical, which was responsible, agreed to establish such a fund for the James, and Sandoz Corporation did the same in the wake of the catastrophic 1986 accident in Basel, Switzerland, which devastated marine life in the Rhine.

Areas in Need of the Global Commons Trust Fund

That brings us to the functions of the GCTF: what would the funds raised be used for? To begin with, the GCTF would pay the costs of the Guardianship system I have described. Any number of potentially critical treaties, including the 1972 London Dumping Convention, the 1973 Convention on International Trade in Endangered Species, the 1987 Basel Convention on the Movement of Transboundary Wastes, and the 1992 U.N. Resolution on Driftnetting, are simply underpoliced; the GCTF would make policing viable. The monies would support improved scientific monitoring and modelling of the commons areas, and underwrite the transfer of environment-benign technology to developing nations. They could also promote institutional readiness to respond to various sorts of crises with the global equivalent of "fire fighters." To illustrate, no single nation anticipates enough incidents in its own waters to warrant keeping on alert a full-time staff trained and equipped to contain oil spills with oil-eating bacteria, etc. But a force with global responsibilities, financed out of the fund, might well be cost-justified. It has been estimated that $150 million a year would underwrite an effective world-wide system to ensure early detection of major new viral diseases—so that the next AIDS-type epidemic does not catch us off-guard.

Notwithstanding the mutual and widespread value of such measures, not every country would blithely submit. One can anticipate resistance among the already struggling developing nations, in particular. But they do not face the highest levies, and the fund therefore does not depend on them. For the developed countries, the four-five billion or so is a lot more realistic than many of the figures that have been bandied around in the wake of Rio.

Some countries will object to any tax on activities within their territories, or, in the case of the coastal states, within their self-proclaimed Exclusive Economic Zones (EEZs). However, the charges are not for what nations do within their sovereign "territories"; they are levied largely for the effects of their activities on the "outside" world.[18] Moreover, many noncoastal, landlocked nations—along with many scholars—continue to regard as semi-legitimate, at best, the coastal states's proclaimed EEZs of 200-miles and more from their coasts. Allowing the coastal states to supply exclusive management across these zones makes a certain amount of sense; some management of ocean resources is better than none. But allowing the coastal states to snatch all the wealth without any accounting to the rest of the world, just because it happens to be closer to them, is questionable. That is why I would incline to tax activities such as fishing and oil production undertaken anywhere beyond the traditional territorial boundaries of three or twelve miles from the coastline, and not merely in the smaller region beyond their EEZs.

Many people will object to the pollution charge component of the proposal, calling it offensive to permit pollution-for-pay. The answer is that some pollution is inevitable, and it is more of an outrage that we let the polluters get away with it, as they presently do, free of charge.

Indeed, if there is a real objection to the proposed GCTF, it is that the initial rates I have suggested are probably too paltry. One can argue that, viewed as a strategy for reducing environmental damage, the levels advanced for discussion—ten cents a ton for carbon usage—are unlikely to confront the polluting nations with the full costs of the damage they are causing, and therefore will fall short of inducing the "right" amount of conservation and pollution control.[19] Viewed from the reverse side, as a strategy for maximizing revenues for the environmental infrastructure, the proposed rates will often fall short of extracting the full value of what users would pay if they were required to bid for restricted rights at an internationally conducted auction.

It is true that superficially similar proposals have been advanced in the past, without making much political headway. But the GCTF can be distinguished from the some other like-sounding plans—distinguished in ways that may make the GCTF both more effective and more 'salable' politically.

First, the GCTF can be differentiated from a host of plans, such as that put forward by the late Rajiv Gandhi of India, to tax each developed nation a fraction of its Gross National Product and to distribute the funds to less-developed countries. While Gandhi called his proposal a Planet Protection Fund, the transparent intent was to redistribute wealth from rich countries to poor. The aim may be noble. But it ought not to be confused with the GCTF, which would link levies not to each nation's wealth per se, but to its *use of the Commons*, and would restrict application of the revenue raised to the *maintenance and repair of the Commons*.

Second, most proposals have been limited to a single source or activity. Recently the focus has been on carbon use. Years ago, during the Law of the Sea negotiations were advanced, unsuccessfully, to tax users of ocean space. While the ocean tax proposals failed, the public atmosphere, in terms of environmental consciousness, is more sympathetic today than twenty years ago. The proposed ocean taxes, moreover, were designed to pay off third world countries, rather than being earmarked to repair the ocean environment. And by contrast both with the carbon and ocean tax, the idea of the GCTF is comprehensive: to bring all economic uses of the commons under an overall plan, from uses of the ocean to uses of the atmosphere and of space.

CONCLUSION

It is true that the GCTF, by focusing on the Global Commons, would leave unaffected many pressing problems that occur wholly within sovereign boundaries. The answer is that these "internal" problems, bad as they are, are better attended to by existing institutions. In fact, the International Development Agency (a subsidiary of the World Bank) has had no trouble collecting a $3 billion "earth increment" to provide virtually free grants to help poor nations protect their internal ecological systems.[20] To some extent, the relative disadvantage of the commons is a question of out of sight, out mind. And partly, while dolphins may have friends in Greenpeace, they don't vote or form potentially irksome alliances. For both reasons, the Commons goes, once more, to the end of the line.

The guardianship proposal would help fill the void. It would establish a "police" mechanism for the global commons areas—an international public service for an international public good. The GCTF is the mechanism to pay for it. The Global Commons Trust Fund is not merely a roundabout scheme to take wealth from the rich nations and redistribute it to the poor. It simply seeks from users of the Global Commons a reasonable fee for their use of the Commons so as to apply it back to the Commons, for their maintenance and repair. What could be more reasonable? Or, given the afflictions of our planet, more crucial?

ENDNOTES

1. As explained more fully below, this is the prevailing view, at least as long as there are no substantial spillover effects across frontiers. In terms of the Stockholm Declaration "States have, in accordance with the Charter of the United Nations and the principles of international law, the sovereign right to exploit their own resources pursuant to their own environmental policies, and the responsibility to ensure that activities within their jurisdiction or control do not cause damage to the environment of other States or of areas beyond the limits of national jurisdiction." 1972 Declaration of the United Nations Conference on the Human Environment, chapter II, Principle 1, reprinted in 11 *International Legal Materials* 1416-69 (1972).
This position is echoed in the 1992 United Nations Framework Convention on Climate Change, which, while calling for "the widest possible cooperation by all countries and their participation in an effective and appropriate international response," makes clear that "states have "the sovereign right to exploit their own resources pursuant to their own environmental and developmental policies...." Preamble, reprinted in 21 *International Environment Reporter Reference File (BNA)* 3901-9 (1992).

2. For example, the Biodiversity Convention that issued from Rio declares the conservation of biological diversity to be "a common concern of humankind." 1992 United Nations Framework Convention on Biological Diversity, Preamble, reprinted in 21 *International Environment Reporter Reference File (BNA)* 4001-10 (1992).

3. *Trail Smelter (U.S. v. Canada)*, 3 R.I.A.A. 1911 (1941).

4. See Stephanie Simon, "Fears over Nazi Weapons Leaking at Bottom of Baltic,"; *Los Angeles Times*, Jul. 18, 1992, p. A3.

5. See (7 May, 1990) "Atomic Waste Reported Leaking in Ocean Sanctuary off California,"; *New York Times*, p. B12 (about one-fourth of 47,500 55 gallon drums dumped between 1947 and 1970 off San Francisco had ruptured, threatening to contaminate local fish resources). How much alarm the potential leakage warrants is controversial. *See* F.G.T. Holliday, "The Dumping of Radioactive Waste in the Deep Ocean" in David E. Cooper and Joy A. Palmer (Ed.) *The Environment in Question;* (New York, Routledge, 1992). [pp. 51-64, 56-9.] In all events, contracting parties to the London Dumping Convention agreed to a moratorium on marine disposal of radioactive wastes in the 1980s; the moratorium is due for revision in 1993. See "Opponents to Nuclear Waste Dumping Ban Want Global Action, Senior IMO Official Says"; 15 *International Environment Reporter (BNA)* 353 (1992).

6. Tyler, Patrick E (4 May, 1992) "Soviets' Secret Nuclear Dumping Causes Worry for Arctic Waters"; *Los Angeles Times*, May 4, 1992, p. A1. Impatient Soviet sailors got the canisters to sink more quickly by punching holes in them.

7. Non governmental organizations were invited to make submissions to early human rights cases before the PCIJ in the 1920's.

8. See 40 C.F.R. (1990) §§ 300.600, 300.615(a)(1).

9. United States v. Montrose Chemicals, Dkt. No. CV 90-3122 AAH, D.C.D. Cal. 1990.

10. Seehunde v. Bundesrepublik Deutschland (Verwaltungagericht, Hamburg, 15 August 1988).

11. See Food and Agricultural Organization, *Fishery Statistics 1989*, vol. 69; (Italy: Food and Agricultural Organization, 1991). [Tables A-2 and A-4.] "Export value" averaged $1.10 a pound. The figures are for 1989, the most recent year for which reports are available.

12. In 1991, 7 billion barrels of oil and 13.5 trillion cubic feet of natural gas were extracted from offshore sites, worth approximately $160 billion. The global data is not gathered in such a way as to enable us to separate the amount produced within traditional 3 and twelve mile limits from amounts produced within the (extended) reach of the EEZs. Our illustrative calculations are based on the assumption that 50% of the yield is beyond traditional territorial waters. In regard to fish, the only break-down available is between national fisheries (95%), on the one hand, and the high seas areas beyond (5%), on the other. See Agenda 21, Chapter 17 (Protection of the Oceans, All Kinds of Seas, Including Enclosed and Semi-Enclosed Seas, and Coastal Areas and the Protection, Rational Use and Development of Their Living Resources)(Draft Version), §17.47, reprinted in 22 *Environmental Policy and Law* 281-90 (1992). Our calculations include all fish. The rationale is explained in the text below.

13. World Resources Institute et al. *World Resources 1988-89;* (Oxford, Oxford University Press, 1990). [p. 330, Table 22.3].

14. A tax on most uses of the ocean has been proposed, but taxing those who take advantage of the sea just because they *use* it makes no more sense than taxing people for making "use" of sunlight: as long as the use is nonconsumptive and nonrival, why drive people to other, depletable resources? At present, sea traffickers do not fully internalize risks to third parties through oil spills. The 1971 International Oil Pollution Compensation Fund provides for compensation, but only up to $84 million per incident. In any disaster of greater scale, such as the wreck of the *SS Braer* off the Coast of Scotland in January 1993, the taxpayers (there, British) will presumably be left to foot the balance of the clean-up bill. If ships were charged a full-coverage level of premium, and no more, the charge would not be a naked fee on the privilege of ocean use (and a deadweight loss), but would internalize some of the costs of ocean transport; the charge would be earmarked to support emergency clean-up operations as explained elsewhere in the text.

15. Humankind added 8.49 billion metric tons carbon of CO_2 to the atmosphere in 1987. World Resources Institute et al. *World Resources 1990-91;* (Oxford: Oxford University Press, 1990). [p. 346, Table 24.1.] Measuring by mass of carbon dioxide, not carbon, the figure is over 22 billion metric tons. Note that inasmuch as the biosphere

continuously withdraws carbon dioxide from the atmosphere, these figures overstate the net annual contribution to atmospheric carbon dioxide attributable to human activities.

16. Annual emission figures for methane and chlorofluorocarbons are found in World Resources Institute et al., *World Resources 1990-91;* (Oxford: Oxford University Press, 1990), p. 346, Table 24.1]; similar figures for nitrogen oxides from U.S. Environmental Protection Agency *Policy Options for Stabilizing Global Climate;* (Washington, D.C., U.S.E.P.A., 1990). [p. II-18.] The emission figures were then multiplied by global warming potentials for each greenhouse gas relative to carbon dioxide., using indices from Ellington R. et al., "The Total Greenhouse Warming Forcing of Technical Systems: Analysis for Decision Making," 42 *Journal of the Air & Waste Management Association* 422-28 1992).

17. In the text I have gathered together resources that in fact present quite distinct features from the perspective of tax policy. For example, depositing waste in the sea and atmosphere present negative externalities that the right level of tax would presumably "correct." By contrast, seabed oil and minerals, as well as satellite slots (barring congestion) present no pollution externalities, but, depending upon costs of exploitation, afford the potential for considerable economic rents that the state *might* be able to peel off without loss of efficiency. Of course, the authority charged with setting the level and style of charge would have to be sensitive to the traps of "deadweight loss" that occur in any severance tax context. That is, if the seabed should turn out to be a low-cost source of cobalt, the authority would have to be cautious not to put cobalt, and, in particular, sea-bed cobalt, at a disadvantage relative to substitutes. The taxation of fisheries or any other regenerative resource presents yet a third type of problem: the right tax will not only raise revenue, but improve the long term yield of the fishery by preventing excessive entry (and do so more efficiently than fishing seasons). These differences would have to be accounted for in any detailed implementation of the GCTF, as would the choice between a tax and alternative policy instruments, for example, auctions of tradable quotas.

18. And, in part (as regards the levies for resources taken from the EEZs, for example), to compensate other nations for an otherwise unjustifiable unilateral partition of commonly-owned areas.

19. Note that the modest carbon tax proposed for the GCTF is not inconsistent with—in fact, it would leave plenty of room for—stiffer carbon and gasoline taxes that have been proposed in the EU and in the United States. Indeed, it ought to be emphasized in general that the two principal proposals in the text are in no way to be understood as displacing various other measures on environmentalist's agenda.

20. "Europeans May Propose Forestry Protocol Under Climate Treaty, EPA Official Says," *International Environment Daily (BNA)*(19 November, 1992).

CHAPTER 5

REFLECTIONS ON
"SUSTAINABLE DEVELOPMENT"[*]

"SUSTAINABLE DEVELOPMENT"

"Sustainable development" is emerging as a central concept in international law and diplomacy. With increasing frequency it is invoked in speeches and declarations, and enshrined in international agreements—25 in the past five years alone.[1] The 1992 "Earth Summit" at Rio gave birth to a new Commission on Sustainable Development. Yet, for all the tribute, no one is quite sure what the term means.

Indeed, the artful vagueness of "sustainable development" partially explains its broad appeal. Any statesmanlike manifesto, such as the 1987 Brundtland Report,[2] which thrust the term into prominence, is faced with the task of building coalitions, particularly in the early (framework setting) stages. A little ambiguity provides cover for a failed consensus, permitting negotiations to move forward while differences get, hopefully, resolved. In this light, the fact that "sustainable development" means different things to different people is understandable, even an asset.

On the other hand, "sustainable development" is not vague the way "heavy" or "bald" are vague. We may disagree, at exactly what point in weight gain or hair loss someone has become heavy or bald; but there is no uncertainty over what makes someone heavier or balder—or, more to the point of international negotiations, whether we have more carbon congestion in the atmosphere or fewer species in the forests. By contrast, although billions of dollars will be submitted to the test of sustainable development, across a considerable range of outcomes it is not clear—even if we agree on the facts—which of two states of the world is more sustainably developed. Would we be more sustainably developed if we were to decrease pressures on ocean resources (reduce fishing) at the cost of increased pressures on land re-sources (convert more forests to croplands)? The fact is, "sustainable development" functions to gloss over unresolved, even growing conflicts among the variety of factions that it has drawn together into a fragile alliance.

In this paper I want to identify the tensions that the term may artfully or unwittingly suppress and clarify some normative aspects of those tensions.

---

[*]   The 1994 Hart Lecture at the University of London, School of Oriental and Asian Studies. The author would like to acknowledge the comments of Scott Altman, Per Ariansen, Marshall Cohen, Greg Keating, Michael Knoll, Ed McCaffery, and Richard Warner.

The Underlying Geopolitical Strains

Even the conflicts underlying "sustainable development" are ambiguous and fluid. The Brundtland Report, *Our Common Future,* originally defined the tension along an intergenerational axis: "Sustainable development is development which meets the needs of the present without compromising the ability of future generations to meet their own needs."[3] But how are needs to be defined, and by whom? In particular, how does one "compromise" the immediate claims of the contemporary desperate—define their needs in such a manner that all available funding is not exhausted on their behalf, leaving nothing for the future?[4]

It soon became apparent that conflicting responses to these questions were forthcoming from the Rich and Poor. Hence, sustainable development, although launched in contemplation of conflicts over resources and opportunities through time, quickly became drawn into long-standing conflicts across space.

For one thing, the Rich and Poor ("North" and "South") offer competing views of what is most important to sustain for our descendants. In general, the diplomacy of the Rich, if not their actions,[*] put more emphasis on sustaining the global-life support system: the ozone layer, atmosphere, biodiversity and ocean environment. They (particularly North-led NGOs) also stress preservation of environmental amenities such as endangered species, wildlands, and an unsullied Antarctic.

The Poor, for their part, can only wish they had the luxury to fret over menaces a century off, such as rising sea levels. Their priorities are on local and immediate challenges such as eradicating poverty, reducing illiteracy and building infrastructure. Accordingly, the environment enters as part of the near-term economic worries—as a factor in improving health and productivity. Hence, insofar as the Poor's agenda is environmental, it tends to emphasize such problems as dirty water, desertification, and the over-taxing of renewable resources.

Diplomatic rhetoric and agenda part accordingly. Although each side acknowledges the legitimacy of the other's concerns, there is a feeling among the Rich that the South would go a long way towards local sustainability if it would only adopt rational resource pricing—and get a grip on burgeoning populations. The Poor rejoins that, for the global-scale problems which the North stresses, there is only the North, with its opulent life-styles, to blame. After all, the charge goes, the inhabitants of the developed countries, who make up about 23% of the global population, consume about 80% of the world's papers, metals and energy.[5] In the Poor's eyes, it is the North that is not developing sustainably.

---

[*]   Although much of the impetus for restrictions on substances that impair the long-term health of the planet come from the Rich, it is also the Rich who, particularly on a per capita basis, are the source of the damage—as the Poor lose no opportunity to remind.

From this one might imagine that the South would be clamoring for the North to consume *less*, perhaps even that "sustainable development" is an endorsement of zero-growth coupled with redistribution. But there is no such unified message coming out of the South. The states that produce the raw materials—the copper and oil—are less agreed that we reduce our profligacy, as that we pay a higher price for it.* At Rio, let us remember, the offensive against deforestation came from the timber-devouring North and was resisted by the South.

The fact is, contentions over sustainable development have to be viewed in the context of the longer standing North-South dissension from which talk about sustainable development is an outgrowth: the thorn of wealth disparity. The Poor seek to catch up; and catching up means producing their power and driving their own cars and having their own traffic jams someday. While the adverse effects of transition to modern economies can undoubtedly be tempered (technology transfer can help them avoid levels of damage we caused in our transitions), no one has found a way to grow and preserve the environment on net; surely not, if population in the Third World continues to explode.

The Moral Quandaries

The fabric of tensions and coalitions are so complex and fluid that one hesitates to generalize. On the one hand there are those who emphasize the "development" part of the term, with its connotation of accelerating productivity to raise the immediate standard of living with relatively low anxiety over environmental amenities and long term perils. This group—"developmentalists," we might call them, certainly includes that part of the world that is poor and getting poorer and laboring to repay international debt and feed itself from day to day. But it is too simple to identify "developmentalism" as defined with the Poor. Resource extraction from tropical forests lines up the poorest indigenous peoples, who find their forest sanctuaries imperilled, on the side of the environment, against Rich interests on the side of development. And, of course, as (as the Poor charge) Rich nations that race through nonrenewable resources and lead the world in carbon emissions are equally discounting environmental amenities and the future—and are developmentalists, in this sense.**

By contrast, those who emphasize the sustainability part of the term—we might well call them "environmentalists," although, again, the term is not perfectly tai-

---

* A South position on North consumption can be stated more plausibly by focusing on the *investment* implications: Considering the whole world as the relevant unit, there is a case to be made that the rich industrialized North's heavy consumption means it is underinvesting; higher-than-market prices can perhaps be regarded as an indirect mode of investment.

** Although the Northern developmentalists, while unprepared to rein in carbon emission, are not pressing for developmental assistance to the South.

lored—are typified by many environmental NGOs, mostly from the Developed Countries. In general, they seek to add to their own enjoyment of the environment, and their own attitudes towards future risks, the projected pleasures and perils of the unborn, of those who will inherit the earth in 2200. After all, we, the living, in stripping the globe of its richest and most ancient forests, eradicating species, and tampering with the atmosphere, are affecting *them*. We are pillaging the oceans of their marine life, and depositing, in a mean return, plastic, garbage, oil, nuclear waste and the detritus of war, much of which will persist for hundreds of years. In permitting the decay—even looting—of civilization's trove of great cultural artifacts, we are violating a great trust. It is easy to see how decisively these grievances pleaded on behalf of the vast unborn may help tilt the scales away from the grievances of the smaller number of living.

The issues so joined, which group deserves our funding priorities? The facile—although important—answer is "both-at-once": we should seek out opportunities that the goals of both factions are, or can be made, congruent.

For example, everyone, I trust, agrees on the need for improved environmental accounting such as the U.N. has recommended, which debits resource consumption against conventional indices of national productivity. In some countries such an accounting will illuminate an imbalance that is grave in all eyes.[*] Measures can be taken to arrest further deterioration. For example, we know from sad experience that massive water projects can be a set-back for local economies at the same time they were devastating the environment.[6] Both sides can profitably ally in rejecting the worst of such lose-lose proposals.

And there are win-wins opportunities to be identified. Carefully managed game preserves, with incentives properly structured for indigenous peoples, promise to draw a steady stream of tourists and hunters to underwrite the conservation of otherwise endangered game animals for the benefit both of impoverished local peoples and of posterity. It has been reported that the environmentally injurious flaring of natural gas in the Western Siberian oil is so colossally wasteful—at current prices the flare is worth perhaps US $1 billion a year—that a $1.3 billion loan from the world bank to exploit the flare commercially could be repaid in four years.[7]

Indeed, searching out such win-win strategies presumably forms the paradigm for "sustainable development" as the Brundtland Report conceived it, economic development for the living that does not compromise the needs of the future.

The idea of sustainable development as compromise—particularly if it suggests mutual advantage—sounds promising. But the fact that an outcome is of mutual advantage does not satisfy all the moral qualms. Are we satisfied if the most powerful

---

[*]   *See* "Green Economics," Scientific American, July 1994 p. 102. An important and difficult query, however, is to what extent should a rational accounting be concerned with losses at local levels that are compensated in global growth (with transfer payments)?

party get the lion's share of the cooperative gains? Would an outcome that advantaged the poor but disadvantaged the rich, thus failing the economist's test of pareto-superiority) be preferable, if it led to a more ideal distribution?

One can perhaps visualize the dynamics of compromise-seeking by imagining a Ven diagram. One circle represents the set of projects that promise to advance productivity and the true standard of living as the beneficiary nations would define it.* The other circle represents the set of projects favored from an environmentalist-futures perspective that ascribes high values both to environmental amenities and to the well being of future persons.** The overlap represents the win-win options, the projects that lie within both choice sets. Lose-lose is a set-back for both.

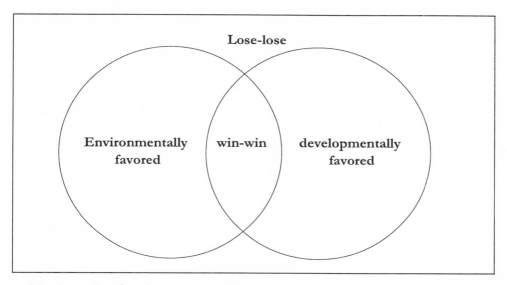

Tensions arise, first, because given the limitation of resources, there are differences over the rankings within the set of mutually acceptable choices. Some win-win alternatives will be more attractive to one group than to the other. Second, there are tensions emanating from the areas beyond the overlap: alternatives that are members of one set, but not the other—projects that are acceptable to the developmentalists but are environmentally suspect, and vice-versa. From the Developmentalist (here, typically South) perspective, why should a project that offers welfare benefits to a hundred persons and preserves a hundred tigers (a member of the "win-win" set) dominate a project that preserves no tigers but alleviates the suffering of, or even saves the lives

---

*   In other words, when gains in productivity are offset by the social costs of pollution, etc. to the living, the projects are on net positive.

**   Calculations here would be driven by, for example, high existence value for species and wilderness areas, and a low rate of discount (and high risk aversion) for time-remote calamities and their costs.

of, thousands who live in the shadows of famine, thirst, and disease (a member of the developmental set only)? On what normative basis can one defend handing over whales to future generations rather than wheat to Somalis? To say we don't have to choose is simply wrong. We are witnessing the establishment of a globe-spanning structure of nongovernmental and governmental organizations that face making or fudging such choices continuously.

Present Versus Future

One major element of the conflict, that implicating future generations, can be dramatized this way. Imagine that some of the economically advanced nations, such as the United States and European Union, were to establish a Beneficence Commission (BC). In essence (I will fill in some details in a moment) the BC is funded with a fixed endowment—say, $1 billion. It is told it is to consider two classes of beneficiaries: strangers in space (Spatial Strangers, or SSs) and strangers in time (Temporal Strangers, or TSs). In disbursing the $1 billion on behalf of these two groups it is to do "the (morally) best it can" with the amount. All strangers, present and future, are to be regarded as inherently worthy of equal respect; and in making the distributions, the donors' own self-(and national) interests are not to be considered a factor.

Determining the right rule is of course quite complex. Leading candidates would certainly include: *Rule 1*: giving first priority to succoring those in dire peril; *Rule 2*: assuring that each successive generation inherit resources and technology adequate to provide the same average welfare per capita as the preceding generation; and *Rule 3*: assuring no reduction in the utility level of the least well off (following John Rawls's maximin).[8]

Interestingly, there are reasons to believe that, whichever of these rules the BC were to adopt, the BC would likely tip resource transfers in favor of Spatial Strangers over the Temporal Strangers.

First, imagine they were to follow *Rule 1*. Considering the marginality of so many present lives—millions dying annually of dirty water, dirty air and malaria—we might fairly conclude that even if the most wretched of the future are equally bad off, they cannot be worse off than contemporary needy or they would be dead. Therefore we should give to the living. The only objection might take the form that the future might hold a larger number of equally destitute people.

On the basis that each person is of equal inherent value, the BC might feel compelled to divide the funds (somehow) accordingly: that is, to make some current expenditures for relief of contemporary sufferers and put aside an investment the interest from which would care for the future "bottom." But unless the BC adopts some such dismal-projection plus strong egalitarian tack, it is hard to imagine any other-regarding fund that would not be exhausted just in trying to buffer existing lives—Spatial Strangers—from extreme misery.

Similarly with regard to *Rule 2*: Wealth on earth, even per capita, has been increasing with time. If history is a guide, average wealth will be higher without any special efforts at all—simply if we have no BC and let the economy flow its course. For the same reasons, if we consider *Rule 3*, the utility level of any lowest group tomorrow (say the bottom 5%) is unlikely to be lower than that of the lowest 5% today. If this trend continues, and future generations, including the bottom group, should be better off than today's bottom, then withholding from the present poor—from succoring them and developing their economies—is distinctly the wrong moral strategy.

There would be no justice in tilting our beneficence towards the worst off among the now living. Assuming marginal utility of wealth, each dollar distributed to a poor person represents more utility than the same dollar placed in the hands of a richer recipient. Hence, the BC should distribute to the living.

Suppose, though, this line of reasoning is wrong: that some group of worse off in the future will, on some basis of calculation, be more deserving of our succor than the worse off of today.*

Even so, the case for aiding them over the present poor runs into a practical consideration. The fact is, we simply have less ability to *monitor and control* dispositions to the temporally distant than we do aid to spatially remote strangers, (Similarly, on utility-based theories we have less information about the utility function of the spatially remote than on the temporally remote.) True, we have a hard time delivering relief to contemporary nations in civil turmoil, such as Somalia. Our would-be deliveries of aid are often intercepted and exploited by war lords. But just imagine the problems the BC would have trying to assure delivery to the wretched of 2100. We could set up an escrow account in their name, with instructions to compound the interest, etc., and to distribute aid among those who fall below the designated level. But we can have no confidence that the intended beneficiaries will receive it, particularly in view of the fact that we have no confidence that the leaders of 2100 will share out taste for succoring the wretched. They may be, if not thieves, elitists.

Moreover, if the BC concludes that some share of our beneficence is available and should go to the wretched among the unborn, transferring funds to Spatial Strangers may be the best way to benefit the future. The reason is that the most likely group of ill-off in the near term are the progeny of the neediest SSs. Hence, any transfers of wealth to them that is not expended in immediate consumption will be a good way to boost investment in the infrastructure and well-being of the future neediest.**

---

*   Perhaps because we may conceive ourselves to be the cause of the plight of our progeny, while our remote coinhabitants' problems are not of "our making." (They may trace to our colonist forebears for example, not us.).

**   On the other hand, our progeny might wish us to invest not in the least developed countries, which offer rather low rates of return at present, but in areas offering the highest rate of return, so as to increase their legacy.

It seems to me, therefore, that in those circumstances in which the ambitions of the Developmentalists and the (Preservationist) Environmentalists conflict, there is a strong presumption in favor of the Developmentalists—those who would succor the contemporary and near term poor and lift them out of their deep poverty.

In Defense of Preservationism

Yet, there are undoubtedly countervailing arguments that we ought, in some circumstances and in some ways, to discount the strong arguments slanted towards today's poverty-stricken masses and favor the future. First, the Preservationist may be able to marshall arguments from utility based on the weight of sheer numbers. To illustrate, each person on earth may get only slight utility from the continued existence of the Sphinx. Why not inundate it (says the Developmentalist) if doing so would feed many starving? But first, the Preservationist rejoins, if humankind can maintain the monument for an additional thousand years, the aggregate satisfaction of all the generations that will enjoy its existence (even if few of them ever actually visit it) might outweigh in some scheme of things considerable present suffering of a lesser number.[*]

Second, utilitarianism is hardly the only basis for moral action. One might derive from competing moral viewpoints an obligation to preserve nature, or other things, even in the face of utility. For example, there is a liberal conception of human welfare, richer than and outside utilitarianism, that could portray the preservation of pristine natural spaces, etc. as a prerequisite to human flourishing. (J. S. Mill believed exactly that.)[9]

Third, a Preservationist, building upon rights-based arguments, can maintain that future generations have rights against us (or, at least, we have duties towards them). And among these duties there might be duties to preserve certain things.

This third position, the notion of future generations as rights-holders in this context raises more questions than it answers. The most common philosophical objection—that we can have no duties to the unborn because they are not in existence—we can dismiss as casuistry. From the principle that one ought to avoid deliberate harm to others, I have no difficulty deriving a strong duty not to bury nuclear waste in unmarked containers that will burst in 300 years even if (as the critics say) the obligees are at present an undetermined (open) set.[10] But even if we grant in principle the plausibility of generation-leaping rights and duties, the devil, we shall, see, is in deriving specific details. If future generations have a right, what is it a right to? To a minimal standard of ecological integrity? To the same wealth as we inherited? To

---

[*] One must grant that the aggregation of utilities, if admitted as a general guideline for future-affecting conduct, leads to awful problems well examined in the literature. For example, their interests, aggregated, would impel us to consume at the bare subsistence level on their (much greater) behalf.

whales? And even if they (shall) have rights, what do we do when plausible rights of future persons (to tigers?) conflict with equally plausible rights-claims of our own contemporaries (to raise their standards of living above the abysmal?)

There is a fourth ground on which the Preservationist can stake a claim. Whether or not our posterity is deemed to possess moral clams against us, and whether or not we have moral responsibilities towards them, a decision to enhance their well-being can find support without ranging beyond the welfare of those presently living. That is, most living people will regard some sacrifice to insure the well-being of future persons as a positive public good (in their own welfare functions). Put otherwise, just as people get benefit from assurances that their homes will not be robbed, so they get benefit from assurances that their descendants will be provided for.

To illustrate, we would not pay an infinite amount to preserve the Antarctic intact. But we might expend more to preserve it *from consideration of them* than we would *from consideration of us alone.* That is, we could employ a contingent valuation that asked each person now living (1) what each would pay to conserve the Antarctic; (2) what each would pay if they believed that all human life would end with the life of the last surviving child of the last survivor of the living. One would imagine that (1) exceeds(2); the difference represents what it is worth to us to include an intact Antarctic in our bequest to the future.[11]

Let me emphasize that I am not trying to evaluate or weigh each of these four platforms for reinforcing future well-being. But taken together they suggest that what I will call "Preservationism" deserves a closer look.

The issue Preservationism leads to is this. Let us suppose that the justifiable priorities of the living (including Spatial Strangers)—whatever theses claims amount to—have been attended to. Suppose, too, that the welfare of future persons is a lingering matter of present concern (for any or all of the rationales immediately above). Committed, on these assumptions, to make the future better, or at least no worse off, the questions then becomes *how* that commitment (whatever its magnitude) should be implemented. To put it simply, if we are going to do something for them, what should be the currency of our altruism?

One common approach is to draw the distinction between what David Pearce calls Sustainable Economic Development (SED) and Sustainable Use of Resources and the Environment (SURE).

Those who subscribe to SED (sustainable development in a "weak sense")[12] are committed to turn over to the future no less capital than they themselves enjoyed. But under SED there are no constraints on the form in which the capital is conveyed, only the quantum: the corpus of our legacy, whatever the "basket" of its goods, must be adequate to assure that our progeny can enjoy the same level of consumption we have enjoyed, without undermining their obligation to leave a similar bequest to their successors.*

By contrast, SURE (sustainable development "in a strong sense") captures the idea that among the many assets we have inherited and produced, there is a subset of natural resources, including soil, species, forests, ores, and the safe-level assimilative capacities of the oceans and atmosphere, that it is our special responsibility to conserve. We might understand the responsibility to attach *tout cours* (meaning we were obliged to make whatever sacrifice conservation required), or to bind us with the more moderate obligation to employ preservationist-skewed accounting when we do cost/benefit analyses. Under the moderate approach, the living would be under no obligation to impoverish itself to maintain a critical habitat. But we might, for example, be obliged to assign a project to preserve the habitat a negligible discount rate (a controversial tactic which would skew capital towards the habitat preservation by making it appear relatively more favorable than competing investments).

Before comparing the merits of SED with SURE let us take a closer look at SURE. It asks us to make the future better off by singling out certain natural resources for preservation. But natural resources are only one form of capital stock. It is not at all clear that a future regarding policy, if it is to privilege any form of capital at all, should single out natural resources as distinct from, for example:

- man-made capital, including the pyramids, railroads, water systems, and technology;

- human capital, including levels of education and skills;

- institutional capital, including safeguards for public order and liberty.

The argument for preserving capital in each such form will vary, since each is a response, at some level, to our conception of the good life, which a fuller treatment would have to examine and specify. An environmentalist, prizing continuity in life forms, would presumably favor preserving biodiversity over preserving the pyramids; the pyramids, in turn, would be favored by those who sought to transmit a feeling for the continuity of civilization. And, in terms of the inter-agency competition, the environmentalist would presumably favor funding the Global Environment Facility (GEF); the civilization-preservationist, the Cultural Heritage Foundation.

---

*   Note the affinity between SED and John Rawls' "just savings principle." Economists vary over the optimal savings rate. See the discussion of the "Golden Rule" of capital accumulation in W.H. Branson, Macroeconomic Theory and Policy 3d ed. 611-626 (1989). There is in all events some ambiguity in SED: is the commitment to assure the succeeding generation the same amount of wealth in gross or per capita? If the latter, population increase alone means we would be compelled to turn over more than we received. Someone might defend the per capita position on the grounds that we (collectively?) are responsible for the size of the next generation's population, not them.

Indeed, a general treatment of this question—what policies ought we to adopt to shape the future?—would have to go beyond considerations of capital-transfer and the development of institutions appropriate to those tasks. The unfolding of the world can be described in many ways, and each vision of the good life would yield its own descriptors and maximands. Insofar as we valued life-style, or health, we might incline to maximize proxies such as leisure hours or mortality measures, respectively. We might choose for our descendants political liberty, and therefore do what we can to increase the expected number of people who will live under democratic rule. For example, we could direct more resources into the United Nations Human Rights Commission, erect statues of Jefferson and others associated in various areas of the world with promoting liberty; we could more systematically condition economic assistance to countries that are democratic, and deny loans to nations that deny human rights.

Hence, in a general discussion of investing with an eye towards the future, we should keep in mind that humanity faces a choice of SED versus, not SURE alone, but a broader category that includes both SURE and other, nonresource descriptors. We might refer to the more inclusive policy as SID: Sustaining Ideal Descriptors. SID can be viewed as the more inclusive, inasmuch as the singling out of favored natural resources can always be phrased in terms of specially favored descriptors. For example what SURE would refer to as more whales can be brought under SID as "a more whale-laden planet" just as SID might include a more democratic or a more literate planet.

In all events, both SURE and SID raise similar questions about how we should plan, as it were, our estate. First, do we want to transmit our wealth in a particular form (skewing our legacy towards certain natural resources, great human artifacts, institutions of liberty, etc.)? And, a subsidiary question (of "dead-hand control," if you will), is any such commitment to leave part of our estate in a particular form so strong that we are prepared even to reduce the economic value they would place on their inheritance, i.e, give them an unimpaired ozone shield even if they would prefer the added cancer risks and unrestricted cash in the amount that allowing the ozone to deteriorate would save?

A. The merits of SED

Insofar as we are committed to benefit the future, why should we do so through a strategy of specific natural resources (or other special descriptors) rather than, as SED would have it, wealth?* In weighing the relative merits of these strategies for benefitting the future, the best start is to mark the strength of wealth as compared with the weaknesses of "special" legacies. For one thing, history shows how commonly assets

---

*   Wealth is of course a descriptor as well. But it is the most "general" category.

highly prized in one epoch (frankincense, amber, myrrh) are subject to devaluation as tastes and needs and substitutes evolve. We could curtail our use of copper, at our expense, only to find that the inhabitants of the earth in 2100 had little use for it. Indeed, they might well wish we had run through it more quickly and productively, amassing that much more (general) capital to deposit in their legacy.

The fragility of many specific assets, and the virtue of a wide investment portfolio will often strengthen the case for SED as well. A forest "tagged" for a privileged existence may, despite our best efforts, be ravaged by fire or flood or blight. On the other hand, by disinvesting in the forest, the wealth produced can be reinvested into various forms of man-made capital (factories and technology), human capital (through schools and education), and so on, as needs evolve. One would imagine that our unfettered liberty to disinvest and reinvest at highest returns is generally just what the future would have us do. After all, we have no clear idea what problems they will face, as they will define them.* For example, it is common to worry on their behalf about global warming; but their prime worry may be global cooling—or an AIDS-like virus or asteroids. The core of the SED approach is that the best way to prepare them for these unforseen challenges is to give them the flexibility of wealth—in other words, to pursue a course of development that does not sacrifice the amount of wealth transferred on account of self-imposed, well-intentioned but quite possibly misguided limitations on the form of the wealth conveyed.

B. The Arguments for SID

This prima facie case for SED over SID appears so compelling, that it is useful to put the policy question in the form of a presumption: under what circumstances, and pursuant to what theories, is there a basis to privilege certain assets (or other descriptors) by "tagging" them for a specially prolonged existence?

One answer is that the endogenousity of tastes makes SID unavoidable. That is, the value persons remote in time place on the existence of marine mammals and tropical birds is not a *given*, but will be a function of the legacy we leave them. I personally would regard their eradication as a terrible loss for my remote progeny. On the other hand, one must grant that if we (let me put it this way) accelerate our disinvestment in these natural biological resources and reinvest in accelerating advances in electronics, our progeny will have, if fewer wild creatures, more electronic stimulation. We have to face the fact they may be as "happy" with their enhanced

---

* We can regard this as an illustration of state-dependent utility. That is, lacking market interchange, it is hard enough to estimate how much a contemporary person values a forest or lake or the ozone shield, even though we know, in principle, both his basket of goods and the circumstances in which he lives. But consider how much more difficult it is to conjecture the value future persons will attach to such goods, when the utility they will derive is so highly dependent on the state of the world they live in—the social and environmental context in which the lake, etc. is situate, factors that are simply beyond our ken.

electronic stimulation as they would be with the wildlife. But the reverse is also true. Hence, we cannot say we are simply deferring to a notion of their welfare in making the very decisions that will, inescapably, form their basic wants. We have the responsibility of deciding (within some range) what those wants will be, i.e., what sort of people they will be.

The point is, SED cannot arbitrate between some subset of policy options. Within that range the SID advocate, in tagging certain resources, etc., for preservation, is engaged in a normative battle over what sorts of persons our progeny will be. And SED—within some range—offers no solutions.

Indeed, it is hard to make SED intelligible without serious thought to what might be called "taste legacy." SED assumes leaving additional wealth. But the indeterminacies in the meaning of "wealth" are exacerbated in an intergenerational context, being a function of opportunities and perceived needs. If our progeny became less needful, they might have fewer resources but (in this context) no less wealth. Hence, as many environmentalists have suggested (in various terms) one of the best legacies we could leave our progeny is a reduced taste for conspicuous consumption.

Moreover, there is a special class of cases in which arranging to preserve specific assets is an efficient strategy in furtherance of SED. Consider, for example, resources that are likely to have a high option value over long time horizons,[13] or those of known high value which, if replaceable at all, require high reinvestment costs. Public works projects such as sewage systems illustrate one prosaic set of examples. Maintaining and improving them is vital (particularly if sea levels rise). Moreover they require long construction periods, so that handing over a fully depreciated system and a bundle of cash equivalent to our savings from allowing depreciation is not the equivalent of leaving them the system in repair. Almost certainly we do right by them to leave them a well-working infrastructure.* The same is true of the ozone shield and other critical life support elements. True, destroying the earth's life support system would fail to meet the SED constraint without any further SID gloss. (We cannot imagine intelligibly claiming to a future person, "you'll be overwhelmed by cataracts and cancer and there's no potable water, but we've so multiplied the stock of marine resources and artifacts that you'll be better off—wealthier—than we were.") The point is, the likelihood of their need for the most critical resources is so high, and the costs of repairing damage so great, that our forward looking commitment should be charged with some level of maintenance costs of keeping these systems from deteriorating.

On the other hand, these arguments all amount to saying that SED policies and SID policies are not inconsistent. The most challenging question Preservation raises is this: When is it defensible to retain a specific asset *even at the cost of a reduction in wealth*

---

* Long term public finance bonds may be thought of as a way to enable the present to pass some of the costs along to the future. The now unborn will continue, rightly, to pay the interest.

transferred? Why would we leave them an amount of biodiversity that (our marginal efforts and alternative investments considered) leaves them less well off?

Perhaps the most widespread arguments for actually subordinating SED arise from commitments to values other than human welfare. At one extreme, such values can take a rights-based form—for example, that whales, as a species, have a right to exist. Accordingly, if measures to conserve whales and dolphins were to reduce the living standards of future humans, so be it.

A related position conceives the living as stewards of (some ideal vision of) the earth. The motivation here is not to prevent a wrong to the whales and dolphins, but to further the appropriate vision. To illustrate, at present over 40% of the land surface's Net Primary Product (NPP) has been arrogated by (or displaced or wasted by) humankind. A "stewardship" advocate would argue that we are morally bound to take present steps to foreclose that figure from rising to 70%, even if we were convinced that our progeny's average utility would be discernibly higher under that humankind-monopolizing alternative. (Such steps would presumably include curtailing population, freezing deforestation, and increasing R&D aimed at fostering growth without further encroachments on other living species.)

Of course, the familiar environmentalist arguments have counterparts in other descriptors. There are certainly those who would take steps to conserve liberty, or the nuclear family, or a belief in God, even if our efforts to secure them made the future less well off materially. Indeed, this accords precisely with the position that John Rawls takes in *A Theory of Justice* regarding liberty: it is the first principle, and to be distributed (I presume through generations) even at sacrifice, if need be, in material wealth.[*] And note that advocates of conserving preferred goods are not apt to be moved by the supposed virtues of flexibility that liquid wealth offers: on the contrary, they will want their "investment" to be relatively sturdy in the face of risks that future persons might try to reject their values.

C. The Rights of the Present Generation

But are we entitled to make the future, by our deliberate choice, less well off materially, so as to foster our own (and our predecessors' ideals)? Is there a good argument that we the living have, as well as the power, a morally justifiable prerogative so to shape the lives of our descendants?

---

[*]   *See* John Rawls, A Theory of Justice 60-65 (1971). Indeed, Rawls, in discussing intergenerational requirements specifies a "just savings rate," *id.* at 284-93. Later, Rawls clarifies that the rate of savings is constrained to whatever level each generation requires "to preserve a just basic structure over time. *Once these conditions are reached . . . net real savings may fall to zero.*" John Rawls, Justice as Fairness: A Restatement 129 (1990) (emphasis added). Query, what of those in the original position were to specify their expectations not merely as to political lives (Liberty, the Difference Principle, etc.) and include as basic goods wilderness area, etc.? In the vocabulary of SED and SURE, would it be unreasonable to imagine the original parties agreeing to the conservation of certain natural assets—even if it meant a reduction in savings transmitted to the future?

The whole project smacks of what lawyers have debated for years under the heading of "Dead Hand Control": ought we to allow creation of estates that single out specific devises with restrictions against alienation ("Greenacre to my daughter Mary and the issue of her body forever"). This is a form of devise disfavored (and severely restricted) by Anglo-American courts, e.g., as per the Rule Against Perpetuities. Should we react otherwise when our attention shifts to what might be called generational estate planning?

In the present context there is this difference. If an entire generation singles out certain species or statues or forests to leave its progeny, there is no way to assure that *their* institutions will honor the restriction as much as courts can be counted on to honor restrictions, say, in charitable trusts. The most we can do is to furnish some of our progeny with a portfolio of options. No future person is forced to go to a rain forest or pyramid. And of course collectively they are free (within the limits of our taste-control over them) to liquidate whatever we leave them.

The fact that our actual influence is limited may be viewed as further support for our liberty to nudge civilization along the track we like——at least absent a strong counter-argument, as that certain moves would be leaving them in peril.

But that is not quite the end of it. While they have no "right" that constrains our interests in preserving, and inviting them to conserve, those artifacts of nature and civilization that we value,[14] we are not excused from consideration of their welfare and (more broadly) well-being.

Some hypothetical calculations will illustrate the predicament we face if we are to take concern for future generations seriously. We the living generally value the untouched beauty of the Antarctic and, in hoping that our progeny will be like us (if not even morally and aesthetically better), want them to enjoy it, too. Indeed, the desire to affect future generations is one reason why the continent's vast stock of buried resources are presently under a moratorium. The moratorium will, however, face increasing pressure if mineral demand increases and extraction technology improves. Let us suppose that, over the next few decades, as the feasibility of extraction improves, the then living persist in favoring the moratorium. But someone points out that, compounded at 3%, each $100,000,000 pumped from the Antarctic into the global economy as investment* will represent an additional $37 billion two hundred years in future. (At 4% the figure soars to $255 billion). And $100 million is the annual yield from a mere 275,000 barrels of oil per day (at $1/bbl. net)—a mere fraction of the Antarctic's economic value. At these prices, is it not likely that our progeny in 2195 would rather we develop the Antarctic even at disruption and sacrifice of its ecology and pristineness? I am not sure that we are bound to honor their preferences. But I do feel we are obliged at least to try to construct and account for their likely

---

* Some of the wealth would presumably be consumed with minimal influence on investment.

attitudes—particularly insofar as our motivation claims not to be our own well-being, but theirs.

CONCLUSION

The deeper we delve into "sustainable development." the more we uncover problems and paradoxes, some practically impenetrable. As a matter of geopolitics, multilateral funding agencies unfortunately find themselves competing for distinctly declining funds as the developed nations tighten their budgets. Some of these efforts emphasize assisting the world's poor to grow in environmentally benign ways; others stress preserving resources, even economically unproductive resources, for the future. Sometimes, and across some margins, the goals overlap. But the tensions are greater than is ordinarily acknowledged. Exposing and analyzing these tensions is the province of philosophy. For all their toughness, they deserve redoubled attention.

The risks of eco-collapse may be exaggerated (and may have to be exaggerated to catch popular and political attention). But in the whole of the universe our planetary habitat *is*, as the environmentalists say, the only spot we know of that harbors intelligence. A bit of alarm about our tamperings with Nature is hardly out of place; on the contrary, one would think provisioning for the future to be a moral imperative. And, so, for the developmentalist's charge about the immorality of our abandoning strangers in space, there remains to answer the environmentalists' reproach: are we doing right by those strangers who will follow in time?

In the last analysis, the strains between sustainability and development ambitions could be, while not eliminated, generously reduced, if we only we would find it in our hearts to give to each its due. Right now we are leaving both camps starved for resources, to spar over scraps.

ENDNOTES

1. Search conducted Jan. 3, 1995, of "sustainable development" in LEXIS in the INTLAW library, ILM and BDIEL (Basic Documents of International Economic Law) file; and in WESTLAW in the USTREATIES database (equivalent of TIAS).

2. WORLD COMMISSION ON ENV'T & DEV. OUR COMMON FUTURE (1987) (Gro Harlem Brundtland, Chairman) [hereinafter Brundtland Report] (1987).

3. *Id.* at 43.

4. The Brundtland Report recommended a lexical ordering: in the case of conflict, "overriding priority should be given to meeting" the "essential needs of the world's poor." *Id.*

5. United Nations Institute for Disarmament Research (UNDIR) and United Nations Environment Programme (UNEP), Disarmament, Environment, and Development and their Relevance to the Least Developed Countries 35. (Research Paper No. 10, Arthur H. Westing, ed. 1991).

6. *See* Fred Pearce, The Dammed 181-202 and *passim* (1992).

7. The flare-off, 16 bcm of natural gas a year (out of a production of 600 bcm), is roughly the equivalent of the flaring of the Kuwait wells that caused such concern during the Persian Gulf War, but on a continual annual basis. A $1.3 billion project could capture for exploitation an estimated 6 bcm., worth $375 million a year. *See* Carey Goldberg, *Flaring Siberia Gas: Torches Light Way to Eco-Disaster*, L.A. Times, July 25, 1993, at A1.

8. John Rawls, in A THEORY OF JUSTICE (1971) imagines that people in an "original position," blind to the details of their own actual lives (which I am imaging to include, in which generation they would be born), and bargaining as to what would be fair, would select a maximin constraint: to avoid the unpleasant likelihood of being on the bottom of the social pile, no one would accept any deviation from an *equal* distribution of his primary goods *unless* the rule permitting the deviation operated to the advantage of the least well-advantaged group. Inequalities that can be so justified are "permissible." Rawls' actual treatment of intergenerational justice is more complex, as indicated in the text.

9. J.S. Mill, PRINCIPLES OF POLITICAL ECONOMY 750 (Ch. VI, Bk. IV, §2; W. J. Ashley, ed. Longmans, Green 1926) (1848).

10. The person who puts explosive material on a raft and sets it floating down the river should not be able to plead he had "no duty" to a child who became its victim on the grounds that at the time of the launch the child was not a person in being. What a nonsensical way to try to shirk our moral obligations. *See* Per Ariansen, *Sustainability, Morality and Future Generations*, 17 Future Generations J. (No. 3, 1995) 20: "The essential morally relevant aspect of the situation is that I [be] aware [of the] high

probability that action voluntarily initiated by me would hurt someone who had not consented to being exposed to the damage."

11. The problems of designing a contingent valuation procedure that would satisfactorily measure the preferences the paragraph describes are obviously challenging, to say the least.

12. DAVID PEARCE, BLUEPRINT 3 (1993) 16-17 suggests degrees of sustainability from weak to critical. In this vocabulary, "weak" presumably corresponds with SED, and "strong" with SURE, below.

13. *See* Kenneth J. Arrow & Anthony C. Fisher, *Environmental Preservation, Uncertainty, and Irreversibility*, 88 Q. J. Econ. 312 (1974); Anthony C. Fisher & W. Michael Hanemann, *Option Value and the Extinction of Species*, 4 ADVANCES APPLIED MICRO-ECON. 169 (1986).

14. Per Ariansen (U. of Oslo) has suggested to me that the Spanish might want to preserve bull-fighting and the Norwegians whaling not in order to shape future generations as much as to make a statement of our times and our identity. He says, "the kind of self-sacrifice associated with mulling out our own cultural preferences and identity statements [on their behalf] cannot be universalized. If all generations should lay low in order not to paternalise the next generations, then no generation would be given the opportunity to bloom."

CHAPTER 6

THE CONVENTION ON BIOLOGICAL DIVERSITY[*]

GENESIS OF THE CONVENTION

The Convention on Biological Diversity (CBD)[1] is not the law's first effort to deal with the earth's biological assets. Hammurabi's Code,[2] the laws of the Hittites[3] and the Old Testament[4] laid down rules ranging from agricultural practices to the protection of enemy fruit trees in time of war. International agreements providing for the conservation of fish, migratory birds and marine mammals trace back at least a century.[5] With the passage of time, such efforts have expanded. Some of the modern conventions focus on particular species, such as the Convention on International Trade in Endangered Species of Wild Flora and Fauna (CITES)[6]; others assume as their focus particular geographic areas, such as the Antarctic Treaty[7]; others seek to regulate particular environment-threatening activities, such as the International Convention for the Regulation of Whaling.[8]

But in 1980 the seminal "World Conservation Strategy," co-produced by the World Conservation Union (IUCN), the World Resources Institute, and others, identified biological diversity as an independent global asset, one whose accelerating decline demanded attention in its own right.[9] This influential report recited the value of genetic resources, identified the many pressures on them (from human encroachment on habitats to pollution and the introduction of exotic species) and outlined a strategy for strengthening and coordinating global and local-level responses.[10]

As the decade unfolded, various scientific studies—for example, satellite-generated reports of forest decline and revised estimates of species loss—confirmed the peril. By 1984 the IUCN, through its Commission on Environmental Law and its Environmental Law Centre, began promoting a series of draft articles towards a treaty.

Formal, broadened efforts were initiated in November 1988, with a succession of meetings of "expert groups" convened by the United Nations Environment Programme (UNEP). Within the next two years a number of working groups were created to examine various subjects including conservation of wild and domesticated species; access to genetic resources and technology; safety implications of released genetically-modified organisms; and financing.

---

[*] Published in French as "Convention de Rio, 1992, sur la Biodiversité," in Strategiques Energies Biosphere & Societe (SEBES) 1996 issue on "Le Droit International Face à l'éthique et à la politique de l'environment," Geneva. The author wishes to acknowledge the research support of Steve Harris.

119

The Convention was opened for signature at the Earth Summit on 5 June 1992. By the close of 1995 it had been ratified by 136 nations,[11] with the conspicuous exception of the United States. President Bill Clinton signed the agreement, but efforts to obtain Senate ratification, as required under the U.S. Constitution, have stalled—and prospects for approval in the near term are poor.

The Political and Economic Setting

Several factors converged to make the CBD an unusually open-textured agreement dominated by commitments (discussed below) that are typically vague, hedged ("as far as possible and appropriate") and unbacked by any sanction. First, a considerable degree of softness was inevitable—and tolerable—within the ambition to produce a supple "framework" convention, roughly comparable to the Vienna Convention for the Protection of the Ozone Layer (1987), and to the Framework Convention on Climate Change that was being negotiated contemporaneously. The negotiators hoped that missing details would be fleshed out over time. A second factor contributing to the CBD's vagueness was the relative rapidity with which the text was prepared. With the Earth Summit rapidly approaching, the Intergovernmental Negotiating Committee (INC) was forced to race through highly complex and relatively novel issues to have a document ready for presentation a little over a year from its first meeting.

But even if the negotiators had had more time, there is a third reason why a higher than average level of obscurity and equivocation—not merely in detail but in sense of institutional mission—was probably unavoidable. The explanation is to be found in the Rich-Poor tensions which have left their mark on all the recent international environmental accords, but perhaps affected the CBD in particular.

One hesitates to generalize about there being two "sides" to the negotiation: Rich and Poor. Many parties participated—Non-governmental organizations (NGOs) as well as nations—injecting many multi-faceted and subtle areas of difference, and agreement, into the process. For example, the NGOs sensitive to the needs of indigenous peoples were as staunchly "conservationist" of forest homesites and ecosystems as any pro-conservation Rich country. But overall, and not to overlook the commonalities of interest and the willingness to seek common grounds, the Rich and Poor brought two different perspectives to the table. The Rich are more preoccupied with risks to the global life support system. The Poor, for their part, share in these concerns. But their priorities are understandably concentrated on local and immediate challenges such as eradicating poverty, reducing illiteracy and building infrastructure. As for the long-term threats, they are for the most part traceable to the activities and life-patterns of the developed world. If the greenhouse blanket has been thickened and the ozone layer thinned, that was the Rich's doing; in justice (as well as economic necessity) let the Rich pay to repair them.

It was against this general background that the CBD negotiations took place. The Rich (to pursue this coarse caricature) entered the negotiations with topmost concern for the predominantly conservationist agenda that the IUCN had outlined as early as 1980. The Poor were wary. Nature had allotted them a disproportionate share of the planet's biological diversity. Hence, talk of conservation threatened disproportionately to question *their* sovereignty over local policies on which *their* economic development (and debt service) depended, from forests to fisheries. Successful conclusion of a broad multilateral agreement required assuring the Poor, first, that their sovereignty would not be infringed; second, that any appreciable financial burdens would be borne by the Rich.

And third, winning the support of the Poor required carrots. As with other framework conventions, the Poor saw in the CBD a potential conduit for transferring "new and additional" wealth from the Rich. In addition, as in so many other negotiations, the door to some sort of undefined "technology transfer" was opened. And perhaps most significantly, the Poor were encouraged to believe that their forests were fabulously rich storehouses of genetic resources that Rich-country firms, pharmaceutical houses in particular, armed with the latest biotechnology techniques and apparatus, were eager to "mine" to their own benefit. If the CBD were to offer the Poor little else, it was seen as a way to insure that they received a goodly share of this supposedly imminent wealth.

These divergent motives, the persistent tensions, and efforts alternately to ease and ignore them, have all left their imprint on the text and on the ensuing progress of the Parties.

General Aims and Objectives

The Convention is launched with a Preamble that sounds both chords—preservationism and development—without acknowledging the inherent disharmonies. Biological diversity is honored both for its intrinsic and its instrumental worth. It is affirmed to be a common *concern* of mankind.[12] But the Convention stops short of endorsing a common heritage viewpoint, which, in the eyes of some, might warrant the world community forcing a government to preserve a species-rich forest. To leave no doubts on this score, the sovereign rights of states over their biological resources is explicitly affirmed.[13] And the Convention even goes so far as to record the undoubted truth: that "economic and social development and the eradication of poverty are the first and overriding priorities of the Developing Country Parties."[14]

The Convention then declares itself to have three "objectives": "conservation of biological diversity", 'the sustainable use of its components"; and "the fair and equitable sharing of the benefits."

The Institutional Structure

The Conventions establishes a Convention of the Parties (COP) as the crucial ongoing body with continuing powers to review data, monitor, adopt new protocols,[15] and, by consensus or 2/3 majority, amend the Convention or any of its protocols.[16] Under the COP there is a Subsidiary Body on Scientific, Technical and Technological Advice (SBSTTA)[17] to handle technical issues. The Global Environment Facility (GEF), originally designated the "interim funding mechanism" continues to serve in that provisional basis. In general, the industrialized nations want to make the GEF the permanent mechanism, but a final decision is being blocked by several LDCs, which continue to insist on reforms in the GEF (including a larger voice in management) before they acquiesce. As for formal dispute settlement mechanisms, there are none. Indeed, the obligations are predominantly so aspirational and discretionary (even the interval for Article 26's periodic reports is undetermined) that it is unclear what sorts of *disputes* could arise; but if any do, the disputants are enjoined "to seek solution by negotiation."[18]

Convention Obligations

Conservation measures. The response of the Convention to its conservationist constituencies is decidedly "soft." Each Party undertakes to prepare its own national strategy plan with no further constraints than to "reflect *inter alia* the measures set out" in the CBD[19]; and each undertakes ("as far as possible and as appropriate") to "integrate conservation and sustainable use of biological diversity" in its national decision processes.[20]

In early negotiation, the conservation forces had hope that a list could be composed of particularly critical biodiversity areas, in parallel with CITES' listings of endangered species. But some countries presumably imagined they might come under pressure to leave listed areas untouched. Therefore, in keeping with the "softer" tone of the Convention, each Party was entrusted to identify and monitor important areas on their own "having regard to" the safely vague guidelines of Annex 1.[21] "As far as possible and appropriate" each party is to establish a system of protected areas in which "special measures" to protect biodiversity shall be implemented.[22] Additionally, each Party is to adopt measures to advance *ex situ* methods of conservation, such as germ storage.[23] Each Party is to consider incentives for conservation,[24] establish technical and research programs,[25] and to enlarge public awareness.[26] Environmental impact assessments and other governmental measures to limit adverse impacts are encouraged.[27]

Resource measures. In response to the resource claims, the sovereignty of each Party that is the site of potentially valuable biodiversity resources is reaffirmed. But the resource host is at the same time encouraged to facilitate access by others. Facilitation does not extend to complete openness: specifically, no nation may access the resources without the prior informed consent of the host.[28] This requirement is aimed at forcing prospectors to strike a bargain with the host, and therefore to share with it, in some degree, the benefits of commercial exploitation (discussed more fully below). Article 16 amounts to asking the technologically advanced countries to transfer biotechnology (and Article 19, to share the benefits produced by the application of biotechnology to genetic resources) on "fair" and "mutually agreed terms." Articles 17 and 18 encourage the exchange of information and technical and scientific cooperation.

Ethical Issues

The CBD rises out of, and its unfolding will implicate, five sorts of ethical conflicts. These are: (1) International Equity (regarding the division of benefits and burdens of genetic resources among nations); (2) Intranational Equity (regarding the division of the benefits and burdens within nations, particularly in regard to indigenous peoples and communities proximate to resource areas); (3) Inter-Species Equity (regarding the division of conservation efforts among competing species and ecosystems); (4) Inter-generational Equity (regarding the obligations of the living to future generations); and (5) Planetary Equity (regarding how much of the Earth's surface, or its Net Primary Energy, *homo sapiens* are entitled to exploit in competition with other species).

Each of these presents independent complex issues. In this space, the author is limited to a few observations on the first three.

(1) International Equity: Justice among Nations

International Equity, at least in its division of benefits aspects, is addressed principally in Arts. 15-16. These provisions, by fostering bargaining (principally through the prior informed consent mechanism), assure that host countries will receive the *market value* of access for bio-prospecting. Moreover, the cautious recognition of Intellectual Property Rights[29] is calculated to raise that value at least marginally. (By protecting the biotechnology industry's investments, the firms will bring more to the table when bargaining with the host country for access.) However, there is little doubt that the less developed host countries mean by "fair and equitable sharing" something over and above an elevated market price. They anticipate, ideally, leveraging their disproportionate holdings of biodiversity into a foundation for reducing global wealth disparities.

There are several problems, however. First, recent studies of the commercial value of biodiversity suggest that the contentiousness over "equitable sharing" is almost certainly disproportionate to the probable booty.[30] If these studies are anywhere near correct—and no rush of pharmaceutical houses is materializing to cast doubts on them[31]—one is reminded how the Law of the Sea negotiations were complicated and prolonged by heated efforts to divide up the riches of sea-bed manganese nodules—riches that have even today failed to materialize.

Second, whatever the actual magnitude of the wealth—only time will tell—the *moral* case for awarding the host countries more than the market price is uncertain.

How does one divide *equitably* among suppliers, processors and others? Countries that have had the good fortune to harbor biological hot spots are as entitled to some reward as are states that turned out to harbor oil and other natural resources. On the other hand, it is equally true that it is the expanding technological capacity of the DCs, specifically, the increased ability to process specimens and synthesize molecules, that is enhancing the value of the forestland. Without the DCs' biotechnology, the biodiversity assets would be leaves and bark. Moreover, in exploiting genetic resources, First World firms are hardly committing "bio-piracy." The probability of any plant resulting in a *marketable* pharmaceutical product has been estimated at between 1 in 1,000 and 1 in 10,000.[32] Even when a promising drug has been located, the costs of bringing it to market are substantial.[33]

Hence, unlike piracy on the high seas, which involves taking wealth at sword point, and which can be unambiguously and universally condemned, bio-prospecting is a cooperative, wealth increasing activity. Both sides enter into the agreement willingly. Each makes a contribution it can point to. Under these circumstances, with no consensus of moral intuitions that one side is acting evilly (like mistreatment of prisoners of war, or genocide), I am not sure how one is to divide the fruits "equitably"—other than by market negotiation. If one nation, *A*, is willing to make one of its hot spots available for bio-prospecting for $1/hectare per year, while others insist that nothing less than $10/hectare is "fair," is anyone really prepared, in the name of morals, to deny *A* the sovereign power to strike up a deal at $1? The CBD, as presently written, provides no basis for forcing such a result.

Granted, leaving the outcome to the play of market forces is not fully satisfactory. The Nash solution to a bilateral negotiation between two parties of unequal wealth demonstrates that the richer, less desperate party will come away with more than half the cooperative potential expressed in terms of *wealth*. (This outcome is driven by the fact that the rich party has less to lose by walking away from the table, thereby terminating the negotiations.) But it can be shown from the same assumptions that prove the wealthier bargainer will get a larger share of the *wealth* that the division of *utility* is apt to be 50-50.[34] Some may believe that a 50-50 division of wealth is more equitable than a 50-50 division of utility—but it is hardly an easy case. After all, it is the same principal, the declining marginal utility of wealth, that the Poor invoke to justify "differential responsibilities", that is, not requiring the Poor to pay as much under the framework conventions, on the view that each dollar they contribute would "cost" them more (utility) than it would the Rich.

In all events, realistically, the more critical moral question is the other side of the coin: not how to divide the (easily exaggerated) bounty that biodiversity will yield, but how to apportion the burden that effective biodiversity conservation will certainly require. On a theoretical level, one can put the issue of burden-sharing in its largest frame:

"if a duty to conserve the environment exists . . . does it rest on all humankind as a corollary of the . . . Biodiversity Convention [designating] biodiversity a 'common concern of humankind'? Or does the duty rest upon states in whose territory the biodiversity is found, as a consequence of the fact that the Convention [makes states] 'responsible for conserving their biological diversity and for using their biological resources in a sustainable manner'?"[35]

But as a practical matter, in a world marked by gross disparities in wealth, the safeguarding of valuable ecosystems and species, particularly those that cannot "pay their own way" from bio-prospecting, eco-tourism, and other sustainable uses, will require a transfer of funds from Rich to Poor nations. Such transfers are anticipated in Article 20, which mandates that the developed countries pay the undeveloped countries the latter's "agreed full incremental costs" of meeting the Convention's obligations.

The introduction of equity in this form only raises further questions, and not merely the obvious one, how "agreed full incremental costs" are to be measured. Inasmuch as there are not nearly enough funds to pay for a fraction of the things that poor countries may be "obliged' to do, the most urgent question is on the fund-raising, not the fund-distributing side. What division of the costs is fair as among suppliers of the financial resources? How much should Germany contribute, and how much Japan?

To answer this question, the ethicist may be inclined to adopt the perspective of welfare economics, and conceive the problem as one of public goods provision—that is, of perpetuating areas that display widely-radiating nonrivalrous benefits beyond their commercially appropriable value. What is "fair" (as a start) is that each benefitter should contribute for conservation of a critical habitat in proportion to that nation's willingness to pay—essentially, its benefit from conserving the marginal area in question.

However, driving the supply of public goods by willingness to pay tilts conservation efforts towards the preferences of the wealthy. And, worse, the fact that all contributions are purely voluntary means that global conservation efforts are fated to be under-funded.

(2) Intra-national Equities: Justice within Nations

The financial benefits of bio-prospecting may be overblown, but there is enough there to make an appreciable difference to many communities. Whatever the benefits, should they go to the general national account or should some share be targeted to local communities from whose region it came? Regarding each nation's obligation to share its benefits with indigenous peoples and local communities the CBD opens the issue by declaring that "subject to national legislation" each Party shall "encourage the equitable sharing of the benefits of [the] knowledge, innovation and practices" with them; even this slender reference appears only in a subsection of Article 8, dealing with *in-situ* conservation.[36] Should the COP press for something firmer? If it were to press in this direction, it would not have much international law behind it. International law almost uniformly takes nation states as the units of significance, disregarding internal impacts. If an international treaty swells a nation's coffers, well and good; but, for better or worse, the state is virtually free to spend the additional monies as it sees fit. Yet, as a moral matter—as opposed to a legal matter—there is more to be said. The plight of indigenous peoples across the world remains scandalous, and perhaps the CBD "biodiversity resources" context should be exploited as a foundation for focusing world attention.*

(3) Inter-Species Equity: Justice among Species

In this, the third equity issue, humankind is viewed, not as competing with Nature (below), so much as serving as an arbiter. Imagine two species or two habitats/ecosystems towards which humans are on balance utility-indifferent. That is, as far as we are concerned, neither can be judged better *for us*. But assume one of them has to make way, either because of conflicting "natural" evolution, or because of some unchallengeable human imperative to advance to the detriment of one or the other. (Imagine that without a new water project *here* or *there* millions of people will suffer from malaria and drought). In making such choices, which species should we favor? The World Charter for Nature proclaims that "every form of life is unique, warranting respect, regardless of its worth to mankind."[37] But it is far from clear how one "respects" an ecosystem. Actions that perturb one equilibrium promote its successor. Fewer whales, more krill. And what if one is forced to choose among species, because we cannot respect *all* equally? Do we conserve the one that is the oldest, or most rare, or highest on the food chain? What account is to be made for sites and species that occupy important places in the life of a culture?

This area is replete with dauntingly complex questions—not merely to answer, but even to pose coherently. Nonetheless, it might be wise to empower the Subsidiary Body on Scientific, Technical and Technological Advice (SBSTTA), perhaps in consultation with some environmental ethicists, to try to devise something in the way of listings or at least criteria. After all, if the Parties cannot agree on priorities it will fall to the GEF to do so, on an ad hoc basis, without the same level of visibility and expertise.

---

*   Pursued as a question of ethics, the issues are quite complex: Should choreographers, composers and film-makers have to compensate every Balkan village whose steps and costumes and harmony they have copied and portrayed over the years? The world would be a poorer place.

CRITIQUE

Any critique of the CBD has to make allowances for the circumstance in which the Parties are operating. It is a hard time for the international environmental movement in general. The 1992 Earth Summit at Rio provided the movement a brief center stage, and sent it off with added optimism and heady talk of spending $400 to $600 billion a year to mend the Earth. But the glow of the meeting has been replaced with the sober realization that Rio was to some degree (in the rest of the world's eyes) a show. National leaders do not share the delegates' fervor, and the new funds have failed to materialize. Moreover, of all the conventions that came out of UNCED, the CBD may have the most difficulty winning the support of politicians and the public. In a 1993 poll, biological diversity ranked dead last in public awareness among all environmental issues, ranging from wildlife to climate change.[38] Indeed, the constituency for biodiversity has to be considered soft even among many who consider themselves environmentalists. It is easier to rally support for particular biological assets—tigers or wetlands—than for a relatively abstract *biodiversity*. Many wonder, why not simply protect tigers under CITES, wetlands under the Ramsar Convention on Wetlands, migratory birds under migratory bird conventions, and so on.

Moreover, the COP labors under the further burden, already alluded to, that the CBD was born out of two motives which, if not always in conflict, are always in tension. Some of the Parties and influential NGOs put priority on preservation; others see the Convention as an opportunity for transfer of wealth and technology. The interests are congruous—there is room for mutual advantage and cooperation—insofar as there is true economic benefit in conservation. But, as we have noted, the prospects of genetic resource "riches" are not proving sturdy. Hence, the "trades" that might have fueled progress are not there.

Meanwhile, the question of how to finance even the most basic commitments (such as the Environmental Impact Assessments of Article 14) remains unresolved. What will qualify as "agreed full incremental costs" to be borne by the wealthier members (Art. 20)? Limited headway can be expected on such critical funding issues until the deadlock on the financial mechanism is finally resolved. A number of nations continue to "reject" the Global Environment Facility on the familiar grounds that it is too closely associated with the World Bank, inadequately transparent, and subject to a governance too heavily slanted towards the nations that provide its resources. These objections persist, mindless of the fact that there are no alternative funding mechanisms waiting to take over the GEF's role, and that nations that have been bankrolling the GEF thus far, not too generously, are not apt to be more beneficent if their voice in the governance is diluted. Nonetheless, it is almost certain that the Parties will continue to spend a considerable amount of their time in lively ideological debate over the "ideal" fund-allocating mechanism: Should it mimic the Montreal Ozone Fund's double-majority, etc.?

The risk is that a sort of vacuum may develop, in which the delegates, unable to make significant headway on either faction's primary goals, marginalized from the perspective of almost every nation's domestic political agenda, and unwilling to commit to a funding mechanism that would reassure donor states, will move along paths of least resistance—in directions that are safe and costless but which may be therefore of borderline importance.

To illustrate, at the time the Convention was being negotiated, one might well have imagined—and hoped—that forest management would emerge as a central concern. Forest ecosystems are, after all, primary repositories of biodiversity, however defined. But many developing nations are under pressure to convert forest-lands to uses that under-write short term needs: lumber sales finance debt, and so on. As a result, the issue of forest management is politically sensitive—and forests have been scantily, and certainly not productively, discussed under the CBD. The Commission on Sustainable Development (CSD) has stepped in to promote an Open-Ended Ad-Hoc Intergovernmental Panel on Forests (IPF). Even though the new arrangement appears to remove from the CBD one of its original raisons d'etre, it may well be best for the IPF to become the "lead" forum for these sensitive issues.[39] But many Parties to the CBD are prepared to abdicate even a supportive role. At the second COP in Jakarta (November 1995) many delegates and NGOs expressed the advisability of the CBD at least formulating its own forest (biodiversity) perspective to be presented at IPF deliberations. But a proposed CBD panel on forests was rejected ostensibly on the grounds of an "absence of financial resources and the possible overlap of work with the IPF."[40]

Unable to advance on the issue of forests, and at an impasse over the financing mechanism, the Parties have shifted their attention to bio-safety, that is, protection against the imagined perils of living modified organisms. The issue is among those that warrant attention, and, indeed, the Convention specifically invited the Parties to consider devising a protocol (Art. 19).[41] But few in the drafting stage would have imagined that the issue of bio-safety would have been propelled into such prominence as it has enjoyed. There is no recorded instance of any ecosystem having been harmed by the introduction of genetically modified organisms (GMOs) (although there are many illustrations of devastation from exotic (nonindigenous) species, a subject that has excited nowhere near the same amount of attention at the COP). Supporters justify the amount of time spent on biosafety by labeling the issue, "crucial." But it is possible to suppose that bio-safety has been labeled "crucial" because it is something the Parties have been able to spend time on. Talk about forests is an embarrassment to the Poor; those who want to bring bio-safety to the floor tap a widespread enthusiasm for tweaking Science and the Rich.[42]

In the meantime, other business has been pushed further back in time. While the need for "technology transfer" is echoed, there are few ideas what it might look like in practice. Surprisingly little attention appears to have been given to the form for PICs, or indeed, anything to do with access to genetic resources, which loomed so large in the negotiating period. The obligation of the Parties to file national plans has been put off until the 4th COP in 1997; and *then*—after the first reports are filed and presumably based on that experience—the question of what the reports should include will be discussed.

CONCLUSION

It is of course premature to pass judgment on the CBD. And also involved: after all, how does one gage the success of a multilateral treaty? The Convention on Long Range Transboundary Air Pollution, designed to protect the Parties from each others' transboundary fluxes, had the fortunate side-effect of accelerating each Party's understanding of how its own pollution was hurting itself (put aside the effects on others!) and thus led to desirable domestic policy reactions from sheerly domestic considerations.[43] In like vein, we may come to count the CBD a success if it succeeds solely in focusing attention and forming consensus that will be important for long-term policy choices, even though the choices may be made "outside" the CBD framework.

On the other hand, to assess the CBD in terms of its stated aims, it is fair to say that in the four years since Rio, substantive progress on the basic motivating issues has been meager. Those who viewed the CBD as an opportunity to secure the riches of genetic resources have failed even to inject meaningful substance into the trade-in-resource provisions. Although these provisions will be filled out, in time, the economic significance of the access provisions, like the much-touted riches they are designed to secure, has almost certainly been overblown, anyway. And it is unlikely that the CBD will become a perceptible conduit for the transfer of wealth and technology. Thus frustrated in their top priorities, one wing of the Parties and their fraternal NGOs is disposed to exploit the framework as a public forum for the airing of grievances on a collection of issues of deep concern and inconsistent understanding, such as the reverberations of international trade, the ecological insensitivity of the World Bank and WTO, and the widely-rumored wickedness of patent law.

Another, overlapping group has hopes of turning the CBD into a sort of umbrella framework for all biodiversity-touching treaties and agencies. This faction regards the existing institutional landscape as too fragmented and "piecemeal," requiring coordination or consolidation under the CBD. But if one sets out to consolidate, where would one stop? There is no way to draw clear lines between biodiversity, on the one hand, and most of the problems that beset mankind, on the other. Desertification, rivers, toxic waste, and ocean management all impact biodiversity, as do weapons testing, trade, agriculture, mining and auto emissions. Moreover, there is little evidence that great umbrella agencies are in any way more effective or efficient than moderately-sized institutions with more sharply focused mandates. And, in all events, the limited financial and personnel prospects of the CBD would counsel the parties to take realistic stock of their ambitions.

Thus far, the wing emphasizing sustainable use and conservation has been satisfied to yield the floor and accomplish what it can in the background, hoping that with time and sympathetic diplomacy its agenda will get back on track. Of course, the conservationists can mark time only so long before their own frustrations vent. The identification of biodiversity under threat and the formulation of national responses lag. The scientists—whose efforts laid the foundation for the Convention—are enmeshed in procedural haggles over how much independence and authority the scientific arm, the Subsidiary Panel on Scientific, Technical and Technological Advice (SBSTTA) is to be permitted. (Some delegates are suspicious of the scientists as North-oriented and politically naive). For conservationists, alternative fora—outside the CBD-GEF framework—may prove more fruitful. Even now, the bulk of biodiversity financing (in the sense of establishing protected areas, managing reserves, funding *ex-situ* conservation and seed banks, etc.) takes place through the International Bank for Reconstruction and Development (IBRD), the International Development Association (IDA), the Rain Forest Trust Fund, and various major NGO "players" such as Conservation International.[44] If the CBD-GEF dynamic proves too frustrating, these alternate routes will dominate competition for dwindling conservation/aid resources. And there is always the prospect that people seriously interested in whaling, the Antarctic flora and fauna, wetlands, and so on, will redirect their energies to the IWC, the Antarctic treaty system, the UNEP Regional Seas Program, etc.

If this happens, starved of funds and competent enthusiasts, the CBD will limp along in marginal relevance, the delegates having only themselves as audience. This would be a disappointment. The CBD was, and continues to be, the depositary of considerable energies and hopes. The tragedy is, that before the CBD was formed, a viable strategic plan had already been formulated—by IUCN, WRI and others.[45] The question for environmentalists is thus, how to salvage and get that good and idealistic work back on track.

Patience will be required, for one thing. And some patience is deserved. In contrast with new domestic environmental legislation, which can be cloned onto an existing structure of bureaucrats, enforcement agencies, and so on, the governance of each new multilateral environmental regime has to be built from the bottom up, on its own independent foundation, in the most trying circumstances. Long, frustrating, often windy start-up periods are the rule.

In all events, with so many centrifugal forces pulling the COP outwards, it will be all the more important for sober forces within the regime to remind themselves, and others, of the central tasks and opportunities. A wise path for the Parties would be (1) to agree upon the highest priorities for action; (2) to rate which of them are already being moderately well-attended to by alternative regimes, such as CITES, IWC, the Antarctic Treaty System, etc.; and (3) having identified the most significant 'gaps," to structure their own efforts accordingly.

For example, the commitment at the last COP to examine Marine and Coastal biodiversity could evolve into a valuable undertaking, if, instead of duplicating the work of the UNEP Regional Seas Program, the United Nations Convention on Law of the Seas (UNCLOS), and other agreements already in place, the Parties can provide a spark and guidance to get structures already in place to link and operate effectively; that would be useful.

But will those who gravitate to control of the COP be able to define for themselves a limited role? Can the CBD framework be steered to those areas where it will do more good than the same resources channeled through alternate, existing fora? The questions are not rhetorical. But in a world willing to offer dwindling resources for medicating the planet, these are the major questions that remain to be answered.

ENDNOTES

1. Convention on Biological Diversity of the United Nations Conference on the Environment and Development, Jun. 3-14, 1992, U.N. Doc. DPI/1307, *reprinted in* 31 I.L.M. 818 (1992) [*hereinafter* CBD].

2. See H.W.F. SAGGS, CIVILIZATION BEFORE GREECE AND ROME 158 (1989).

3. Id. at 168.

4. *Deuteronomy* 20:19-20.

5. PATRICIA BIRNIE & ALAN BOYLE, INTERNATIONAL LAW AND THE ENVIRONMENT (1992), date the first wildlife protection treaty to the 1885 Convention for the Uniform Regulation of Fishing in the Rhine, but trace "*ad hoc*" whaling understandings to the 16th Century. *Id.* at 425. SIMON LYSTER, INTERNATIONAL WILDLIFE LAW 63 (1985) traces the movement to protect birds useful to agriculture to 1868 (although not eventuating in a Convention until 1902).

6. Convention on International Trade in Endangered Species of Wild Flora and Fauna, Mar. 3, 1973, 27 U.S.T. 1087.

7. The Antarctic Treaty, Dec. 1, 1959, 12 U.S.T. 794.

8. International Convention for the Regulation of Whaling, Dec. 2, 1946, 62 Stat. 1716.

9. WORLD RESOURCES INSTITUTE ET AL., GLOBAL BIODIVERSITY STRATEGY (1992).

10. In the next decade the biological diversity dimensions of the 1980 report was elaborated in Conserving the World's Biological Diversity. INTERNATIONAL UNION FOR THE CONSERVATION OF NATURE (IUCN), CONSERVING THE WORLD'S BIOLOGICAL DIVERSITY (1990). As well as in Global Biodiversity Strategy. WORLD RESOURCES INSTITUTE ET AL., GLOBAL BIODIVERSITY STRATEGY (1992).

11. UNEP Voices Support for Methods that Ensure Greater Diversity, WORLD ENVIRONMENT REPORT, Jan. 3, 1996, at Sec. 1.

12. CBD, *supra* note 2, *preamble*.

13. CBD, *supra* note 2, *preamble*.

14. CBD, *supra* note 2, art. 8, § 4.

15. CBD, *supra* note 2, art. 28.

16. CBD, *supra* note 2, art 29.

17. CBD, *supra* note 2, art 25.

18. CBD, *supra* note 2, art. 27.

19. CBD, *supra* note 2, art. 6.

20. CBD, *supra* note 2, art. 10.

21. CBD, *supra* note 2, art. 7.

22. CBD, *supra* note 2, art. 8.

23. CBD, *supra* note 2, art. 9.

24. CBD, *supra* note 2, art. 11.

25. CBD, *supra* note 2, art. 12.

26. CBD, *supra* note 2, art. 13.

27. CBD, *supra* note 2, art. 14.

28. CBD, *supra* note 2, art. 15.

29. CBD, *supra* note 2, art. 16, § 5.

30. In a recent article, R. David Simpson, Roger A. Sedjo and John W. Reid, using what they label highly optimistic assumptions to estimate the pharmaceutical value of world's top 18 "hot spots," conclude that some areas of Western Ecuador might be worth $20 a hectare as bio-prospecting sites, but their median is only about $2. R. David Simpson et al., *Valuing Diversity for Use in Pharmaceutical Research*, 109 J. Pol. Econ. at 163-185 (1996). And these, remember, are "hot spots". Using a different methodology, Robert Mendelsohn and Michael J. Balick conclude that the world's 3 billion hectares of tropical forest are worth on average $.90 to $1.32 per hectare. Robert Mendelsohn & Michael J. Balick, *The Value of Undiscovered Pharmaceuticals in Tropical Forests*, 49 ECON. BOTANY 223.

31. It is common to refer to the contract between Merck & Co. and InBio as the prototype of many contracts that will follow. But thus far there are few followers; and as of July 1995 Merck reportedly had made no return on its investment. *See* V. Cheng, *Useful Drugs are Said to Lie Hidden in Tropical Forests*, N.Y. Times, Jun. 27, 1995, at § 4, col. 1.

32. Studies of the U.S. pharmaceutical industry indicate a commercially marketable drug requires an average $230 million and 12 years to develop. Walter V. Reid et al., *A New Lease on Life, in* BIODIVERSITY PROSPECTING 47 (World Resources Institute eds., 1993).

33. J.A. Dimasi et al., *Costs of Innovation in the Pharmaceutical Industry*, 10 J. HEALTH ECON. 107 (1991).

34. See BRIAN BARRY, THEORIES OF JUSTICE 15-16 (1989).

35. Farhana Yamin, *Biodiversity, Ethics and International Law*, 71 Int'l Affairs 536-537.

36. CBD, *supra* note 2, art. 8, § j.

37. United Nations General Assembly, *World Charter for Nature* (1983), *reprinted in* 22 I.L.M. 455 (1983).

38. "In a world rife with street shootings, grinding inequity and ethnic wars of extermination, it is hard to get worked up over 'ecosystems.'" Oliver Hauk, *Coming to Grips with Biodiversity*, 8 TULANE ENVTL. L.J. 3. (*preface*, 1994).

39. Although there is no reason to believe the IPF will confront them successfully, either. And while discussions move from one forum to another, huge forests are falling.

40. Bureau of National Affairs, *COP-2 Arees on Biosafety Protocol*, INT'L ENVTL. REP., Sep. 29, 1995, at 897-898.

41. *See* Open Ended Ad hoc Group of Experts on Biosafety, *Report of the Panel of Experts on Biosafety*, CBD/Biosafety Expert Group/2, 12 June 1995 (A subsequent meeting was held in Cairo 11-14 December 1995).

42. The fear is that the protocol, by over-regulating the traffic in genetically modified organisms, could stifle development of crops that may become vital to third world agriculture. Henry I. Miller et al., *Agricultural Production, Innovation and Biological Diversity*, 5 AUSTRALASIAN BIOTECHNOLOGY 238-241.

43. Marc A. Levy, *European Acid Rain: The Power of Tote-Board Diplomacy, in* INSTITU-TIONS FOR THE EARTH: SOURCES OF EFFECTIVE INTERNATIONAL ENVIRONMENTAL PROTECTION 75-132 (Peter M. Haas et al. eds. 1993); Convention on Long-Range Transboundary Air Pollution, Nov. 13, 1979, T.I.A.S. 10541, *reprinted in* 18 I.L.M. 1442.

44. WORLD BANK ENVIRONMENT DEPARTMENT, WORLD BANK, ENVIRONMENT DEPARTMENT PAPER NO. 029 (Biodiversity series) MAINSTREAMING BIODIVERSITY IN DEVELOPMENT: A WORLD BANK ASSISTANCE STRATEGY FOR IMPLEMENTING THE CONVENTION ON BIOLOGICAL DIVERSITY (Nov. 1995).

45. *See id.* Even the drawing up of the much discussed bio-safety protocol has been deferred until 1998. What has been decided, after extensive discussion, is that there should be some such protocol.

CHAPTER 7

AN ENVIRONMENTAL ETHIC
FOR THE TWENTY-FIRST CENTURY[*]

Eventually we have to set off and discover, or construct, an ethical accounting for the environment. Should we establish game preserves for "higher" mammals, such as elephants, even though they have a devastating effect on the natural ecology of their preserve? Can we justify owl habitats, even if it drives up the price of housing for the poor?

The more complex and ambiguous the issues we confront, the fuller and more intricate the ethical accounting we require as guidance. But how much guidance can we demand of an ethical framework? Certainly we cannot be expected to produce a framework capable of persuading everyone to agree on every question we pose. No ordinary (interpersonal) morality can claim that degree of success. What if there are quandaries for which our framework cannot offer a unique, yes-no solution? Have we succeeded if our ethic eliminates some erroneous solutions—and leaves us with a range of resolutions all of which are equally valid from a moral point of view?

Consider an analogy from mathematics. One is asked to solve the value of x in the formula: $[x^2 = 16]$. The solution is: $x = |4|$ —that is, x could be +4 and it could be -4. Other equations can be solved only within a certain range: $[x$ lies between 5 and 9]. Perhaps the answer is 6; or perhaps the answer *is* 5-through-9. In these cases, we have not as fine-tuned a solution as we might have wished for. But we have learned something from the exercise. We have eliminated as answers 1 and 2 and 11. Perhaps that is all that we can expect, considering the nature of the question.

But imprecision is one thing; inconsistency, another. What if a skeptic points out that from the premisses we settle upon we can derive judgments that are worse than vague: they actually conflict. To illustrate, suppose one of the premises on which we base an environmental ethic is an obligation to preserve rare forms of life; the skeptic points out that in applying this principle one can derive that we are morally commanded both (a) to preserve and (b) to destroy the last vial of smallpox virus (because its existence threatens other life). Is the derivability of inconsistent conclusions to be regarded as a fatal flaw, so that the whole framework that permitted it must be torn

*   From a paper delivered at the Philosophisches Seminar, "Ökologisches Ethik und Rechtstheorie," Der Georg-August-Universität, Göttingen, October, 1994. A fuller version appears as "Eine Ökologische Ethik für das einundzwanzigste Jahrhundert" in N. Rümelin, ed., Ökologisches Ethik und Rechtstheorie (Nomos Verlag, Baden-Baden 1995).

down, the way we would reject as incoherent a geometry in which all lines did, and did not cross.

There is a question even more basic than the standards of precision and consistency with which an ethic is to provide answers. What are the questions we expect it to answer? For example, do we expect it tell us what to do—that is, to guide us regarding particular actions? Or, is its ambition to tell us, in a more general way, how to live—what sort of persons we should aim to be?

Let me offer here some preliminary glimpse of my own views—of what demands we should place on, what we should expect of the ethics for which we search.

Rather than to begin with right and wrong, and try too closely to approximate formal systems of thought, let us take "being responsible" as the rudimentary notion of ethics, and ask what that involves. My list, to which others might wish to add, would include the following:

- Responsibility starts with hesitance; the responsible person suspends putting his or her initial desires into action in order to reflect.

- The next step is perception. The responsible person observes phenomena the irresponsible person ignores; more than this, the responsible person looks for certain morally significant features of his environment: other persons (and other creatures), harm, pain, benefit to the social group. (Deciding what is "the group," and which features are significant is part of the larger ethic.)

- A responsible person acknowledges the full range of his freedom. It is in this sense that a person is not responsible if he too quickly claims he "had no choice."

- To be responsible is to make oneself aware of the consequences of one's actions, and to consider and weigh alternatives.

- Being responsible involves reflection in all the above senses, but reflection per se is not enough; the reflection must be structured by reference to the some appropriate moral vocabulary—so as to force judgment on whether the act or character is "good," "bad," "cruel," "just," and so forth.

- One must have, in addition to a moral vocabulary, a moral inclination—a desire, probably as much internalized as conscious, to "do the right thing."

- To be responsible involves being prepared to give good reasons for one's actions. This preparedness to justify, and especially the preparedness to do so in terms that admit of generalization (the Golden Rule, Kant's Categorical Imperative), is an important step toward the socialization of one's actions, inasmuch as it forces awareness of the social setting and the socially sanctified grounds of behavior.

The collective search for an ethic is part of the commitment to build a good society, one in which people seek agreement through reason.

THE HISTORICAL LEGACY

With no further demarcation, for the present, than that, let us move on to this question: What is our present ethic, that some persons are urging we amend it? It is common to say our contemporary ethic is homocentric, and that we need to develop a nonhomocentric ethic. This is close to the truth, but not exactly right.

The inherited ethic is indeed human-centered. But the focus of concern has been less extensive than all *homo sapiens*. Specifically, it is not only animals and trees that have been of peripheral interest; so too have humans who have not yet been born, and those who live beyond the moral agent's own community. To clarify the central focus of conventional ethics more exactly, I use the term *Persons*—with a capital P. By Persons in this special sense, I mean to denote typical adult humans not of unsound mind, associated in a common community—neighbors both in space and in time.

The point to emphasize is that the texture of our inherited law and morals has been a response both to the properties of humans (that they experience pleasures and pains, possess dignity, are capable of practical reasoning, and so on) and also to the properties and possibilities of community (the ways in which its inhabitants can best relate to one another).

Now, of course, like any other broad generalization, this one—that conventional morality is fundamentally Person-regarding—warrants enough qualifications to fill a book. Some accounting had to be made for creatures that did not fit the conventional mold but were of too much interest to ignore entirely. These peripheral entities, ("Nonpersons," as I shall sometimes call them) ranged from natural persons of "special" sorts (infants and lunatics deemed incapable of participating in communal decisions) to various sorts of aggregate or corporate bodies, including nations, tribes, and municipalities.

There is no way fairly to summarize how some provision was made for each of these entities in various contexts across the sweep of history. In general, wherever it has been considered necessary to provide—or begrudge—a Nonperson some accounting, the aim has been to do so with such minor tamperings as would preserve the Persons orientation as intact as possible.

A California legal case that came up a few years ago will illustrate. A lady had provided in her will that if she should predecease her dog, the dog should be destroyed. She died first, but before the dog could be destroyed such a public outcry was raised that an animal group brought suit to enjoin the dog from being killed. The California legislature was even drawn into the controversy, eventually enacting a special "private bill" preserving the dog's life. But the bill, closely read, evidences no genuine break from the Persons orthodoxy I am describing. The lady, the legislators reasoned, had not really wanted her dog to be destroyed. She just did not want it uncared for. Had she known the circumstances (that one of the attorneys would be prepared to offer "it" a good home), she would not have provided for its destruction. Thus, the society labored to make it appear that it was sparing the dog's life not from consideration of the dog, but of the late owner. These mental gymnastics sustained the notion that what really counts are Persons. But in so doing, we let slip the opportunity to think through the value of a dog—not to its master, but intrinsically and to itself.

This sort of legal analysis does no more than mirror orthodox philosophy's response to cruelty to animals: that such cruelty threatens to make us—that is, we Persons—less trustworthy and nice in our dealings with one another. What might have been phrased and examined as a practice objectionable to animals is straightaway recast in more familiar terms of human feelings and human virtues. The thing whose fate gave rise to the original intuition of wrongness or cruelty drops out. It is not just with animals that this strategy occurs. Our obligations to wilderness areas are frequently presented as obligations towards one another "in respect of" enjoying wilderness areas. As a consequence, the originally animating perceptions and sentiments that might, if attended to, have evolved into a new set of principles about Nature are deflected into talk about indirect duties to other persons. Lingering, critical attention is deflected away both from the *thing* that originally motivated our concern and from our conventional modes of thinking.

STRESSES ON THE CONVENTIONAL FRAMEWORKS

For centuries, society (perhaps this statement is more true of Western Societies than of some others) has been able to accommodate the occasional Peripheral Entity ("Nonperson") that seemed to require some legal or moral recognition, without any challenge to the conventional Persons framework deep enough to force an articulation and defense of its philosophical foundations.

Recently, however, and particularly as the present century comes to a close, we are witnessing several developments that, together, raise questions whether there might not be "other ways" — other than the received ways—to think about our relations with these Nonpersons, including qualities of the environment.

Scarcity

First, there is a growing apprehension of impending scarcity. If goods were in unlimited supply, questions of distributional justice—of allocating goods rightly—would not arise. The customs and laws that grow up around a water hole in the desert are not the same as those that develop in regions where water is plentiful. Today, however, it is not just a water hole, but the whole earth that one fears is running dry of basic resources.

This specter of global scarcity, now entered into public consciousness, provides impetus to come up with new principles. For example, what if any obligations do we have to conserve resources and cultural heritage in the interests of remote future generations? This is a concept that is being invoked with increasing frequency in international documents, but is not one with which the conventional Persons framework can straightforwardly deal. To many observers, the very idea of future person having legal or moral "rights" against the living, "rights" that will not spring into being until we, the duties-bearers, are long dead, is incoherent, even paradoxical. Yet, the concerns over scarcity, and the predicaments in which we may leave our progeny, keep alive an intuition that there must be some basis of responsibility to future generations—even if that basis lies beyond the conventional framework.

Technology

The second source of pressures comes from the accelerating advances in technology. Ethical questions arise with choice. Today, technology has offered us a range of choices our predecessors did not have the luxury and anguish of facing—the ability to make power out of nuclear energy (with all its hazards), to sweep the seas of life, to level forests, to weaken the ozone shield, perhaps to alter the climate.

These new capacities not only promise to make our legal and moral lives more complex, in general, but they have specific implications on the position we accord Nonpersons. With increased power to preserve life, we have to face the question, when are we permitted to let it pass away? What is the right, morally and legally, of a severely incapacitated human to die with dignity? With the growing power to create life (even, with genetic engineering, to create new forms of life) there comes in tow the question: What lives and life-forms ought we choose to create? A baby girl is born with a hole in her heart; we can remove her defective heart and replace it with that of a baboon, thereby extending her life a few weeks. Is extending a child's life two weeks worth the life of one baboon? Is two years of her life worth the lives of a thousand baboons? Anyone who follows the philosophy journals, and the law cases, can see that technology is raising hundreds of questions like these at the social horizon—questions that fluster the conventional frameworks.

Globalization

It is commonplace to observe that the world has become a "global village." The image is an exaggeration. But it is part truth. Communications, trade, banking, weaponry—indeed, all the technologies referred to, above—not only increase the range of choices, but they lengthen our shadow. The injury Cain did Abel was done on the spot, at arm's length. But the potential for harm that we have now acquired (one has only to think of toxic effluents) stretches across the earth and lingers well into the future. We have the power to slay unseen brothers, strangers to us both in space and in time. These distances dilute the forces that animate and direct moral thought in kinship groups and small communities—shame, guilt, empathy, anxiety, and the specters of retaliation and reciprocity. And at the same time, the potential universe of our obligees—the very number of persons whom we know our actions do or could affect—seems simply to overwhelm us with the impracticality of extending throughout the world and throughout time the familiar moral demands that evolved to adjust relations among Persons. Can we really subscribe to a morality that impels our being responsible to everyone everywhere and in every generation in the same degree as we are each obliged towards members of our narrower communities?

Moral Maturation

And finally, the moral and legal structures have evolved along with civilization—with the moral maturation of mankind. This is not to make the claim that the history of civilization has been a march towards moral progress, towards people getting better and better every day in every way (which would be a more difficult thesis to maintain). But, as Darwin wrote, history does appear to display a continual extension in the range of objects receiving man's "social instincts and sympathies." Primitive man's concern was predominantly for a narrow circle of family and tribe. Later, "his sympathies became more tender and widely diffused, extending to man of all races, to the imbecile, maimed and other useless members of society, and finally to the lower animals. . ."[1]

There has been, in effect, a widening of the circle. The more we are learning about animals, plants, and, in a way, all of existence, from subatomic motion to cosmic phenomena, the more we have been struck with the sorts of similarities that stir empathy and the often unanticipated interdependencies that cause concern. This appearance, that we are all, even amidst so much conflict, part of one fragile global community, encourages us to provide a clearer and more direct accounting for a wide variety of entities, to make a more safeguarded place for animals, plants, indeed, for the entire planet, in some sense, as an organic whole.

THE CRISIS IN FRAMEWORKS

These pressures have led to what I call a "crisis in frameworks." There is evidence, both in the popular media and academic literature, that moral discourse has to provide at least some PEs a more satisfactory moral accounting that they are presently receiving. Among academics, the acknowledgment that some revisions are in order takes the form of each school's determination to show how it can accommodate some of our Nonperson-sympathetic intuitions according to its own lights. But considering the entire range of peripheral entities, it seems doubtful that any single framework—not one of the conventional frameworks certainly—can successfully make the adaptations without stretching itself so unrecognizably as to risk jeopardizing its original appeal.*

That is why I have maintained that we should abandon the effort to "stretch" one of the familiar ethics to make room for these objects of new or intensified concern, and to seek a new framework (or, as we shall see, frameworks), instead.

A New Framework

Here, understand that when I speak of devising a new framework, I do not mean that we should renounce conventional moral theories. I envision a framework (or frameworks) that will supplement, and not necessarily replace conventional moralities. This openness sets me apart from most moral philosophers, who by and large divide into what might be deemed schools. Each school is monistic and, as a sort of corollary, each is determinate. By monistic, I mean that the enterprise is conceived as aiming to produce, and to defend against all rivals, a single coherent and complete set of principles. By determinate, I mean that the framework is supposed, at least in principle, to yield the One right Answer for All Moral Quandaries. One is either a this or a that: a utilitarian or a Kantian.

The alternative conception to which I have been inviting discussion, what I call Moral Pluralism,[*] takes exception to Monism point by point. It refuses to presume that all ethical activities (evaluating acts, actors, social institutions, rules, states of affairs, etc.) are, in all contexts (in normal interpersonal relations, across large spaces and many generations, between species) determined by the same features (intelligence, sentience, capacity for emotions, life) or even that they are subject, in each case, to the same overarching principles (utilitarianism, Kantianism, etc.). Pluralism invites us to conceive the intellectual activities of which morals consist as being partitioned into several distinct frameworks, each governed by its own appropriate principles.

[**] For example, since utilitarianism can be extended to anything that experience pleasure and pain, it provides a window for drawing animals into the moral community. But species, feeling no pleasure or pain, cannot be sheltered within utilitarianism directly; and utilitarianism's efforts to handle future generations ties it in some awkward if not paradoxical knots. Utilitarians's principal contenders all require, in various ways and with various justifications, putting oneself in the place of the other whose actions one will affect. While such hypothetical trading of places is always problematical, it seems least so when we are trading with (or universalizing across) persons who share our culture, whose interests, values, and tastes we can therefore presume with some confidence. But that confidence erodes the further we venture our imaginations beyond the familiar Persons domain. With what conviction can we trade places with members of spatially and temporally remote cultures, with aboriginal tribes, or with our own descendants in some future century? "How would I feel if I were to be born a river, and ribbed with dams. . . .?"

[*] Moral pluralism ought not to be confused with moral relativism, the view, roughly, that all morals are context- or agent-dependent. A pluralist can be agnostic with respect to the moral realist position that there are absolutely true answers to moral quandaries, as invariable across time, space and communities as the value of pi. There may be "really right" and not just relatively right answers, but the way to find them is by reference not to one single overarching principle, but by reference to several distinct frameworks, each appropriate to its own domain of entities and/or moral activities (evaluating character, ranking options for conduct, etc.).

Certainly, one would expect pain-regarding principles to emerge as pivotal in establishing obligations towards all those things that experience pain. Not pain alone, but preferences of some sort, e.g., the projection of a life plan, has to be accounted for in our relations with humans. Still richer threads (such as a sense of justice, and rights of a sort that can be consensually created, extinguished, traded and waived) form the fabric of the moral tapestry that connects humans who share a common moral community in which the quantity and quality of interactions is high. Other principles, perhaps invoking respect for a natural unfolding, seem fit as a basis for forming our relations with plants.

The implication of pluralism for this task is critical. It means that those trying to compose an environmental ethic are not under the burden of producing one grand system capable of providing one right answer to all quandaries.

THE CHALLENGES IN CONSTRUCTING AN ETHIC

Limiting our quest to an environmental ethic (or ethics) is, in a sense, a more manageable enterprise. It releases us to concentrate attention (at least in the first instance) on one domain, without having simultaneously to worry, as we progress, about how adequately the unfolding environmental morality "fits" interhuman ethical dilemmas. Despite this benefit, the construction of an independent environmental ethic faces considerable burdens of its own. . . .

[See Moral Pluralism and the Course of Environmental Ethics, following.]

ENDNOTES

1. DESCENT OF MAN 119-121 (2D ed. 1874)

CHAPTER 8

MORAL PLURALISM AND THE
COURSE OF ENVIRONMENTAL ETHICS*

INTRODUCTION

With this volume, *Environmental Ethics* concludes its first decade. It may be a good time to ask what the environmental ethics movement has to show for itself, where it is, and where it should be heading. Without doubt, and particularly in view of the short time span, the contributions assembled are impressive. Many (some might surmise all) of the basic issues have been clarified. Perhaps most valuable is the body of literature focusing attention on what I will call "the obstacles" (below).

Good work continues, to be sure. But I fear we have reached a plateau. The signs include a tendency to reiterate the well-worn "need" for an environmental ethics "whose time has come," and then to work over the increasingly familiar themes about the restricted reach of mainstream theories, et cetera. Part of the problem is that we have yet to establish a clearly defined sense of mission. Where does environmental ethics situate itself within the larger world of moral philosophy?

As an applied ethics is one response. But, if so, we still need to ask what such a status entails.[1] Does it mean we are to regard environmental ethics as applying certain invariant fundamental moral principles—"core principles," let us say—to deal with the peculiar properties of nature, the way mathematics's core principles (of algebra and topology) are said to be extended and refined by statistics and probability theory to suit them for application to their special "materials"?[2] If that is the commitment, then certain other questions follow. What are the invariant moral principles that environmental ethics, as an applied field, is applying? (In whose service do we place ourselves?) What leeway do the appliers have to supplement and deform the "purest" and most abstract propositions in the core when they bruise against the concrete riddles of the world?

An alternate, considerably larger ambition is to assemble forces under the banner of a new, independent ethic and proceed to mount an assault on the core itself with an aim either to overthrow and replace the reigning premises or to establish some sort of co-regency.

---

*   From volume 10 of ENVIRONMENTAL ETHICS. With the permission of *Environmental Ethics*.

A third alternative is the most far-reaching. It would use the environmental ethics movement as the occasion to reexamine the metaethical assumptions that underlie all of moral philosophy.

It is my position that each of these mission has some validity, but the third must dominate attention now, for we have not yet made clear, neither to ourselves nor to others, what exactly are the aims and ground rules that govern the composition of an ethical viewpoint.

THE OBSTACLES

Certainly I am not going to presume to summarize the body of literature that has appeared to date. The writers of the past ten years have identified a cluster of obstacles that environmental ethics face. Most of these are familiar to readers of *Environmental Ethics* and require, therefore, only a brief recapitulation here.

First is the question of putting the *objective* into coherent form. On this score the proponent of an environmental ethic is tempted to fall back upon negatives, to speak of what such an ethics is *not*: the aim is to inject into moral reasoning considerations that are not sheerly homocentric, that do not appeal solely or decisively to human preferences or utility. Here the first difficulty appears. Even if the environmentalist can persuade others that trees and trout *have value* (in some sense), only humans *do the valuing*; it is, after all, humankind, not trees or trout, that the environmentalist is seeking to persuade. Does this requirement to appeal to human consciousness and preferences land us in a contradiction, a sort of homocentrism after all?

Second is the related question of the *foundation*. Even if we can intelligibly express an environmental ethic's objective, on what rational basis can it possibly rest? We could conceive ourselves to be working within an applied field, and then figure out which dominant ethic to apply. Subordination to utilitarianism is unappealing because it is an alliance that values nature only so far as it is instrumental to human welfare. Union with the neo-Kantians is rebuffed, for while we are glad that they do not kick their dogs, the justification—duties to their own selves, not to the dogs—is unacceptable. The prevailing mood is to uncover some "good" that is not wholly instrumental either to human welfare or to human virtue, one that is somehow situated outside ourselves in nature. The challenges of identifying and legitimating such an intrinsic or inherent good are substantial, however, and increase the further we wander beyond intelligence or life as its foundation. The animal rights advocate has, at least, some of the goods of familiar moral theory to work with: a life that can be snuffed out, a plan that can be frustrated, a nerve that can transmit pain. The person who supports the moral considerateness of an inanimate object confronts the task of identifying some comparable basis, some "intrinsic worth" of something that cannot be killed, frustrated, or pained.

Third, what is being sought is not just a moral viewpoint that accounts for nature in principle. We need a moral viewpoint detailed and ingenious enough to maneuver us through the *ontological conundrums*. By reference to what principles is the moral and legal world to be carved up into those "things" that count and those that do not? This is a problem that can be approached as one of ethic's *boundaries:* that is, if self-consciousness is not the key to moral considerateness, nor sentience, nor life ... how does one draw the line so that an argument favoring a lake does not apply with equal force to a lamp? The same sort of dilemma crops up in other forms: is the unit of our concern the individual ant, the anthill, the family, the species, or the ant's habitat?

Fourth, suppose that we can do the carving up correctly, that is, identify those objects toward which some prima facie moral regard is justified, e.g., perhaps a certain mountain. There will remain the question, even if moral obligations to a mountain are conceded to exist in principle, how they can be *discharged.* In familiar, interpersonal moralities, the discharge of duties toward another is connected with respect for the other's wants and welfare. But how does one "do right by" a mountain?

Fifth, there are the *distributional dilemmas.* It is not enough to carve up the world, establishing what is to be morally considerable. Nor is it enough to agree how that regard translates into prima facie good and bad acts. What are we to do in the case of conflicting indications? For example, one can imagine a life-respecting moral framework whose basic principle is "more life is better than less." One can imagine, too, support for the preservation of a singular, pristine desert. But then, how do we judge an irrigation project that offers to transform the desert into a habitat teeming with vegetation? In general terms, the problem is the familiar one of weighing: even if the continued existence of a species, or the state of a river is demonstrated to be a (noninstrumental) good, how strongly does that good withstand the moral force of other, competing goods?

While each of these questions is hard–the fact we are in the tenth volume of this journal says as much—we can take some heart from the fact they are, in kind, no more formidable than those with which the proponents of every moral theory have been vexed: how to establish the meaning and legitimacy of moral reasoning in general, to demonstrate that it is cogent and defensible to sacrifice evident ego-pleasures to further something else. Those who appreciate the difficulties of substantiating the human community as that "something else" cannot sniff at those who find some plausible candidacy in the biotic. That granted, the development of an ethic that gives good moral guidance for our conduct respecting nature is not a quantum leap more perplexing than the task of putting together (or discovering) an ethics for our conduct respecting persons.

THE METAETHICAL ASSUMPTIONS

The larger–in all events, prior–questions require further consideration of the implicit metaethical assumptions. What are environmental ethicists trying to achieve, and what are the standards for success? In other words, what, more exactly, is an ethics supposed to look like and do? To illustrate, for years environmental ethicists have been stimulated by Aldo Leopold's conviction that we should develop a "land ethic." But how much thought has been given to what such a project implies? Are the proponents of a land ethic committed to coming up with a capacious replacement for all existing ethics, one capable of mediating all moral questions touching man, beast and mountain, but by reference to a grander, more all-encompassing set of principles? Or can the land ethic be an ethic that governs man's relations with land alone, leaving intact other principles to govern actions touching humankind (and yet others for actions touching, say, lower animals, and so on)?

If we are implying that there are different ethics, then there are a host of questions to face. What is an ethical system, and what are its minimum requirements? Need its "proofs" be as irresistible as a geometry's? Is it required to provide for each moral dilemma that it recognizes as a dilemma one right, tightly defined answer? Or is it enough to identify several courses of action equally acceptable, perhaps identifying for elimination those that are wrong or unwelcome? How—by reference to what elements—can one ethic differ from another? What possibilities of conflicting judgments are introduced by multiple frameworks, and how are they to be resolved?

These are among the questions that, sooner or later, environmental ethicists will have to confront. Upon their answer hinges nothing less than the legitimacy of environmental ethics as a distinct enterprise.

MORAL MONISM

The environmental ethics movement has always known that if it is to succeed, it has to challenge the prevailing orthodoxy. But the orthodoxy it has targeted is only the more obvious one, the orthodoxy of morals: that man is the measure (and not merely the measurer) of all value. Certainly calling that gross presumption to question is a valid part of the program. But the orthodoxy we have to question first is that of metaethics—of how moral philosophy ought to be conducted, of the ground rules.

Note that I am not claiming that we lack controversy at the level of *morals*. There is no shortage of lively contention in the philosophy literature. But underneath it all there is a striking, if ordinarily only implicit agreement on the metaethical sense of mission. It is widely presumed, by implication when it is not made explicit, that the ethicist's task is to put forward and defend a single overarching principle (or coherent body of principles), such as utilitarianism's "greatest good for the greatest number" or Kant's categorical imperative, and to demonstrate how it (the one correct viewpoint) guides us through all moral dilemmas to the one right solution.

This attitude, which I call moral monism, implies that in defending, say, the preservation of a forest or the protection of a laboratory animal, we are expected to bring our argument under the same principles that dictate our obligations to kin or the just deserts of terrorists. It suggests that moral considerateness is a matter of either-or; that is, the single viewpoint is presumably built upon a single salient moral property, such as, typically, sentience, intelligence, being the subject of a conscious life, etc.

Various entities (depending on whether they are blessed with the one salient property) are *either* morally relevant (each in the same way, according to the same rules) *or* utterly inconsiderate, out in the moral cold.[*]

Environmentalists, more than most philosophers, have at least an intuitive reason for supposing that this attitude is mistaken, for it is they whom the attitude is the first to bridle. Environmentalists wonder about the possible value in a river (or in preserving a river), but cannot rationalize those feelings in the familiar anthropocentric terms of pains and life-projects that they would apply to their own situations. By contrast, mainstream ethicists, concentrating on interpersonal relations, constrict their attention to a relatively narrow and uncontroversial band of morally salient qualities. Persons can speak for themselves, exercise moral choice, and–because they share a community–assert and waive many sorts of claims that are useful in governing their reciprocal relationships. Orthodox ethics has understandably tended to identify all ethics with this one set of morally salient properties: the paradigmatic moral problems have historically been interpersonal problems; the paradigmatic rules, person-regarding.

Thus, while vying camps have arisen within the orthodox tradition, none is ordinarily forced to account for the significance of properties that lie outside the common pool of human attributes. It is only when one starts to wonder about exotic clients, such as future generations, the dead, embryos, animals, the spatially remote, tribes, trees, robots, mountains, and art works, that the assumptions which unify ordinary morals are called into question. Need the rules that apply be in some sense, and at some level of generality, "the same" in all cases? The term *environmental ethics* suggests the possibility of a distinct moral regime for managing our way through environment affecting conduct. But in what respects that regime is distinct from other regimes and how conflicts among the regimes are to be mediated are crucial matters that have not been generally and directly addressed.

In default of well-worked out answers, the prevailing strategy of those who represent nonhumans is one of extension: to force one of the familiar person-oriented frameworks outward and apply one of the familiar arguments to some nonhuman entity. But such arguments too often appear just that–forced. Utilitarianism's efforts

---

[*] Consider the argument that a proponent of using animals in medical research throws up to the animals rights advocate: "If all forms of animal life ... must be treated equally, and if therefore ... the pains of a rodent count equally with the pains of a human, we are forced to conclude (1) that neither humans nor rodents possess rights, or (2) that rodents possess all the rights that humans possess." Carl Cohen, "The Case for the Use of Animals in Biomedical Research." *New England Journal of Medicine* 315 (1986): 865, 867. An alternative "pluralist" position would examine the possibility that a laboratory bred animal has rights, but not the same as humans. The rodent might have no "right" to life, but have a "right" to be free from suffering. This distinction could be operationalized by saying that the proponent of an experiment that took a laboratory animal's life painlessly would only have to show a clear likelihood of an advance of human welfare; animal suffering, however, would (alternatively) never be allowed, or allowed only when it could be shown that there was a very high probability that the experiment would result in the saving of human lives or the reduction of human suffering–never because it would alleviate mere inconveniences in human life, such as baggy eyelids.

to draw future generations under its mantle (a relatively easy extension, one would suppose) ties it in some awkward, if not paradoxical knots. Do we include, for example, those who might be born–obliging us to bring as many as possible of them into existence in order to aggregate more pleasures? Nor is it clear that utilitarianism, unqualified by a complex and ill-fitting rights appendage, can satisfy the concerns that drive the animal liberation movement.

The shortcomings of (let us call it) moral extensionism[*] are not peculiar to utilitarianism. Extensions of utilitarianism's principal contenders all require, in various ways and with various justifications, putting oneself in the place of another to test whether we can really wish the conduct under evaluation if we assume the other's position, role, and/or natural endowment. While such hypothetical trading of places and comparable techniques of thought experiment are always problematical, they are most satisfactory when we are trading places with (or universalizing about) persons who share our culture, and whose interests, values, and tastes we can therefore presume with some confidence. But even that slender assurance is destined to erode the further we venture beyond the domain of the most familiar natural persons. With what conviction can we trade places with members of spatially and temporally remote cultures, or with our own descendants in some future century? And, of course, if we wish to explore our obligations in regard to the dead, trees, rocks, fetuses, artificial intelligence, species, or corporate bodies, trading places is essentially a blind alley. It is one thing to put oneself in the shoes of a stranger, perhaps even in the hooves of a horse–but quite another to put oneself in the banks of a river.

Certainly, the fact that orthodox moral philosophies, each with its own ordinary-person orientation, have difficulty accommodating various nonhumans is not, in itself, proof that the conventional moral schools are wrong, or have to be amended beyond recognition. One alternative, the position of an ardent adherent to one of the predominant schools, is that any unconventional moral client that it cannot account for, except perhaps in a certain limited way, cannot (safe in that limited way) have any independent moral significance or standing.

But there is another response to the dilemma, one that is more challenging to the assumptions that dominate conventional moral thought. In accordance with this approach we need to ask several new questions. How imperialistic need a moral framework be? Need we accept as inevitable that there be one set of axioms or principles or paradigm cases for all morals–operable across all moral activities and all diverse entities? Are we constrained to come forward with a single coherent set of principles that will govern throughout, so that any ethic we champion has to absorb its contenders with a more general, abstract and plenary intellectual framework? My own

---

[*]   The term was suggested to me by Holmes Rolston.

view is that monism's ambitions, to unify all ethics within a single framework capable of yielding the one right answer to all our quandaries, are simply quixotic.

First, the monist's mission sits uneasily with the fact that morality involves not one, but several distinguishable *activities*–choosing among courses of conduct, praising and blaming actors, evaluating institutions, and so on. Is it self-evident that someone who is, say, utilitarian in his or her act evaluation is committed to utilitarianism in the grading of character?

Second, we have to account for the *variety of things* whose considerateness commands some intuitive appeal: normal persons in a common moral community, persons remote in time and space, embryos and fetuses, nations and nightingales, beautiful things and sacred things. Some of these things we wish to account for because of their high degree of intelligence (higher animals); with others, sentience seems the key (lower life); the moral standing of membership groups, such as nation-states, cultures, and species has to stand on some additional footing, since the group itself (the species, as distinct from the individual whale) manifests no intelligence and experiences no pain. Other entities are genetically human, either capable of experiencing pain (advanced fetuses) or nonsentient (early embryos), but lack, at the time of our dealings with them, full human capacities. Trying to force all these diverse entities into a singe mold–the one big, sparsely principled comprehensive theory–forces us to disregard some of our moral intuitions, and to dilate our overworked person-wrought precepts into unhelpfully bland generalities. The commitment is not only chimerical; it imposes strictures on thought that stifle the emergence of more valid approaches to moral reasoning.

MORAL PLURALISM

The alternative conception toward which I have been inviting discussion, what I call *moral pluralism,** takes exception to monism point by point. It refuses to presume that all ethical activities (evaluating acts, actors, social institutions, rules, states of affairs, etc.) are in all contexts (in normal interpersonal relations, across large spaces and many generations, between species) determined by the same features (intelligence, sentience, capacity for emotions, life) or even that they are subject, in each case, to the same overarching principles (utilitarianism, Kantianism, nonmaleficence, etc.). Pluralism invites us to conceive the intellectual activities of which morals consist as being

---

*   Moral pluralism ought not to be confused with moral relativism, the view, roughly, that all morals are context-dependent. A pluralist can be agnostic with respect to the moral realist position that there are absolutely true answers to moral quandaries, as invariable across time, space, and communities as the value of pi. There may be "really right" and not just relatively right answers, but the way to find them is by reference not to one single principle, constellation of concepts, etc., but by reference to several distinct frameworks, each appropriate to its own domain of entities and/or moral activities (evaluating character, ranking options for conduct, etc.)

partitioned into several distinct frameworks, each governed by its own appropriate principles.

Certainly, one would expect pain-regarding principles to emerge as pivotal in establishing obligations toward all those things that experience pain. Not pain alone, but preferences of some sort, e.g., the projection of a life plan, have to be accounted for in our relations with a second level of creature. Still richer threads (such as a sense of justice, and rights of a sort that can be consensually created, extinguished, traded, and waived) form the fabric of the moral tapestry that connects humans who share a common moral community. Other principles, perhaps invoking respect for life, for a natural unfolding, seem fit as a basis for forming our relations with plants.[*] Indeed, should we pursue this path, we would multiply subdivisions even within the interpersonal realm. The Kantians, emphasizing the place of nonwelfarist duties, make rightful ado about our not saving our child from drowning because it is "best on the whole." But this does not mean that classic utilitarianism is wrong. Maybe it is of only limited force in parsing out obligations among associates and kin. Utilitarianism strikes me as having considerable validity for legislation (an activity) affecting large numbers of largely unrelated persons (an entity set) who are therefore relatively unacquainted with each other's cardinal preferences.

That monism should have become so firmly established in morals is understandable (it echoes one God, one grand unified theory), but is hardly inevitable. Geometers have long relinquished the belief that Euclid's is the only geometry.

> This discovery led to the pluralization of mathematics (itself already a strangely plural noun); where we once had geometry, we now have geometries and, ultimately, algebras rather than algebra, and number systems rather than a number system.[**]

A comparable partitioning has taken place in the empirical and social sciences. The body politic is commonly viewed as being comprised of groups: groups of humans, each of which is made up of more groups, groups of cells, molecules, atoms, and subatomic particles, and/or waves. What happens at one level of description is undoubtedly a product, in some complex way, of what is occurring at another. Many,

---

[*]   See Paul W. Taylor, RESPECT FOR NATURE, 1986); J.L. Arbor presents a coherent and persuasive plea for plants in "Animal Chauvinism, Plant-Regarding Ethics, and the Torture of Trees." 64 AUSTRALASIAN JOURNAL OF PHILOSOPHY, 335 (1986).

[**] Steen, "MATHEMATICS TODAY," pp. 4-5. To pursue the mathematical model for a further moment, Godel and others have laid to rest the hope of ever producing a complete and consistent formal system powerful enough to prove or to refute every statement it can formulate. Although what happens in math is hardly a conclusive model of what should go on in morals, it does make one wonder how much of moral philosophy implicitly proceeds on the assumption that a morality not only has axioms (or even solider starting points), but that they are actually more powerful than math's! And if that is not the assumption, what takes its place?

perhaps most scientists feel that "in principle" there is a single unifying body of law–the laws of nature–that at some level of simple generality hold throughout. If so, one may harbor the hope not only of abolishing all lingering pockets of ignorance and chaos, but of connecting phenomena on every plane with phenomena on another, of someday unifying, say, the laws that particles with those that govern social conduct. But we are far from it. What we actually work with, for all intents and purposes, and to almost everyone's satisfaction, are separate bodies of law and knowledge.

The issue I am raising is this. If, as I maintain, ethics comprises several activities and if it has to deal with subject matters as diverse as persons, dolphins, cultural groups, and trees, why has ethics not pursued the same path as the sciences–or, rather, paths? That is, why not explore the possibility that ethics can also be partitioned?

Perhaps the analogy is simply too weak. However free science may be to partition, one might argue, ethics appears to be under peculiarly strong constraints to remain monistic. The argument might go like this. Alternative descriptions of how the world is (or might be) can peacefully coexist over a broad latitude without logical conflict,–e.g., in most contexts, one can indulge either in a particle or a wave version of light without chafing. And even where apparently irreconcilable conflict does erupt at one level (say, at the subatomic) the participants at other levels (those doing cellular biology) can ordinarily remain agnostic. By contrast, ethics (one is tempted to say) is not merely descriptive. It has as its ultimate aim choosing the right *action*. Unlike describing, in which subtly overlapping nuances of adjective and predicate are tolerable, acting seems to lend itself to, if not to demand, binary yes/no, right/wrong alternatives.

If this is the argument why morals require monism, it appears to me unpersuasive. There is, to begin with, the question of agenda: one wants from moral reasoning not merely the verdict, whether or not to do act *a*, but also what the choice set is: *a, b, c, ...*? Moral thought is a service when it is populating and clarifying the range of morally creditable alternatives. Hence, attention to plural approaches would find justification if, by stimulating us to define and come at problems from different angles, it were to advance our grasp of alternatives.*

Perhaps most importantly, let us remind ourselves that actions are in the physical world; the evaluation of them is intellectual. Many persons (are these the "moralists"?) would probably be pleased if our moral reasoning had the power to map a unique, precise moral evaluation for each alternative action. It would give us much the same

---

*   Note that this rationale for pluralism could be endorsed on heuristic grounds by a monist, even by a moral realist who presumed (as I do not) not all the candidates for truth *disclosed* by this many-angled attacked on the problem will in the end be submitted to a single adjudicatory principle to decide which of them is *uniquely and truly right*. Compare the position Paul Feyerabend adopts with respect to the natural sciences, viz., that the history of sciences reveals an incompleteness and even inconsistency of each framework which should be regarded as routine and inevitable, and that a pluralism of theories and metaphysical viewpoints should be nourished as a means of advancing on the truth. Feyerabend, *Against Method* (London: Verso, 1978): 35-53.

pleasure (tinged with a note entirely ingenuous surprise) that mathematicians derive from confirmation that the world "out there," while theoretically at liberty to go its own haphazard way, is conforming in general to the elegant inventions of our intellects.[3] Why, when we set out to apply our best moral theories to the unruly world of human conduct should we confidently expect more–a more meticulous isomorphism, more freedom from inconsistency, more power of resolution?

Specifically, it may be a (not terribly interesting) truth that an act can be defined in such a way that we are left with no alternative but to do it or not–a feature of the world that makes monism superficially attractive. But even if so, it is a fact about the world that our best moral reasoning may just not be able to rise to or to map. The rightness and wrongness of some acts may lie beyond our power to deduce or otherwise discover. Key moral properties may not lend themselves to produce a transitive ordering across the choice set.

THE VARIABLES

If we are to explore bringing our relations with different sorts of things under different moral governances, then we face the question: by reference to what intellectual elements might governances vary domain to domain?

(a) *Grain of description.* Morals is concerned with comparing actions, characters, and states of affairs. To compare alternatives, as a logical first step, we have to settle upon the appropriate vocabulary of description. For example, in evaluating our impact on humans, we consistently adopt a grain of description that individuates organisms: each person counts equally. In evaluating other actions, there is often intuitive support for some other unit, e.g., the hive or the herd or the habitat. I am not claiming that these intuitions are self-validating, only that they, and their implications, merit sustained and systematic attention. Each vying grain of description is integral to a separate editorial viewpoint. Suppose that a bison naturally (of its own action) faces drowning in a river in a national park. Should we rescue it, or let "nature take its course"? One viewpoint emphasizes the individual animal; another (favored, apparently, by the park service)[4] consigns the individual animal to the background and emphasizes the larger unit, the park ecosystem. Another viewpoint emphasizes species. Each focus brings along its allied constellation of concepts. In invoking the finer grain, focusing upon the individual animal, we scan for such properties as the animal's capacity to feel pain, its intelligence, its understanding of the situation, and its suffering. None of these terms apply to the park. Instead, the ecosystem version brings out stability, resilience, uniqueness, and energy flow.

(b) *Mood.* What I mean by mood may best be illustrated by a contrast between morals and law. Law, like morals, often speaks in negative injunctions, e.g., "Thou shalt not kill ..." and "Thou shalt not park in the red zone...." But the law always proceeds to specify, in each case, a sanction which expresses the relative severity of the offense, viz., "... or face the death penalty," "...or face a $12 fine." The result is a legal discussion endowed with fine-tuned nuances. By contrast, much of moral philosophy, inspirited with monism, is conducted at a level of abstraction at which every act is assumed to be either-or, either good or bad; there is either a duty to do x or a duty not to do x; a right to y or no right to y. Monist moral discourse, then, lacks the refinements of expression that enrich legal discourse. As long as monism reigns, significant distinctions between cases, distinctions marked by nuances of feeling and belief that moral reflection might investigate and amplify, lack a semantic foothold.

By contrast, pluralism welcomes diversified material out of which moral judgments can be fashioned, particularly as we cross from one domain to another. Moral regard for lakes may seem silly–or even unintelligible–if we are required to flesh it out by reference to the same rules, and express our judgments in the same mood, as those that apply to a person. But there are prospective middle grounds. Our lake-affecting actions might have to be judged in terms of distinct deontic operators understand to convey a relatively lenient mood, perhaps something like "that which is morally welcome" or that which will bring credit or discredit to our character.

(c) *Logical (formal) texture.* Every system of intellectual rules is girded on a number of properties that endow it with a distinct logical texture. These range from whether it is subject to closure (whether it is capable of yielding one unique solution for each question that can be opened within it) to its attitude on contradictions and inconsistencies. As to closure, the monist implicitly assumes that morals must be modelled on ordinary arithmetic. There is one and only one solution to 4+7; so too there should be, for each dilemma of morals, one right answer. And monism rejects, too, any system of ethical postulates from which we could derive conflicting and contradictory prescriptions. After all, what would we think of a system of geometry from whose postulates we could derive both that two triangles were, and that they were not, congruent?

Pluralism is not so dogmatic–or perhaps one should just say not so "optimistic"–about the prospects of assimilating morals to (slightly idealized conceptions of) arithmetic or geometry. We simply may not be able to devise a single system of morals, operative throughout, that is subject to closure, and in which the laws of noncontradiction* and excluded middle** are in vigilant command.†

---

*   The law of contradiction holds that it cannot be the case that both a proposition *p* and its negation *-p* are true.

**   The law of excluded middle maintains that either a proposition *p or its negation -p* must be true; there is no middle possibility.

†   See Freidrich Waismann, "Language Strata," in *Logic and Language,* ed Anthony Flew (New York: Anchor Books, 1965), p. 237. The notion I present of multiple conceptual planes with systematically varying formal requirements owes much to Waismann's musings about "language strata."

RECONCILING THE DIFFERENCES

There are many problems with this pluralistic approach. Many of the stumbling blocks—those that I could identify by myself, or with a little help from my friends—are dealt with in *Earth and Other Ethics*.[5] It can be defended from the obvious charge that it must stumble into moral relativism of the rankest sort.[6] But it faces comparable problems that are not so easy to dismiss. It would appear that a pluralist, analyzing some choice situation in one framework (say, one that accounts for species in an appropriate way) may conclude that act *a* is right. The same person, analyzing the situation in another framework (one built, say, from a person-regarding viewpoint) concludes *b*. Are not such conflicts paralyzing? And do they not therefore render pluralism methodologically unacceptable?

To begin with, the fact that morals might admit of several allowable viewpoints does not mean that each and every dilemma will require several competing analyses. Assuming that remotely probable and minimal consequences can be ignored, some choices may be carried through solely within one framework. For example, whatever morality has to say about whether to uproot an individual plant could be provided, presumably, by the appropriate one-plant framework. No excursion into the agent's obligations to the plant's species, or to mankind, or to kin or whatever would be called for.

We can anticipate myriad other circumstances in which thorough analysis requires defining and processing the situation in each of several frameworks. But in some subset of those situations each of the various analyses will endorse the same action. We all know that vegetarianism, for example, can be supported both within a framework that posits the moral considerableness of animals and one that values humans alone, viz., that by eating animals the planet uses protein inefficiently, therefore reducing aggregate human welfare, even robbing badly undernourished persons of a minimally human existence. (What we do not know—and ought to examine—is why approaching such a question from several angles, a technique well-accepted in other areas,* should be indicted as an ignoble and impure way to go about doing philosophy).

There is a third set of cases in which more than one framework will appear appropriate, and the different frameworks, rather than mutually endorsing the same result, reinforce different, even inconsistent actions. The potential for conflicts is there—but no more so than in any moral system that deems the proper choice to be a function of several independent criteria: welfare maximization, duties to kin, respect

---

* I do not mean only lawyers, who do this sort of thing unabashedly all of the time. As for the natural sciences, see Feyerabend, *Against Method*. In mathematics, Gorg Polya, HOW TO SOLVE IT (1957) is a classic exposition of how mathematicians may stalk a single problem with widely assorted techniques (indirect proofs, reductio ad absurdums, analogy), ultimately to be convinced of the truth of a solution by the dual standards of formal proof and intuition.

for life, the values of community and friendship. How do we "combine," where rights analysis says one thing, utility analysis, another?

One possibility is to formulate a lexical ordering rule. For example, our obligations to neighbor-persons, as determined on a framework built on neo-Kantian principles, might claim priority up to the point where our neighbor-persons have reached a certain level of comfort and protection. But when that level has been reached, considerations of, say, species preservation as determined per another framework, or of future generations per another, would be brought into play.

One might claim, with partial justification, that in those circumstances in which we accepted mediation by reference to a master rule, we are reintroducing a sort of monism "after all." But even in these cases, it is an "after all" significant enough to keep pluralism from collapsing into monism. Under monism, a problem is defined appropriately for evaluation by the relevant standard, in such a way that all the "irrelevant" descriptions are left behind from the outset. The problem, so defined, is worked through to solution without further distraction. Under pluralism, a single situation, variously described, may produce several analyses and various conclusions. If a master rule is to be introduced, it is to be introduced only after the separate reasoning processes have gone their separate ways to yield a conflicting set of conclusions, *a, b, c, d*. The master rule is brought to bear on that set, none of whose members would necessarily have been constructed had the procedure been subjected to the monist stricture that a single standard, such as utilitarianism, had to be applied consistently and exclusively from the start.

Finally, and most troublesomely, there are quandaries for which each of our multiple analyses not only endorse inconsistent actions, but for which no lexical rules is available, and for which further intuitive reflection[*] reveals no further, best-of-all, alternative. We can imagine as a "worst case scenario" an outcome not merely of the form *a* is mandatory per one framework and *b* is mandatory per the other (and we cannot do both), but rather of the form *a* is mandatory and *-a* is mandatory (*a* is impermissible). One must, and must not, pull the trigger. What then?

This much is clear: those two edicts, taken together, tell us (logically) nothing. We would say of the total system of beliefs that it had *disappointed us in the particular case*. We would have to agree, too, that if such out-and-out conflicts were in each and every case endemic to pluralist methodology, the whole system we constructed would have to be abandoned. But suppose that such outcomes, while possible, should prove exceptional. Then we could regard their occasional occurrences as a particularly poignant indication of the total system's indeterminacy.

---

[*]   I mean by intuitive reflection a process of analysis that leads to a right-feeling judgment, but one for which, even after the conclusion, we cannot offer any proof, perhaps not even specify the premises.

This prospect illustrates one of the principal monist-pluralist dividing lines referred to earlier: How fatal is it to a system of moral rules if it fails to furnish a single unambiguous answer to each choice we recognize as morally significant? If we cannot devise a whale-regarding moral framework that gives us one confident right answer to every action affecting whales, do we have to withdraw whales from consideration (except as resources in a human-oriented framework) entirely? If our whale-regarding and our person-regarding edicts conflict, does one or the other or both of the systems responsible have to be dismantled?

As I have already indicated, such a standard, if to be applied with an even hand (and fin) throughout, would cramp the range of morals significantly. Better to come right out and consider the alternative: that we may have to abandon the ambition to find perfect consistency and the "one right answer" to every moral quandary, either because a single answer does not exist, or because our best analytical methods are not up to finding it.*

In some circumstances, if we can identify and eliminate the options that are morally unacceptable, we may have gone as far as moral thought can take us. It may be that the choices that remain are equally good or equally evil or equally perplexing.**

This does not mean that as a moral community we are relieved from striving for a higher, if ultimately imperfect consensus on progressively better answers.† Nor does it mean that, as regards the indeterminate set, one can be arbitrary—as though, from that point on, flipping a coin is as good as we can do. It is by the choices we affirm in this zone of ultimate uncertainty that we have our highest opportunity to exercise our freedoms and define our characters. Particularly as the range of moral considerateness is extended outward from those who are (in various ways) "near" us, people who take morals seriously, who are committed to giving good reasons, will come to irreconcilably conflicting judgments on many issues. But the main question now is this: what model of decision process provides the best prospect for constructing the best answers reason can furnish?

---

* As Hilary Putnam puts it. "The question whether there is one objectively best morality or a number of objectively best moralities which, hopefully, agree on a good many principles or in a good many cases, is simply the question whether, given the desiderata ... [of] the enterprise ... will it turn out that these desiderata select a best morality or a group of moralities which have a significant measure of agreement on a number of significant questions." Hilary Putnam, *Meaning and the Moral Sciences* (1978), p. 84.

** See Leibniz's stumper: "It is certain that God sets greater store by a man than a lion; nevertheless it can hardly be said with certainty that God prefers a single man in all respects to the whole of lion-kind." *Theodicy,* trans. E.M. Hoggard (1952, sec. 118.

† One might even expect this endeavor to take the form of integrating, or at least striving to integrate, originally independent "plural" frameworks into something grander and more unified– much as the theoretical physicist will continue to scout about for a grand unified field theory. But in the meantime, the practical and even playful work of significance will take place on humbler levels.

ENDNOTES

1. See J. Baird Callicott, "Non-Anthropocentric Value Theory and Environmental Ethics," *American Philosophical Quarterly* 21 (1984): 299-300.

2. See Lynn Arthur Steen, "Mathematics Today," in *Mathematics Today,* ed. Steen (New York: Springer-Verlag, 1970), pp 7-8. Note that in the model of mathematics Steen presents the flow of ideas and valuable information runs in two directions: the inventory of the most highly abstract ideas in the core are available for equipping application in the outer regions; in turn, the core is fueled with the new ideas that concrete application sends back from the field.

3. See E.P. Wigner, "The Unreasonable Effectiveness of Mathematics in the Natural Sciences," in Wigner, *Symmetries and Reflections* (Cambridge: M.I.T. Press, 1970).

4. See Jim Robbins, "DO NOT FEED THE BEARS", *Nature History,* January 1984, p.12

5. Christopher D. Stone, *Earth and Other Ethics* (1987).

EPILOGUE

"TREES" AT TWENTY-FIVE

. . . continuing

As I was saying in the Introduction, I had not been an environmental lawyer when *Trees* came out, and the focus of my energies turned to other things, including the control of organizational behavior and energy policy. But the environmental movement was swinging into high gear. A number of lawyers began to file suits in the name of nonhumans, including, in a fairly short space of time, the Byram River, No Bottom Marsh, Death Valley National Monument, and an endangered Hawaiian bird (the Palilla)—many of which have now threaded several appearances throughout the text.

In New York, a lady sued as "next friend and guardian for all livestock now and hereafter awaiting slaughter," to challenge as "inhumane" and unconstitutional an exemption to the Humane Slaughter Act in favor of the orthodox Jewish ritual which prescribes that cattle be conscious when knifed, shackled, and hoisted.[1] In Hawaii, a young laboratory assistant "liberated" two dolphins from the university's tanks into the Pacific Ocean so that they could "exercise their freedom of choice" whether to return to captivity. Tried for first degree theft, he defended on the grounds that the dolphins were jural "persons" whom he was saving from slavery—a defense that won him considerable sympathy slightly tarnished by testimony about marijuana use and the opinions of marine biologists that, left to fend for themselves in the open seas, the bred-in-captivity dolphins were as good as dead. The liberator wound up with six months in jail and five years probation.[*]

---

[*] State v. LeVasseur, 613 P.2d 1328 (Int. Ct. App., Hawaii 1980). (Rejecting defendant's interpretation of Hawaiian law that dolphin was "another [person]" under statute). For another early unsuccess, see Anthony v. Commonwealth, 2 D & C 3d 746 (1976) (challenge to action of Department of Environmental Resources resulting in the encasement of a stream instituted by non-riparian with environmental sympathies, but whose property was not affected by the actions complained of. Held, plaintiff's interest as a user of downstream parks was too remote to support standing, the court observing in dictum that "perhaps one day the environment will have standing to sue on its own behalf through a guardian appointed as trustee . . . [citing *Trees*]. However, the Pennsylvania courts by which we are bound, and for that matter the federal courts, are a long way from recognizing that concept of standing." 2 D & C 3d 753 note 1.

THE AFTERMATH IN LAW

If young people I meet in airports are to be believed, *Trees* continues to pop up in colleges and law schools, perhaps to inspire. But what has been the impact *within* the law, if not of *Trees* itself (for the environmental movement had an inertia of its own well before and quite independent of my own little contribution) at least of the "Nature's own rights" thesis for which it spoke? Let us take the original three elements of legal personhood that *Trees* set forth: (1) that suit be permitted in the object's own name and interest; (2) that the calculation of damages (or balance of equities where damages were inappropriate) include an accounting for the interests of, or nonintrinsic value of, the object (not limited to commercial economic value); and (3) that judgment be applied for the benefit of the object. To what extent have they been realized?

(1) "Standing in its own name and right . . ."

Cases continue to be brought, sporadically, in the interest, and often the name, of nonhumans.One group of cases names endangered species as plaintiffs, alleging failures to protect their habitat as required by the Endangered Species Act. This group begins with the Palilla litigation (1979),[2] and runs through the Northern Spotted Owl (1988, 1991),[3] the Mt. Graham Red Squirrel (1991),[4] the Hawaiian Crow ('Alala 1991),[5] the Florida Key Deer (1994),[6] and the Marbled Murrelet (1994).[7] In all these cases except Hawaiian Crow ('Alala), standing was granted (and indeed, the plaintiff continued to meet some success on the merits). But in no case was the species the sole plaintiff. Plaintiff's counsel typically cover their bets with one or more conventional plaintiffs whose standing is less vulnerable to challenge. As a consequence, the species's standing in its own right has usually gone unchallenged by the defendant and not dwelt upon by the court.

In *Hawaiian Crow ('Alala)*, in which the defendant did make a specific objection to the species' appearance as named plaintiff, the suit in the name of the species was dismissed. The *'Alala* court took note of the Ninth Circuit's statement that the Palilla "also has legal status and wings its way into federal court as a person in its own right"[8] but labeled the statement mere dictum in light of the presence there of conventional plaintiffs. The judge also observed that there was no reason why the Audubon Society and other conventional plaintiffs could not press ahead for the relief sought and thus tossed out the 'Alala on the square holding that the bird was not a "person" as that term should be understood in the ESA's citizen suit provision.[9] By contrast, the district court in *Marbled Murrelet*, in the course of enjoining the challenged logging operation, took the species-standing language of *Palilla* as more authoritative, expressly declaring that the marbled Murrelet, as a protected species under the Endangered Species Act, "has standing to sue in its own right."[10] The Court of Appeals took no issue in affirming; but there was a back-up plaintiff in Marbled Murrelet, EPIC (Environmental Protection Information Center), which means that future courts may, if pressed to decide the capacity of a species itself to bring suit, follow *Hawaiian Crow ('Alala)*.

Litigation naming species as clients has not been confined to the United States. In 1988, when harbor seals of the North Sea began dying off in huge numbers, a suit was instituted in Germany in the name of the seals to arrest the flow of toxic metals into their environment. The administrative law court in Hamburg dismissed it with the pithiest opinion.[11] In Japan, a suit was filed in 1994 in the name of an endangered rabbit, the Amami, whose sole surviving habitat is being threatened by construction of a golf course; as in the U.S. cases, an environmental group and several individuals were named as additional plaintiffs.[12] The court, noting that only humans were permitted to file suit, demanded that counsel supply the names and addresses of the plaintiffs to assure they were humans. This order counsel could not do, and the suit in the name of the species was dismissed.[13] In 1995, another suit was filed in the name of rare migratory bean geese (among the world's largest geese), to force the government to declare its choice wetlands a sanctuary. The complaint was marked with a goose's webbed footprint; it, too, was rejected.[14]

Another group of cases has involved particular animals (as distinct from the species), and originate with what might be called the animal rights bar, as distinct from environmental law bar. Unsurprisingly, the cases that include, or come closest to including, animals as parties in interest appear limited thus far to "higher" mammals, viz., dogs, monkeys and dolphins.

No dog, to my knowledge, has yet appeared as plaintiff. But the notion of rights-like treatment for them, once ridiculed,[15] has successfully been raised in actions in which the dogs were in jeopardy—defendants, as it were. In Detroit, authorities impounded a prize sheep dog with plans to destroy it for having killed an 87 year old woman. The dog's owners rejoined that the woman had died of a massive heart attack. The dog was tried, even allowed "character witnesses" to testify about its "gentle disposition." After a hearing that, according to press reports, took on "all the trappings of a murder trial" the dog was ordered defanged, neutered, and confined to home.[16] In Virginia, a dog sentenced to death for barking was reportedly given a reprieve by an appeals court, the death penalty being considered too harsh a punishment.[17] My sense, however, is that, technically speaking such protections as dogs have received in these and similar cases derived not from the dog's own due criminal due process rights, but from the owner's right not to be deprived of *their property* without due process of law.

As far as (nonhuman) primates are concerned, the closest approximation to a test of animal personhood arose in a complex series of lawsuits known as the Silver Springs Monkeys Case. The case grew out of revelations that a group of research monkeys had been subject to shockingly abusive conditions.[18] Several animal welfare organization, including People for the Ethical Treatment of Animals (PETA), the International Primate Protective League (IPPL), and the Animal Law Enforcement Association (ALEA) filed a complaint in Montgomery County alleging violations of various animal cruelty laws. In the original complaint the plaintiffs claimed that they spoke, as well as for their own and class interests, as next friends of seventeen non-human primates (macaque monkeys).[19] The cause was removed to US District court for the district of Maryland. The defendant Institute of Behavioral Research moved to dismiss for lack of standing. The federal court did so, ruling that the plaintiffs had failed to demonstrate that they had personally suffered any actual or threatened injury as a result of the putatively illegal conduct of the defendant, and in all events, holding that the Animal Welfare Act does not authorize private suits (presumably whatever the plaintiff's species).[20] In light of the disposition, no specific attention was given to the "best friend" theory, which was the closest approximation to an argument that the animals has their own legal interests.

The plaintiffs having failed to gain custody in Maryland, the monkeys were transferred by court order to the National Institute of Health (NIH) which lodged them at Tulane. In 1988, when NIH announced that it was going to euthanize three of the monkeys, essentially the same organizations filed state law claims in Louisiana to prevent the killing and assume custody, alleging standing, inter alia, as attorneys for the monkeys. The state court issued a temporary restraining order halting the euthanization, whereupon NIH removed the cause to federal court. The U.S. District Court continued the state court's temporary restraining order and NIH appealed to the Fifth Circuit.

On appeal, the Fifth Circuit rejected all the plaintiff's theories of standing, including the claim that the handling of the monkeys imperiled their mission as advocates for the rights of the Silver Spring Monkeys, who had no means of protecting themselves.[*] To the court, this boiled down to arguing that plaintiffs should be allowed standing because to deny it would leave the monkeys unprotected. "The assumption that if respondents have no standing to sue, no one would have standing, is not a reason to find standing. . . . [T]he mere fact that the monkeys would be left without an advocate in court does not create standing where it otherwise does not exist."[21]

Two cases naming marine mammals as plaintiffs have been brought in U.S. District Court in Boston. Both were precipitated by efforts to transfer dolphins from the New England Aquarium to Naval Centers; in both, the crux of the complaint was the alleged failure of all parties concerned to acquire the permits that the federal law allegedly required to make the transfers lawful.[**] The first case, in 1992, was filed when

---

[*]   Note that counsel drew back at the edge of arguing the rights of the monkeys. The argument was still homocentric to the extent of being based on the humans' rights to their missions. In addition to this theory, plaintiffs pointed to (1) personal relationships with the monkeys; (2) long standing, sincere commitment to preventing inhumane treatment of animals.

[**]   The Marine Mammal Protection Act requires certain permits for the "taking" and importation of marine mammals. 16 U.S.C. § 1374. Plaintiffs' substantive claim was that the transfer, albeit of a dolphin already in captivity, was a "taking" requiring a permit from the Secretary of Commerce, a claim that borrowed support from a subsection that could be read to suggest that for these purposes "taking" might extend to the

the Navy sought to transfer Rainbow, an 11 year old bottlenose, to the San Diego Naval Center, where dolphins were being trained for naval warfare. Rainbow's "own" resistance was joined with objections of a group called Citizens to End Animal Suffering and Exploitation (CEASE), a Massachusetts non-profit corporation. CEASE's claim was that among its 4000 members were many patrons of the New England Aquarium who would, if the Navy were to take Rainbow from the Aquarium, "be unable to observe Rainbow further." The case was settled with the Navy and Aquarium calling off the transfer by stipulation.[22] Thus, no opinion was ever issued in the Rainbow matter.

But in 1993 continuing disagreement among the parties came to a head over another New England Aquarium dolphin, Kama, who had been born in captivity (in Sea World) in 1981, and transferred to Boston in 1986. Kama, the Aquarium maintained, never "fit well into the social climate of the Aquarium,"[23] and he was transferred, without permits, to a naval station in Hawaii to be studied for his sonar capabilities. CEASE, once more joined by its animal client, Kama, sued to nullify the transfer. This time, however, the Aquarium, Navy and Department of Commerce fought back.[24]

On the issue of Kama's standing, could Kama be, legally, "a person" suffering legal injury, as federal law would appear to require for him to appear in court in his own right?[25] U.S. District Court Judge Judge Mark. L. Wolf began by noting the parallel efforts to designate species as "persons" under the Endangered Species Act (ESA). The *Palila* opinion, he granted, had favorable language, but the defendants there had not challenged the species's standing. But he correctly noted that in the only ESA case in which the species's claim was contested, *Hawaiian Crow ('Alala)*, the species was dismissed. Turning to the Marine Mammal Protection Act, on which Kama's claims were based, the court would "not impute to Congress or the President the intention to provide standing to a marine mammal without a clear statement in the statute."[26] In essence, a dolphin could be made into a (legal) person with standing; it was at least an open question. But Congress would have to expressly provide before the Court would entertain such a claim.

One further case deserves note at this point. Soon after *Trees* was published, several correspondents raised the question of standing for the unborn. After all, like animals, future generations were unrepresented in the processes that were shaping the world they would inherit.[27] In 1993, in a landmark case in the Philippines, plaintiffs, all minors, sued on their own behalf *and on behalf of unborn generations* to cancel timber licensing agreements so as to (in the terms of the complaint)

---

transportation, purchase or sale of a marine mammal. See 16 U.S.C. 1374(4).

"Prevent the misappropriation or impairment [of Philippines rainforests and] arrest the unabated hemorrhage of the country's life support systems and continued rape of Mother Earth."[28]

The Philippines Supreme Court upheld the complaint on a basis that included the infringement of the rights of the unborn.

Where Do We Stand on the Standing Element?

While it is fascinating (and gratifying) to follow these developments, the sum of cases is insubstantial and the substance unclear. Only a scattering of claims have been brought on behalf of a nonhuman (animal, species, or nonsentient natural object), and of these few, fewer still have been filed in the name of a Thing only, unjoined by a natural person or association of humans as back-up co-plaintiff.[29] That is to say, the lawyer may name a river lead plaintiff, so that in the official reporters the case bears a title like *Byram River v. Village of Port Chester* or *Marbled Murrelet v. Babbitt*, the lawyers instigating them are leery of placing all their chips on the unconventional plaintiff. As a consequence, in those instances when the suit has proceeded to the merits, one cannot know how the courts would have decided the standing issue if standing had rested on the nonhuman plaintiff exclusively. Indeed, to judge from the author's communication with counsel in most of the cases cited, favorable media attention has been as significant as any other consideration in the decision to list the natural object as lead plaintiff. And in at least two cases where the naming of the unconventional plaintiff was confronted—one under ESA, the other under MMPA, trial courts have thrown the unconventional plaintiff out (above).

There are several reasons for the paucity of litigation in the name of nonhumans. Even those who get over the first impression—that the idea is simply wacky—move on to raise practical objections. A common worry is that voiced by our lawyer-poet (above):

> *Our brooks will babble in the courts,*
> *Seeking damages for torts.*

Once the concept should be admitted, how would we stem a flood of litigation? This problem, I believe, is exaggerated. Lawyers value their time too much to throw it away on a brook—certainly not on any brook that has nothing to babble about on the merits. Brooks cannot cover the Xeroxing costs of modern litigation, much less the hours.* Moreover, the range of guardian need not be open-ended. Guardian-ward

---

* Environmental and animal-rights lawyers typically depend on scarce public donations for support, and occasionally court-awarded fees. My sense is that they, and most public interest lawyers, file fewer cases that

relationships, peculiar to certain "objects", may develop de facto. The Hudson River has a "Riverkeeper" who is the client of the Pace University Law School Litigation Clinic; the clinic at Widener University Law School has taken on the Delaware Bay Keeper as its principal client; Boalt Hall (U.C. Berkeley) law school works for the San Francisco Baykeeper.[30] Or, statutes can be drafted (and treaties negotiated) that authorize standing in the name and interests of certain designated nonhumans. Such provisions can also circumscribe, in advance, the group authorized to represent them. In Germany, some of the states (Länder) have by special regulation constituted approved environmental groups to serve as in effect guardians for certain forests.[31] In the United States, the National Oceanic and Atmospheric Administration (NOAA) is designated trustee for fish, marine mammals, and their supporting ecosystems within the U.S. fisheries zone. NOAA has authority to institute suits to recover restoration costs against any party that injures its "ward."[32] The notion of having guardians for natural resources has become so familiar, that under the Superfund Acts the President is authorized to appoint, from among governmental and state agencies, "natural resource trustees" with power to sue wrongdoers for restoration costs.[33] The supposed "practical" problem of court-clogging strikes me as, where not illusory, surmountable.

At the other end of the spectrum of objections there are philosophical criticisms. "The only stone which could be of moral concern, and thus have legal rights, and thus deserving of legal rights," one Canadian commentator gibed, "is one like Christopher."[34] But as I have pointed out above,[35] this challenge is largely based on a common error, to suppose that a thing's having *legal rights* (being a person in a legal system) has to stand or fall on the thing possessing *moral rights* underneath. (We assign corporations independent status in the legal system, such as the capacity to sue and be sued in their own name, but we do not do so because anyone believes that corporations are moral agents).

Thus, I do not believe that the commonly cited practical and philosophical conundrums are anything near fatal. I suspect that the principal reason why *Trees* has had so mixed an impact has been, ironically, the growth, the success, of environmental law. Throughout the seventies, as the social climate grew more sympathetic to the environment (even in face of the "energy crisis"), several developments reduced the value of *Trees*'s "standing" thesis as a tactic for environmental lawyers.

Most important was judicial liberalization of standing, in which the courts, by relaxing the traditional standing requirements (such as that the plaintiff have suffered "injury in fact,") made it easier for a human to bring a case in her own name on the homocentric theory that the damage to the environment was a cognizable injury *to her*. Environmental lawyers were thus provided an alternate, and in most cases equally

---

might be called "frivolous" than are filed by "regular" lawyers who rely on client fees.

satisfactory key to the courthouse door. In the *Mineral King* controversy the Sierra Club Legal Defense Fund simply redrafted its complaint to accentuate how injury to the area would infringe the Club's "associational interests" and be detrimental to individual members' interests in hiking and aesthetics. It was a pithy amendment, but the trial court bought it.

There is no more striking illustration of the improving climate for conventional, human-based standing than the South African seal litigation. In 1976 several animal welfare groups joined in an action to restrain the Secretary of Commerce from issuing permits for U.S. firms to import South Africa sealskins. They charged that the methods employed to separate the seals from their skins (for transference to humans whose needs for them was in all events quite less urgent) violated the Marine Mammal Protection act of 1972. To satisfy the standing requirement, the groups alleged—in lieu of injury to the seals—injury to the recreational, aesthetic, scientific and educational interests of individual group members. The U.S. District Court dismissed the action on the basis of *Sierra Club v. Morton*, noting that, like the Sierra Club, the groups before it, "however great their interests," were not "on any different footing from any other concerned citizen." In fact, one might say that their homocentric claims were weaker than those of the Sierra Club in *Morton*. In the seal case, South Africa was not only so far away that the chances of any plaintiff ever traveling there were frankly remote: the area of the Cape that the seals inhabited was accessible only with the special permission of the South African government, a permission not likely to be given to U.S. seal watchers!

Hence, considering itself bound by the standards the Supreme Court had laid down in *Morton* (1971), the District Court felt bound to reject jurisdiction. But by the time the seal case reached the Court of Appeals (1977), the court, "in the light of rapidly developing case law," seized upon an affidavit by one of the groups' expressing a plan to go to South Africa in the future to uphold standing and invalidated the permits.[36] Indeed, in 1973 the U.S. Supreme Court had upheld the power of an unincorporated group of law students to challenge Interstate Commerce Commission's approval of freight rate increases without filing an impact statement examining the impacts of the new rates on the environment.[37]

In the *American Cetacean Society* litigation, the Society, to thwart Japanese whale hunting, sued to compel the United States to invoke trade sanctions against Japan for "undermining the effectiveness" of the International Whaling Convention.[38] The defendant, insinuating (not without merit) that a suit essentially on behalf of whales was a doubtful mechanism for plunging the judicial system into imbroglios of foreign relations that are best left to the Executive, invited the courts to invoke the Society's tenuous connection to the controversy as basis for extricating themselves. In an editorial titled "Do Whales Have Standing," The *Wall Street Journal* opined hopefully not. But the courts did not rise to the bait, ruling that the plaintiffs were "sufficiently aggrieved" because the harvesting of whales interfered with their interests in whale-watching.[39] Clearly, liberalized (human) standing was entering a golden age—one in which the need to persuade courts to hear suits on behalf of Nature itself was becoming less crucial. Just about any human or human group, with any plausible connection, would do.[40]

At the same time the courts were extending human standing through expansive interpretation of existing rules, legislatures were engaged in a parallel process. With increasing frequency, new enactments were drawn to include provision for "citizens' suits," in which courts were expressly authorized to hear challenges to environment-disrupting actions by parties whose own personal injury, if any, would have been otherwise inadequate to confer standing. Other legislation has fortified and expanded the government's right to sue private environment-despoilers through a revival of ancient public trust concepts.

(2) ". . . accounting for its own interests or damages . . . "

For me, the second element is most problematical (and interesting) condition of legal personhood: having the law account for the nonhuman's "own 'injury'." In an ordinary lawsuit—arising, say, out of a car accident, measurement of the plaintiff's damages invites no serious theoretical challenges: the owner of the wrongfully wrecked car is entitled to $X, viz., the amount of money required to make her indifferent between being (i) owner of undented car and (ii) owner of badly dented car plus $X (the damages). In other words, orienting ourselves to the imagined interests of the plaintiff (or of a reasonable person in the plaintiff's position) the law makes the defendant compensate to a point that restores the victim to her original welfare position.

But when we venture to admit into the law nonhumans (even unborn generations of homo sapiens), fundamental notions of *interests* and *equivalent welfare* become difficult to apply, even all but incoherent, depending upon the particular "thing" bringing suit. The difficulties need not derail the extension of legal protection of individual animals—particularly of the higher animals such as nonhuman primates and marine mammals.[41] And of course as we move downward through the "chain of being," passing through creatures possessing decreasing degrees of sentience, and onto inanimates (such as mountains and lakes) one is inclined to become increasingly leery of our ability to fit the object into the legal system.

To illustrate, a Florida electric utility diverted the flow of a small river through its plant for cooling purposes. The water was then reintroduced into the river no dirtier than before, but somewhat warmer (referred to as thermal pollution). The elevated river temperature turned out to be blissful for the manatees, who multiplied as the population of marine plants, the manatees' choice diet, exploded. But other population declined. If we imagine now that the river, through a guardian, were to sue the utility, what would she argue: is the elevated temperature good or bad for her client, conceived as the river?[42] There is a large and fascinating literature on conservation biology dealing with ecosystems, that might give courts good guidance in some cases.

But the learning it offers is subtle and often ambiguous. The long-term health of an ecosystem, measured for example by its resilience, and even the proliferation of species, may depend on exposing ecosystems to (certainly not buffering them from) stresses.[43] And in all events, the argument cannot be grounded on what the client prefers. Humans prefer; not rivers.

How can the law respond to the challenge of interest-less plaintiffs? My answer, (which is elaborated in the text above)[44] has been this: as in any situation in which a guardian or trustee is empowered to speak for a ward, what she argues will depend upon what the legal rules provide. In relevant cases in "ordinary" law, such as child custody matters, the rules are linked to the ward's "best interests." But inasmuch as an inanimate object like a river can neither be benefitted nor detrimented in any ordinary sense, the state of the river for the preservation or attainment of which the guardian speaks, will have to be some state the law *decrees* to be the legally mandated one, defined without reference to the rivers own best interests.[45]

The best proof that we can, meaningfully, assign legal rights to interest-less things, is that the law has already done so. It is done in civil recovery actions. Units of the federal or state governments are authorized to sue polluters as trustees for the environment, to recover and apply the costs of restorations, *even if those costs exceed real market value*. For example, when a mismanaged oil tanker ravaged a Puerto Rican mangrove swamp the operators had to pay what was liberally estimated as the costs of "make the swamp whole."[46]

And we have done so as a matter of property law. What "having a property right" comes down to, in the ordinary case, is that no one can trespass upon our land or oust us of our possession simply because the invader can put the property to a more socially beneficial use than we are doing. This is just what the Endangered Species Act does for a species, every time it protects a critical habitat from invasion: it is giving the species a property right, much as the law gives each of us a property right in our houses. The society as a whole might pay a value the timber of some forest acreage more highly than it values the owls that depend on it. But once the owls are "listed," the owls prevail. And note that the law is not merely protecting the endangered creatures from *harm*. The Supreme Court rejected such an argument in *Babbitt v. Sweet Home Chapter of Communities for a Great Oregon*, emphasizing that their habitat is protected (as are our homes and lawns) from having *modifications* imposed upon them.[47]

This idea of nonhumans enjoying a strict property right (no-balancing of interests) has found explicit expression under the Marine Mammal Protection Act (MMPA). In a challenge to purse-seining for tuna in a manner that imperiled the optimal sustainable population of porpoises, the D.C. Court of Appeals observed:

> "We accept as sufficiently demonstrated that the tuna fleet would be
> seriously harmed by such a ban. The arguments, however, properly should
> be addressed to Congress rather than to the courts. Balancing of interests
> between the commercial fishing fleet and the porpoise is entirely a
> legislative decision, dictated at present by the terms of the Act."[48]

And note that while the court's allusion to the "interests" of the *porpoise* might be assailed (an individual porpoise may have interests, but has the "optimal sustainable population" such?) we have no trouble following his reasoning.

On the other hand, to say it is coherent to assign such entities legal interests protectible by tort or property mechanisms is not to say in what circumstances to do so is *wise* or *right*. To illustrate, suppose we give owls in effect "property rights" that their habitat remain as-it-is. This is a much more solemn step than assigning property rights to humans. If we make the wrong assignments initially to humans—if you inherit an apartment building that I can manage more efficiently than you—our capacity to trade interests with one another keeps the allocation moving in the direction of the community's greater needs. But when rights are assigned to the owls, some institutional arrangements are required if we are to avoid a worrisome inflexibility. Indeed, lots of problems are introduced that the law must address. Giving the owls rights would presumably oblige us humans to refrain from deliberate interference, such as clear-cutting. But what about changes that occur independent of identifiable human agency? For example, if an exotic predator invades on a wind current, threatening to upset the area's balance of life: are we obliged to intercede to eliminate the intruder? If, in the face of drought, the habitat began to go perilously dry, can the owl guardian sue for more water?

Similarly, and for similar underlying reasons, there are complications, and understandable resistance, to forcing the defendant to pay for full restoration when the costs of doing so exceed the lost market value occasioned by the injury. The Department of Interior proposed Regulations that would have limited compensation to the lesser of restoration costs and diminution in use value.[49] This is a solution that would have conformed to the way the common law treats ordinary injuries to property: if your car worth $15,000 is "totaled", the person who did it does not have to pay you $100,000 to restore it piece by piece. But Interior's "lesser-of" rule for natural resource damages was challenged. The court envisioned the critical issue as follows:

> [Imagine] a . . . spill that kills a rookery of fur seals and destroys a habitat for seabirds . . . . The lost use value of the seals and seabird habitat would be measured by the market value of the fur seals' pelts (which would be approximately $15 each) plus the selling price per acre of land comparable . . . to . . . the spoiled bird habitat . . . ."[50]

Reviewing the legislative history the court found that "Congress established a distinct preference for restoration costs as the measure of recovery."[51] Nice for Nature! But what if the costs of restoring the habitat are far out of line with its robustly estimated value, not just its use value but its "existence" value and "bequest value", too?

In the essays above I have addressed such questions—with what success I leave it to the reader to judge. Here, in the course of surveying the path the law has taken, my claim is only that the second element is not only intelligible, it has gained a solid foothold.

(3) ". . . recovery to go to its own benefit."

Of all three elements, the third, the creation of environmental repair and mitigation funds, has become the most commonplace. The authority for the funds has derived from a variety of legal sources. An early basis was for courts to arm-twist "charitable contributions" out of convicted wrongdoers, as a condition of mitigating their sentences. In the mid-1970sAllied Chemical Company was convicted for its role in discharging tons on the pesticide Kepone into the James River. The judge announced a fine of $13.24 million—but reduced it to $5 million on condition that Allied make a contribution of $8 million to a Virginia Environment Endowment Fund that in turn would, among other things, monitor the wounded river.[52]

Today, as the notion of the trusts has become more familiar, an increasing number (perhaps five to ten per cent) of Environmental Protection Agency enforcement actions are settled on condition that the defendant or respondent undertake a "supplemental environmental project" (SEP).[53] Under EPA guidelines, the purposes may include restorations and improvement of the affected ecosystem.[54] In 1991, in the wake of the wreck of the *Exxon Valdez* in Prince William Sound—with release of millions of tons of petroleum into the ecosystem—the federal government and state of Alaska settled natural resource claims for $1.15 billion, payable over eleven years.[55] Under the Comprehensive Environmental Response, Compensation, and Liability Act (CERCLA), amounts recovered by the Presidentially appointed natural resource trustees are earmarked "only to restore, replace or acquire the equivalent" of the damaged environment.[56]

But the most prevalent route to environmental funds has almost certainly been through private negotiated settlements of citizen's suits, principally under the Clean Water Act (CWA). There have to be at least a thousand cases instituted under the CWA citizen suits provision in which the plaintiff sought a "consent decree" in lieu of the civil penalty provided.[57] These decrees, in turn, often involve payments for some sort of environmental mitigation, ordinarily managed by some existing institution, such as the environmental group plaintiff, or a university, that agrees to apply it to environmental purposes.[*]

---

[*] It is often hard to disentangle which consent decrees are for the repair of the environment in a conventional sense, for example, $13,000 to Murray State University for the purpose of breeding injured bald eagles and reintroduction of the species in depleted habitats (Sierra Club v. Vanderbilt Chemical Corp., settlement) or to a cause where human motivation is more traditionally "consumptive," for example, $15,000 to a Cook College research fund for oyster culture (New Jersey Public Interest Research Group (NJPIRM) v. Public Service Elec. and Gas Co., settlement) both cited in Marcia R. Gelpe & Janis L. Barnes, *Penalties in Settlement of Citizens Suit Enforcement Actions under the Clean Water Act*, 16 Wm. Mitchell L. Rev. 1025, 1032 n.35 (1990). Because of our

Although widespread, the practice of having defendants pay damages into a fund to be managed for the benefit of the environment is not uncontroversial. Environmentalists of course favor "returning the purse to the victim."[58] But the Department of Justice has objected that, absent specific congressional authorization, anything that looks like a fine or penalty should (like a penalty for narcotics violation) go to the general treasuries. Presumably deficit reduction is a concern, of course. But government officials have also argued that courts are poorly equipped to monitor, over time, whether the funds (and interest) are being expended for the intended purposes.[59] And there are fears that environmental groups may institute suits with an eye towards funding pet projects they cannot underwrite through contributor donations.

WHERE DO WE GO FROM HERE?

The past twenty-five years have shown steady if slow progress towards giving the environment its own legal voice and status. Most dramatically, the liberalization of citizen suit standing, and the creation of public trusteeship powers for natural resources suggest that some of *Trees'* original agenda have been either adopted or overtaken by events. But progress has been only partial. The successes should enable us to get a better fix on areas that remain to be addressed.

(4) ". . . entities remaining voiceless . . ."

First, there are situations in which nature may be in peril, but there are no citizen suit or equivalent mechanisms in place. Generally, standing via citizens' suits hinges, at a minimum, on a federal or state statute that can be construed as touching the controversy, preferably a specific law, such as the Endangered Species Act. In many circumstances no such provision will be applicable. When the Navy proposed slaughter of the goats on Catalina Island where the military has an installation, an animal rights group raised a challenge. The goats, however, were neither members of a "listed" species nor marine mammals, and the would-be plaintiffs could not show themselves to be persons "adversely affected," the key term of the Administrative Procedure Act. Suit was rejected for want of standing.[60] If protection of animals in such circumstances is to go forward, it will likely require a legislatively authorized expansion of permissible "citizen suits," legislation which is not likely in the present atmosphere.[61]

To my mind, the most significant total "gaps" in coverage are areas of the global commons, especially the high seas. These are the areas outside any national jurisdic-

---

ignorance of the long-term environmental effects, over time the distinction blurs between repairs that are made for Nature's "own benefit" and those justifiable in terms of Nature's services for human benefit.

tion, and which therefore are most vulnerable to unprotected and excess exploitation. In the essay, *How to Heal the Planet*, I propose a system of guardianships for critical global commons areas.[62] I am chary of empowering any would-be guardian of a global commons resource to step forward and bring suit before the World Court or other agencies. What I suggest instead is a system in which an existing international agency or institution with special competence over living marine resources, etc., be designated guardian in advance. This has the advantage of assuring continuous and expert monitoring; it also mitigates the dilemmas of legal ontology (are we to protect every sea worm, a species, an ecosystem?), and puts some valve on the flow of potential litigation.

Another area of gap involves the interests of future generations of persons. The vaunted "voicelessness" and "bad deal" of future generations are easy to exaggerate. The overlapping of generations, and intergeneration empathy, assure a certain guardianship of interests "naturally"; and any qualified accountant would suggest we are primed to leave our descendants, as our ancestors left us, a pretty nice legacy on balance. But just as there are externalities in space (U.S. utilities spew pollutants with little accountability into Canada) so too there are undoubted externalities through time. We the living are projecting risks on the unborn, in the form of nuclear waste and an uncertain climate. In the essay, "Should We Establish a Guardian for Future Generations?"[63] I examine the proposal, in particular, the institutional qualities that a Future Generations Guardian would have to have.

The Implications of Lujan

A second gap is reopening closer to home. I have referred to the liberalization of citizens' suits. Certainly the court-rooms opened wider in the 1970s and early 80s. But then, in 1992, came the U.S. Supreme Court decision in *Lujan v. Defenders of Wildlife*,[*] which questions protection of animals and natural resources even where there is a citizen's suit in place. *Lujan* arose as a challenge by environmental groups to the Department of Interior's failure to issue guidelines insuring that U.S. funded actions not imperil endangered species outside the United States. Interior responded by challenging the standing of the groups and its members to question regulations that would affect animals on other continents; its argument rested on the unlikelihood of the plaintiffs suffering any cognizable injury.

A majority of justices agreed. The several opinions in *Lujan*, while somewhat cloudy in aggregate detail, send a distinct signal that a plurality of the justices are

---

[*] 504 U.S. 555 (1992). The court, by a 4-3-2 vote, denied standing to an environmental group claiming that decimation of Asian species would harm one of their members who had future plans to embark on a Sri Lankan wildlife viewing expedition.

prepared to arrest, even to constrict, liberalization. The court labeled as "novel" and rejected several theories of standing that did not appear inconsistent with rulings in some of the earlier cutting edge cases, such as *Kreps* (the South African seal case) and *American Cetacean Society* (the Japan whaling case). Justice Scalia, speaking for the Court, specifically ridiculed several grounds of standing including one

> "called, alas, the 'animal nexus' approach, whereby anyone who has an interest in studying or seeing the endangered anywhere in the globe has standing; and the 'vocational nexus' approach, under which anyone with a professional interest in such animals can sue. Under these theories, anyone who goes to see the Asian elephants in the Bronx Zoo, and anyone who is a keeper of elephants . . . has standing to sue because the Director of AID did not consult with the Secretary [of Interior] regarding the AID-funded project in Sri Lanka.[64]

To Justice Scalia, moreover, standing was not merely a matter for Congress to decide—to confer standing on this sort of plaintiff or not, as it choose. Most pertinently, Article III, which is the ultimate source of judicial authority, bars Congress from empowering the courts to entertain cases in which the purported plaintiff's injury is so remote and conjectural that there is no constitutional "controversy." To put it otherwise, "injury in fact" is a limitation on congressional power.[65]

Lujan did not close the door to citizens' suits. But it looms as a sort of double-gate-keeper—constitutional and statutory—for which environmental organizations have to find the right "nexus." Indeed, the effort to find a qualified plaintiff (which means, to get the "right affidavit") leads, repeatedly, to ironic if not downright contorted arguments.

Consider the post-*Lujan* efforts of the Animal Legal Defense Fund (ALDF), an outstanding animal rights group, to challenge the actions (inactions) of the Secretary of Agriculture under the Animal Welfare Act. The law provides that the Secretary must promulgate regulations to improve the treatment of certain animals, where "animal" means any . . . dog, cat, monkey, guinea pig, hamster, rabbit, *or such other warm blooded animal as the Secretary may determine is being used, or is intended for . . . research . . .* (emphasis added).[66]

In promulgating regulations implementing the provision, the Secretary expressly excluded birds, rats and mice, even though they are, obviously, warm blooded.

Another provision of the law provides for such matters as exercise regimes for dogs and cages for monkeys. The Secretary, rather than to promulgate federal minimum standards, chose to leave it to each research facility to adopt its own "written standard procedures" for dog exercise, and to develop its own plans for housing nonhuman primates.

ALFD and other organizations brought two cases against the Secretary of Agriculture. The first (rats & mice)[67] sought to force a judicial ruling on the Secretary's interpretation of the ambiguous language: were not mice, as clearly warm-blooded animals, within the statute, so that the only discretion the secretary had (the italics above) was to determine which flow of them were intended for research, etc.? The second case (dogs & monkeys)[68] challenged the abdication to individual research institutions of the power to make up their own exercise and housing rules.

In both cases, the federal district court reached the merits to set aside the Secretary's interpretations. In both cases, however, the Secretary appealed on the basis of plaintiffs' failure to tender adequate basis for standing. Indeed, the plaintiff's evidence of personal "injuries" required some stretching. One retired lab psychobiologist alleged that "the inhumane treatment of these animals will directly impair her ability to perform her professional duties as a psychologist," in part because "she will be required to spend time and effort" to convince the facility," should she return to one, "of the need for humane treatment." Another plaintiff, a lawyer and member of a research facility's animal care and use committee (mandated by federal law) complained that the Secretary's failure to promulgate standards "left him without guidance." And so on. In both cases, the D.C. Court of Appeals reversed, dismissing the plaintiffs for failure to have satisfied *Lujan's* standards for standing.

I find these cases troubling. It is not so much that I fault the D.C. Court of Appeals (or Scalia and the Supreme Court in *Lujan*) for being dubious about escalating thin claims into law suits. Indeed, what strikes me is that none of the affiants *was* appreciably harmed by the Secretary's actions. The "persons" who were *really* harmed—who deserved, at any rate, a day in court—were the mice and monkeys. Surely *someone* should be able to secure judicial review of these clearly shaky administrative interpretations. Why shouldn't it be the animals, letting the suit be brought in their name, the object of judicial focus being their welfare, their pain and suffering, rather than the discomfort and inconvenience of the researchers? The D.C. court of Appeals had reason to doubt there was "a congressional intent to benefit the organization," that is, ALDF. But there was a relevant intent of Congress—it is an Animal Welfare Act, after all—to benefit the animals. If the researchers are outside, or only peripheral to, the "zone of interest," this is a situation in which the animals are clearly within it. Why isn't this the clearest opportunity to talk about *them*? Indeed, in an intriguing (if slightly enigmatic) hint, Chief Judge Mikva, concurring in the dogs and monkeys case, wrote separately to emphasize his view that "had the public interest organizations . . . alleged an interest in protecting the well-being of specific laboratory animals (an interest predating this litigation), I think [they] would have had standing to challenge these regulations as providing insufficient protection to the animals."[69]

Back to Trees: Does Nature Count?

Let me persist. ". . . [I]nsufficient protection to the animals." What I believe Chief Judge Mikva had in mind is something like the difference between suing in your own (strained) right and—what is being lost sight of—suing as a true Guardian. Even if the

174

courts were to retract *Lujan* and "reliberalize" standing in the sense of relaxing the requirements of "causality," "injury-in-fact" and so on for humans, it would not be the same as creating standing for Nature. *American Cetacean Society* (probably no longer good post-*Lujan* law?) was "liberal" in that it recognized the right of a group to go to court and at least stir up some conversation about whether Japan was undermining the International Whaling Convention. But to force a decision whether Japan is abiding the Convention—the human community of nation's agreement among themselves as to the rate and conditions under which whales can be killed—is not the same as empowering someone to speak *for the whales.*

In a case currently pending to challenge the new Secretary of Agriculture's failure to promulgate adequate guidelines for zoos under the Animal Welfare Act, one of the plaintiffs seeking to tip-toe around *Lujan*, alleges as the qualifying injury that she accompanied her daughter's preschool class on a bus trip to the local zoo ("to cultivate in her daughter [her own] compassion toward and aesthetic enjoyment of animals"). She continues with the allegation that,

> "[a]t the zoo, plaintiff's aesthetic enjoyment of the animals was impaired by the following: when she witnessed an orangutan, "Rusty," who was socially isolated, sitting in the corner of his cage, in a hunched-over position, shielding his eyes from the zoo visitors, plaintiff cried and experienced extreme discomfort. She was also seriously distraught by the primates in the 'monkey house' . . . in [their] small barren cages contaminated with fecal waste, flies, [and inadequately lighted.]

> Outside of the primate house, she saw tigers and other big cats in small cages with metal bars. . . . . The cages were so restrictive that all the animals could do was pace a few feet before reaching the opposites side of their cage, turn around, then pace another few feet. Looking at the cramped size and height of the cages made plaintiff feel claustrophobic. The pathetic growl of the cats reminded her of a child whimpering.

When I read these pleadings recently my mind went back to one of the passages I wrote twenty-five years ago: that when people "argue this way" so as "to play up to and reinforce anthropocentric perspectives, there is something sad about the spectacle. I suspect the environmentalists want to say something less egoistic and more empathic but the prevailing and sanctioned modes of explanation in our society . . . are not quite ready for it."

I wish someone would sue on behalf of the orangutan. Even if they would lose. I have personal sympathy for the distraught would-be lady plaintiff who witnessed these things (but to whom the law will undoubtedly answer that she can stay away from zoos) and I have professional sympathy for the wonderful lawyers who are forced, in the face of their better feelings, to talk the law's language, not their own. But I am still waiting to live in a society in which the courts will lend themselves to a conversation about Rusty's life, not ours.

So: what has it all come to? Things could be better. But they are better than they were twenty-five years ago. I do not know what part *Trees* played in all of this. I am pleased to imagine that the essay has given students and the front line lawyers and environmental lobbyists a little lift. And of course hopeful it will continue to do so.

Los Angeles, June 1996

ENDNOTES

1. Jones v. Butz, 374 F.Supp. 1284 (S.D.N.Y. 1974); Standing was granted to Mrs. Jones and her human co-plaintiffs as taxpayers, consumers, and citizens to challenge the provision, without discussion of the "next friend" rationale, but their claims were denied on the merits.

2. Page vi *supra*.

3. Northern Spotted Owl v. Hodel, 716 F. Supp. 479 (W.D. Wash. 1988); Northern Spotted Owl v. Lujan, 758 F. Supp. 621 (W.D. Wash. 1991).

4. Mt. Graham Red Squirrel v. Yeutter, 930 F.2d 703 (9th Cir. 1991) (steve).

5. Hawaiian Crow ('Alala) v. Lujan, 906 F. Supp. 549 (Hawaii 1991).

6. Florida Key Deer v. Stickney, 864 F. Supp. 1222 (S.D. Fla. 1994).

7. Marbled Murrelet v. Pacific Lumber Co., 880 F. Supp. 1343 (N.D. Cal. 1995), affirmed sub nom., Marbled Murrelet v. Babbitt, 1996 U.S. App. LEXIS 10342 (9th Cir., May 7, 1996). C.V. No. 95-16504.

8. 852 F.2d at 1107.

9. The ESA authorizes enforcement by "any person" 16 U.S.C. Sec. 1540(g)(1) defined as "an individual, corporation, partnership, trust, or any other private entity." The judge denied the defendant's motion to sanction plaintiff's attorney for naming the Alala as a "frivolous filing and misuse of judicial procedure". 906 F. Supp. 549, 552.

10. 880 F. Supp. 1343, 1346.

11. Seehunde v. Bundesrepublik Deutschland, (Verwaltungsgericht, Hamburg, August 15, 1998), pp. 89-90, *supra*. Later, canine distemper was identified as the mysterious virus that was decimating the seals; but the problem persisted, may human activity have altered the marine environment in such a manner as to make the seals more vulnerable? The case is described in Christopher D. Stone, THE GNAT IS OLDER THAN MAN 85-88 (1993). Strictly speaking, it would probably be the more accurate to construe the case as involving a stock of seals, not the species.

12. See "Amami rabbit to be 'plaintiff' in case to stop construction," Japan Times, Nov. 8, 1994. Three other species—all birds—were also named in the complaint. (Correspondence with Takamachi Sekine and Takao Yamada, Esqs., Osaka).

13. "Court seeks animal plaintiffs' details" Japan Times, March 9, 1995. As of mid-1996 the suit in the name of those other than the species was continuing. Correspondence with plaintiffs' counsel.

14. "Geese in Suit over Habitat Protection," *Japan Times* December 21, 1995, and correspondence with counsel.

15. See note page i, *supra*

16. See "Pampered Dog on Trial for His Life in Woman's Death," L.A. Times, pt. 1, p. 22, cols. 3-6, January 17,1985; "Prize Dog Spared in Death of Woman, 87, L.A. Times, January 23, 1985, pt. 1, p. 4, cols. 1-3.

17. L.A. Times, Sept. 24, 1983, pt. 1, at 10, col. 1.

18. The background is in DEBORAH BLUM, THE MONKEY WARS 105-131 (1994).

19. 799 F.2d at 937.

20. International Primate Protection League; Animal Law Enforcement Association, People for Ethical Treatment of Animals, et al. v. Institute for Behavioral Research; et al. [cite district court], affirmed, 799 F. 2d 934 (1986).

21. F.2d 1056, 1060-61. The case was appealed, Primate Protection League and its members, et al. v. Administrators of Tulane Educational Fund et al., 500 U.S. 72 (1991). (U.S. Supreme Court reverses, remanding to state court on the theory that the removal to federal court deprived plaintiffs of the right to sue in the forum of their choice. While the case, on remand, bounced between federal and state courts, the health of the monkeys became more and more pitiful; with the deaths of several of them, the controversy was brought to a close to no one's satisfaction. See Blum, note 18, *supra*. Nothing in the subsequent case history illuminated the standing-of-Nature dimensions.

22. Joint Stipulation and Proposed Order for Dismissal, Rainbow v. New England Aquarium, C.A. No. 90-12207-WF (D. Mass. Nov. 5, 1990).

23. Citizens to End Animal Suffering and Exploitation, Kama, et al. v. New England Aquarium, 836 F. Supp. 45, 46.

24. The Navy also maintained that "Kama is able to associate with wild dolphins on a daily basis, and could swim away if he so desired." 836 F. Supp. 45, 47.

25. The MMPA presumably has to be read in conjunction with 5 U.S.C. sec. 702 which grants standing to "a person suffering legal wrong . . . or aggrieved by" violation of MMPA.

26. 836 F. Supp. 45, 49. The Court also dismissed the claims of the organization to standing on failure to show actual imminent (injury in fact) harm to members' interests in dolphin watching. Claims based on informational harm were also rejected.

27. Edith Brown Weiss develops and explores this theme in IN FAIRNESS TO FUTURE GENERATIONS (1988); and see my essay, *Should We Establish a Guardian for Future Generations?*, Chapter 3.

28. Complaint, Oposa v. Factoran, G.R. No. 101083 (Supreme Court of the Philippines, Jun. 30, 1993). Para 22; see IUCN (THE WORLD CONSERVATION UNION) COMMISSION ON ENVIRONMENTAL LAW, WATCHING THE TREES GROW: NEW PERSPECTIVES ON STANDING TO SUE FOR ENVIRONMENTAL RIGHTS 50 (1995).

29. Perhaps only Death Valley Monument, which was never filed and *Seehunde*, rested entirely on nature's claim.

30. Robert F. Kennedy Jr., and Stephen P. Solow, *Environmental Litigation as Clinical Education: A Case Study*, 8 J. Envtl. L. & Litig. 319 (1994).

31. The number of Länder that provide for some such special group standing has grown from five (of Germany's 17 states) in 1992 to twelve in 1996. See for example, §39a Berliner Naturschutzgesetz, §36 Hessisches Naturschutzgesetz.

32. See 40 C.F.R. (1990) §§ 300.600, 300.615(a)(1).

33. Superfund Amendments and Reauthorization Act of 1986 (SARA), 42 U.S.C. §§ 9607. *seq.*, As of 1994, there had been reportedly forty actions in which the Department of commerce, through NOAA, was seeking damages for injury to natural resources, and an additional twenty in which the Department of Interior was involved. Paul R. Portney, The Contingent Valuation Debate: Why Economists Should Care, 8 JOURN. ECON. PERSPECTIVES 3, 11 (1994). See [below].

34. P.S. Elder, *"Legal Rights for Nature—the Wrong Answers to the Right(s) Question,"* 22 OSGOOD HALL L.J. 285, 288 (1985).

35. See p. 50 and note, *supra.*

36. Animal Welfare Institute v. Kreps, 7 Envmntl Law Reporter 20,617 (D.C. Cir. 1977).

37. United States v. Students Challenging Regulatory Agency Procedures (SCRAP), 412 U.S. 669 (1973). Although the students passed the standing hurdle, they ultimately lost on the merits.

38. Trade sanctions appear to be the required sanction under the Pelly Amendment to the Fishermen's Protective Act, 22 U.S.C. §1978 (1988 & Supp. IV 1992), for undermining a fisheries agreement, but the power of a nongovernmental authority—here, the Cetacean Society—to invoke the courts to force the executive's hand is more problematical.

39. Both the District Court and the Court of Appeals dismissed the objections to standing almost cursorily: "plaintiffs have a clear right to relief." American Cetacean Society v. Baldridge, 604 F. Supp. 1398, 1411; American Cetacean Society v. Baldridge, 768 F.2d 426, 444 (D.S. Cir. 1985). The U.S. Supreme Court reversed on the merits, 5-4, sub nom. Japan Whaling Association v. American Cetacean Society, 478 U.S. 221, 106 S. Ct. 2860 (1985).

40. Other suits notable for the liberality of standing included Citizens to Preserve Overton Park v. Volpe, 401 U.S. 402 (1970) (citizens group successfully challenges Department of Transportation highway plan that would have threatened a park without any challenge to its standing).

41. Even with higher mammals, such as whales, there are complications owing to our limited capacity to construct their preferences in the detail the law ideally would like. See the essay *The Nonperson in Law,* Chapter 2.

42. Note that the posture of the lawyer for the manatees would be less ambiguous than that for a lawyer designated for the river. But that is one of the hurdles facing Trees' position: how to carve up the world into those entities that will count, and those that do not. See the Essay, "Moral Pluralism and the Course of Environmental Ethics," above.

43. See DANIEL B. BOTKIN, DISCORDANT HARMONIES: A NEW ECOLOGY FOR THE TWENTY-FIRST CENTURY (1990).

44. See pp. 59-63, *supra.*

45. Humans, enacting the law which inevitably seizes imperfect benchmarks, might just select a dissolved oxygen constraint.

46. Commonwealth of Puerto Rico v. SS Zoe Colocotroni, 456 F.Supp. 1327 (D.P.R. 1978), *aff'd*, 628 F.2d 652 (1st Cir. 1979), discussed below. Federal statutes such as CERCLA, and the Oil Pollution Act of 1990, 33 U.S.C. §§ 2701-2761 (Supp. 1994) do the same to the extent full restoration costs are demanded, also discussed below.

47. 115 S. Crt. 2407 (1995).

48. Committee for Humane Legislation v. Richardson, 540 F.2d 1141, 1151, n.39 (C.A. D.C. 1976).

49. 43 C.F.R. § 11.35(b)(2) (1993). Although the regulations do not use the specific "lesser of" language, commentators understand this as the nature of the proposal. *See*

Douglas R. Williams, *Valuing Natural Environments: Market Norms and the Idea of Public Goods*, 27 Conn. L. Rev. 365, 384 (1995).

50. Ohio v. United States Department of Interior, 880 F. 2d 432, 442 (D.C. Cir. 1989).

51. *Id.* at 459.

52. The case is discussed in Christopher D. Stone, *A Slap on the Wrist for the Kepone Mob*, 22 Bus. & Soc'y Rev. 4, Summer, 1977.

53. Sometimes, "environmentally beneficial expenditure" (EBE). *See generally*, Donald Stever, *Environmental Penalties and Environmental Trusts: Constraints on New Sources of Funding for Environmental Preservation*, 17 Envtl. L. Rep. 10356 (1987).

54. Leslie J. Kaschak, *Supplemental Environmental Projects: Evolution of a Policy*, 2 ENVTL. LAW 465, 479 (1996).

55. See Paul R. Portney, *The Contingent Valuation Debate: Why Economists Should Care*, 8 Journ Econ. Perspectives 3, 11 (1994).

56. See note 55.

57. For a sampling of relevant decrees, *see* L. Jorgensen & J. Kimmel, *Environmental Citizen's Suits: Confronting the Corporation* (1988) (BNA Special Report).

58. Leslie J. Kaschak, *Supplemental Environmental Projects: Evolution of a Policy*, 2 Envtl. Law 465, 466 (1996).

59. Marcia R. Gelpe & Janis L. Barnes, *Penalties in Settlement of Citizens Suit Enforcement Actions under the Clean Water Act*, 16 WM. MITCHELL L. REV. 1025, 1031 (1990).

60. Animal Lovers Volunteer Association v. Weinberger, 765 F. 2d 937, 938 (9th Cir., 1985).

61. Moreover, any such expansive legislation likely faces a constitutional challenge under *Lujan*, discussed below.

62. See Chapter 4, *supra*.

63. See Chapter 3, *supra*.

64. 504 U.S. at 566.

65. Cass R. Sunstein, *What's Standing After Lujan? Of Citizen's Suits, "Injuries", and Artilce III*, 91 Mich. L. Rev. 163. Professor Sunstein takes issue with the court's analysis, suggesting that the relevant question cannot be understood simply in terms of "injury in fact" but must include whether the law, including statutes, the Constitution, and federal common law can fairly be read as conferring on the plaintiffs a cause of action.

66. 7 U.S.C. § 2132g [supp?]

67. Animal Legal Defense Fund v. Espy, 23 F. 3d 496 (D.C., 1994).

68. Animal Legal Defense Fund v. Espy, 29 F. 3d 720 (D.C., 1994).

69. *Id.* at 726.